*Western Representations of the Muslim Woman*

*Mohja Kahf*

# WESTERN REPRESENTATIONS
# OF THE MUSLIM WOMAN
## *From Termagant to Odalisque*

UNIVERSITY OF TEXAS PRESS    *Austin*

FRONTISPIECE: *Untitled, Self-portrait #3 by Yasmina Bouziane*

Requests for permission to reproduce material from this work should be sent to
Permissions, University of Texas Press, Box 7819, Austin, TX 78713-7819.

∞ The paper used in this book meets the minimum requirements of ANSI/NISO
Z39.48-1992 (R1997) (Permanence of Paper for Printed Library Materials).

Library of Congress Cataloging-in-Publication Data

Kahf, Mohja, 1967–
    Western representations of the Muslim woman : from termagant
to odalisque / by Mohja Kahf. — 1st ed.
        p.      cm.
    Includes bibliographical references (p.      ) and index.
    ISBN 0-292-74336-X (cl : alk. paper). — ISBN 0-292-74337-8
(pbk. : alk. paper)
    1. Muslim women.    I. Title.
HQ1170.K347    1997
305.48'6971—dc21                                    98-41903

*To my parents, with love & thanks*

# Contents

# *Acknowledgments*

Many thanks to Josephine Diamond for guiding me through the labor with wisdom and insight. I am grateful to Elise (Lisa) Salem Manganaro, Mary Gossy, and Diane DeLauro for taking my frantic and ecstatic phone calls and responding with thoughtful attention. I thank Bruce Robbins and John McClure for their encouragement and counsel. Thanks to Steven F. Walker and Janet A. Walker for kindly making themselves available for consultation, and to Ann Lipovsky for her patience and aplomb and making sure all the pieces didn't go flying off the face of the earth. I appreciate the good cheer of my colleagues at Rutgers University and the University of Arkansas. I owe William Quinn thanks for helpful suggestions on the medieval section, whether or not I had the good sense to take them. I thank Sharon Casteel of the University of Texas Press and Amanda Grant of Springdale, Arkansas for editorial services.

Many wonderful friends in New Jersey generously proffered help, child care, home-cooked meals, computer know-how, and much else during the gestation, including Salwa Shishani, Ziad Rida and Zeena T. Rida, Denise and Waleed Soufi, Sohaila Soliman and Muhammad Aburub, Mona Hubbi and Anas Kasem, and Jamal Radwan and Sana Jazara. I am blessed to have had the keen mental engagement of Rabia Harris on my side during the final contractions and Zaineb Istrabadi's delight by my side at the delivery.

While I was working, my brother Yasir came to take care of me; my daughters Weyam and Banah empathized by sitting cross-legged under my desk and composing their own treatises; my parents supported me toward this goal in manifold ways, not least of which was their confidence in my success. My husband, Najib Ghadbian, buoyed me with his humor and lovingly tended the flame so that I could work through the night.

Alhamdulillah.

*Western Representations of the Muslim Woman*

# Chapter One

# INTRODUCTION

A distinct narrative representing the Muslim woman abides in Western culture today. This narrative has formed a central part of Western discourse on Islam ever since the eighteenth century. The expository tenets of the narrative are "that Islam was innately and immutably oppressive to women, that the veil and segregation epitomized that oppression, and that these customs were the fundamental reasons for the general and comprehensive backwardness of Islamic societies" (Ahmed, 152). The core narrative itself, whittled to one sentence for working purposes, is this: the Muslim woman is being victimized. There are variations on the narrative: the woman may be a willing accomplice, or she may be escaping her victimization. But "the Muslim woman is being victimized" is the common axis undergirding a wide variety of Western representations.

The narrative about the Muslim woman is so diffuse as to be part of conventional wisdom in the Western world. A corporate advertiser can appeal to this received image in producing advertising copy precisely because the narrative operates at almost all levels of culture, from high to low.[1] Not only can a television cartoon program churn out a *Heathcliff the Cat*–level, children's version of the stereotype,[2] but a university professor or an article in a major metropolitan newspaper can refer to the basic elements of this narrative without finding it necessary to substantiate them. This narrative is so ubiquitous as to be invisible, except when crises cause it to be deployed in a direct fashion, as during Operation Desert Storm, when the narrative of the Muslim woman was activated to round out the story of the need for a civilizing American presence in the Gulf.

Challenges to Western representations of the Muslim woman, from feminist as well as Islamic apologist starting points, have tended to ignore the "representation" part and instead contest the realities of "the Muslim woman." Those realities are the subject of historians and other social scientists, and require methods different from those of literary research. The actual condition of Muslim women is a serious and complex topic. Its study, however, does little to explain the development of the Western narrative. This narrative has a genealogy and logic of its own, emerging from developments in Western representations of gender, of the self, and of the foreign or Other.

The genealogy of the narrative, the study of its descent, "requires patience and a knowledge of details, and it depends on a vast accumulation of source material" (Foucault 1977, 140). There is nothing essential or timeless behind Western representations of the Muslim woman; they are products of specific moments and developments in culture. Recognizing these developments depends on a broad knowledge of Western cultural history, and familiarity with texts in which nary a Muslim woman surfaces but which are haunted by her presence nevertheless. It depends on the ability to detect the absence of this dominant narrative of the Muslim woman as well as its presence.

This book is a history of Western literary representations of the Muslim woman from medieval times to the period of Romanticism in the early nineteenth century. The value of such a history is that it will open today's narratives of the Muslim woman to new interpretations, allowing us to see them not as "culminations" of a natural truth, but "merely the current episodes in a series of subjugations" (Foucault 1977, 148).

Before the time that Islam appeared on the world stage, "the West" did not exist; the peoples of what is now called western Europe did not conceive of themselves as a community. Memories of the Roman Empire had left traces of some differentiation between Europe and Asia (even though that empire had included parts of both). However, large numbers of European peoples had remained outside Roman civilization and outside Christianity (by then split into Western and Eastern branches). Then the Frankish Empire, allied with the Western Christian Church, emerged dominant.

After clashing with enemies to the north and the south, Christianity became the religion of the European peninsula (later with the significant exception of Spain). From these events came the wealth of legends around which a western European sense of identity coalesced and which later discourse (e.g., of the Renaissance, of Romanticism, of Modernism) bonded into a cohesive history, connected backward with Rome and Greece and forward with the modern European nation-states and their "New World" progeny.

Why then use the word "Western?" I am aware that to speak of "Western" culture, "Western" literature, a "Western narrative," and so forth, is not to speak of one stable unitary field but of a multiplicity of cultures that have been soldered together at various times in history, sometimes violently, for ideological purposes. In each chapter I refer to specific texts and literatures: British, French, Spanish, and so forth. When I review trends and patterns throughout these bodies of literature, I use "Western" as a shorthand. Arthurian romance, for example, is simultaneously a product of England, France, and Germany. And despite the enormous differences between the Italian Renaissance and the English Renaissance, one can still speak of the Renaissance as a development in "Western" cultural history. I do not intend, by this usage, to make essential or exclusive claims about what constitutes "Western."

I examine mainly canonical, male-authored texts in the Western tradition. At times, women have applied themselves to the patterns of Western representation of the Muslim woman which I describe. Even a Muslim woman writer could conceivably author such representations, since the issue is not the identity of the author but the mobilization of the core "Western" narrative.

The same objections can be raised about the term "the Muslim woman." Is it not too nebulous and ahistorical? Who is this creature whose feet never touch earth? Why not speak about representations of Arab women, Turkish women, African women? Such distinctions may be valid when it comes to social science analysis of women in Islam. However, a basic point of this book is to rip apart at the seams the apparent fit between "the Muslim woman" as the object of representation in Western texts and real Muslim women with live cells and nerves and muscle tissue, women whose feet touch earth in Hamah or Rawalpindi or Rabat.

My subject is not "women who are Muslim" but "Western representation of the Muslim woman," a category shaped by the literary conventions,

linguistic tropes, and narrative processes within Western cultural traditions. Using this category makes it possible to analyze representations
across racial, ethnic, and even religious[3] lines which become artificially separated if studied within the confines of the obscuring terms used by the various texts (such as "Macon," "pagan," "Paynim," "Saracen," "Turkish,"
"Circassian"). This is not to belittle the independent significance of the
overlapping categories. "Muslim" and "Islamic" here refer to a general civilizational heritage, in which religious minorities have played an integral
part, more than to the religion for which that heritage is named. The texts
themselves do not refer to these figures as "Muslim women"; I offer the
term as a useful way of seeing patterns in the representations of disparate
literary periods.

The image of the Muslim woman in Western culture has been a changing, evolving phenomenon. Some of the basic elements of her image congealed even before there were any real Muslim women, because the representation builds on conventions of representing alien women (pagans,
foreigners, Old Testament figures) already formed in Western texts before
the advent of Islam. Afterward, the emphasis accorded the female image in
the overall Western narrative of Islam undergoes transformations as that
narrative alters.

The Muslim woman occupies a much smaller and less central place in
that narrative in medieval texts than she does in the texts of the nineteenth
century. Her nature, too, is different. Western concerns about Islam in
medieval texts cluster around concerns other than women. The success of
the world of Islam was the source of resentment in medieval outlooks
which equated success with right. How could blasphemy be allowed to gain
power and glory? Technological expertise, magical knowledge, and superhuman power help explain this conundrum and constitute major elements
in the medieval Western narrative of Islam. The Muslim woman in medieval literature typically appears as a queen or noblewoman wielding power
of harm or succor over the hero, reflecting in this the earthly might of Islamic civilization. These figures are loquacious and transgress the bounds
of traditional femininity, reflecting the failure of their parent religion to in-
culcate proper gender roles. The rhetorical move of many medieval literary
texts involving a Muslim woman is to subdue her, not to liberate her.

The basic plot of the story of the Muslim woman in medieval texts runs
like this: A high-ranking noblewoman becomes attracted to a Christian
man imprisoned by her father or husband and aids him in a battle between

Christians and Muslims. At the end of the battle, the lady converts, transfers the father's or husband's treasures to the Christians, embraces a more passive femininity, and becomes part of the European world. Despite this obligatory transformation, the image that remains dominant is the powerful female figure that was present through most of the text. Sometimes this exuberance is manifested in the physical size of Muslim "giantesses." In other instances, it is expressed as "wanton" or intimidating sexuality of the Muslim woman, who also holds higher social rank than the Christian hero.

"The Muslim woman is being victimized" is the litany of a later age in Western discourse. There is no veil and no seclusion in her medieval representations. There is often an attempt to recuperate her as a Christian or a European, rather than an emphasis on her irreducible alienness. The notion that a (formerly) Muslim woman could enter Europe as an equal—and even more than equal—character in a story, and the desirability of her doing so, is a characteristic of medieval literature; it could never happen so easily in nineteenth-century literature.

During the centuries of early European exploration, commercial expansion, and incipient empire-building, the Western narrative of Islam expands moderately in range and sophistication. Still, interest in the Muslim woman increases only minutely in proportion to the overall discourse on Islam. Traces of the medieval legacy are detectable in some Renaissance literature, but much of the aggressive, exuberant nature of the Muslim termagants and queens in medieval stories has dissipated. The Muslim woman in European literature of the Renaissance is between myths. In some texts, the Muslim female character shows features of the "wanton" queen of old; other texts provide foretastes of the helpless damsel, a type which emerges more fully in later periods. In many texts she is constituted by rather the same gender constraints as her Western counterparts, functioning in a field of similarity and "indifference" rather than in one of "Otherness."

In the seventeenth century, the veil and the seraglio or harem enter into Western representation of the Muslim woman. The veil still appears on European women as well, and has not yet become a prop associated exclusively with Islam. The word "seraglio" surfaces in English in 1581 and "harem" in 1634 (OED). Meanwhile, across the channel, "serails" materialize on the French stage, and Muslim slave women appear in some texts. Although the Muslim woman character is still to some extent "on the loose" early in this period, the "wanton" model drops away bit by bit, and a very diminished figure emerges. Gradually, the seraglio slides into place as her setting. By the eighteenth century—but not before—it becomes the proper space of the Muslim woman in Western literary representation. The odalisque, or concubine, is the character who inhabits this new place, abject and angry or virginal and victimized, but always an oppressed creature. Though only recently confined to this cell, she is held to have always been there.

Historians, who of all folk should know better than to claim timelessness for any concept, still make such assertions as: "The harem has always pricked the imagination of Western people. . . . Students of exoticism and Orientalism have noted the *longevity* of the *topos* of the harem and its endurance in the face of political and cultural changes. From the earliest encounters between Christians and Muslims till the present, the harem as the *locus* of an exotic and abnormal sexuality fascinated Westerners" (Melman, 59–60; emphasis hers). Historians are human and may be excused for making the ubiquitous assumptions of the rest of our kind; still, it is my job here to point out mildly that none of these claims, as a matter of history, is true. Any survey of Western discourse on Islam that goes beyond the last three hundred years will not bear such statements out. The veil and the harem do not exist in medieval representations of the Muslim woman and are barely present in the Renaissance.

And yet, after the beginning of the modern era, a representation of the Muslim woman not linked to veil and harem is almost unimaginable. What causes this fascinating change of paradigm?

It is true that "the issue of women only emerged as the centerpiece of the Western narrative of Islam . . . as Europeans established themselves as colonial powers in Muslim countries" (Ahmed, 150). The "rise" of the subjugated Muslim woman concurred with the build-up of British and French empires in the nineteenth century, which, in subjugating whole Muslim societies, had a direct interest in viewing the Muslim woman as oppressed— even as their policies had oppressive effects on flesh-and-blood Muslim women. However, causally linking the rise of "harem discourse" to colonization proper is too specific and limiting. The question of the liberty, or lack thereof, of the Muslim woman appears as early as the seventeenth century. "I have heard that Christian ladies live with much more freedom than such as are born here," says a Muslim woman in an English drama produced in 1624 (Massinger's *The Renegado*). Ironically, her statement cues a misogynistic satire of English women's "liberties," and I believe the answer to the question lies in this most unexotic, homeward direction. If direct

Western colonialism and administration of Muslim societies were the only factor responsible for the emergence of the narrative of the Muslim woman as victim, this narrative should not begin to emerge so early. To imagine that the first shufflings of European states to establish trading outposts in the Muslim world instituted imperialist domination overnight is to indulge in an overreaching hindsight. Because we are so familiar with the shape of Western global dominance, we may seek it as an explanatory factor in vague ways, over periods when it does not apply.

The beginning of the question of liberty for Muslim women coincides with the beginning of the whole question of liberty in Western political discourse. Before the seventeenth century, the modern vocabulary for discussing individual liberty and human rights did not exist. The dawn of the harem issue also coincides with the beginnings of a gradual but pivotal shift in Western cultural norms of femininity and gender. The position of "man" in the universe seemed to have shifted in Europe, calling everything else, including the position of woman, into question. The middle ranks of the old society were stirring into early capitalist forms of production and reorganizing the sexual division of labor; the Church was losing its grip on society; monarchies were consolidating and centralizing into the form of the modern nation-state; European commercial enterprises across hitherto unknown oceans were flourishing, bringing them into novel forms of contact with multitudes of foreign peoples and civilizations. Europe's sense of itself was changing.

An important change within the West concurrent with the earliest beginnings of its expansion into Islamic lands was the rise of the "domestic woman," the altered, specifically modern criterion for what was desirable in a female (Armstrong 1987a, 3). This new ideology of middle-class female domesticity, coming into circulation in the eighteenth century, pushed against older, aristocratic notions of the female and the family, and against working-class realities. At the same time it pushed a new Muslim woman into the field of representation as a sort of negative female ideal. This discursive tactic allowed disparate groups within changing European societies to articulate common values by giving them a single social image they could agree to disparage. The image helped create the fiction of a Western, a *not-Oriental*, identity—and thus to prepare a supportive culture for colonialism as it began to gather momentum.

Both the external and internal processes, both the domination of foreign lands and the remapping of gender boundaries within European societies, combine to compose the new Muslim woman in the Western imagination. I will explore how the narrative of the Muslim woman is intimately connected to dramas unfolding within "the West," as well as between the West and the Islamic Other, to try to explain this distinct breach between the older model of the exuberant and overbearing Muslim woman—the termagant—and the model of the helpless, inferior Muslim woman—the odalisque.

The explicit association of Islam with the oppression of women does not reach full fruition until the eighteenth and nineteenth centuries. When the Orient was Orientalized (to paraphrase Edward Said), when a vast and complex body of knowledge about the Islamic Other developed simultaneously with Western subjugation of that world, the image of the Muslim woman most familiar in the West today emerged. Relative to the growth of the discourse on Islam in general, the Muslim woman character grows all at once (as if she had eaten one of Alice in Wonderland's distending cakes) into one of the overarching concerns of that discourse. Paradoxically, her figure simultaneously shrinks in subjectivity and exuberance. In the eighteenth century, the Muslim woman character turns into an abject harem slave, the quintessential victim of absolute despotism, debased to a dumb, animal existence. Then in the nineteenth century, this harem slave is rescued by the Romantic hero and recreated as the ideal of numinous femininity. The recurrent drama of incipient colonization, that of a heroic male conquest of a feminized Oriental land, is played out in literature upon the inert body of the Muslim woman. To turn to ironic use a couplet from an earlier century,

And when her city and her state was lost,
Then was her person lov'd and honor'd most.
(Tasso, 6.56)[4]

The Muslim woman character is "loved" and "honored" (to death) by the Romantic hero. The literature which condescends to express the most tender concern over the Muslim woman is the literature in which she is the limp shimmering object of a fetishizing male gaze and absented, if not killed outright. Romanticism inaugurates a portrayal of the Muslim woman in which these new clusters of elements are key: irredeemable difference and exoticism; intense sexuality, excessive ornamentation and association with fetish objects; and finally, powerlessness in the form of imprisonment, enslavement, seclusion, silence, or invisibility. These elements are often manifested in a kind of narrative shorthand by the veil and/or the harem. A basic plotline is the battle between the Romantic hero and a Muslim man over possession of the Muslim woman, often figured as a contest of who can penetrate the harem wall and/or her veil and be master of the gaze over her body.

From bold queens of two worlds who bully, boast, and beckon in the early texts of Western Europe, to helpless harem slaves mutely marking space for two sets of masters at the other end of history, how did the image of the Muslim woman evolve? What caused her textual presence to deteriorate so? The question requires study of the intersection between two broad swathes of Western cultural history: the discourse on Islam and the discourse on gender. At each pivotal moment, what is the contact "on the ground" between the West and the world of Islam, including the variations among differing positions within those two categories? How do these material forms of contact inform Western discourse on Islam? At the same time, what, broadly speaking, are the material conditions informing gender issues within the Western world?

These two questions touch the fundamental issue of Western self-definition, both in relation to other civilizations and in relation to "Woman," who has traditionally figured as the Other within. Against an understanding of the intersection of these two sets, I will study representations of Muslim women in Western literary texts spanning the period from the middle of the eleventh century to the middle of the nineteenth century. There are many cultural questions that may be so answered, and perhaps a personal one. Is there any way that I as a Muslim woman can deflect the debilitating impact upon me of dominant Western representations of "the Muslim woman" through a strategy of wayward readings of texts which contain her? I will suggest openings for such rereadings along the path of her history. Perhaps such a strategy may prove a means of eluding the crushing weight of this heritage while retaining its textured literary pleasures. Or perhaps it may, in the end, only resuscitate the authority of those representations. What is to be done with the history of "the Muslim woman" may emerge only after this history has been done.

## Chapter Two

# THE MUSLIM WOMAN IN MEDIEVAL TEXTS
## *"Dame, ne parlez tant!"*

How is the Muslim woman represented in medieval European literature? What is her significance in the European imagination when she first appears? It is not possible to address these questions today without beginning in the negative, by understanding what the Muslim woman in medieval texts is *not*. She is not what we expect her to be. The very notion of "medieval," first of all, places us squarely in a European perspective because "for all non-European peoples, this much is common: that the concept of a Middle Age has no relevance" (Daniels 1975, 3). To be discussing Muslim women in this category of literature at all gives us a specific perspective. We who live at the end of the twentieth century, who are readers and writers of English or French or Spanish or German or Italian and who are, directly or indirectly, heirs to the cultural traditions of Europe, expect the Muslim woman to be represented in certain ways. The development of these expectations and these ways is precisely the subject of this work.

When we travel backward to the entrance of the Muslim woman into Western culture, there is a risk of burdening these first representations with later accretions—much as someone might attribute the current meaning of a word, with the sum of its accruals over the years, to its medieval cognate. Students asked to describe the role of Bramimonde in *La Chanson de Roland* after she has been introduced as a woman on the Muslim side have responded that she is submissive and secluded. This response has not the slightest connection to the text itself.[1]

The accretion with which the reader is likely to load medieval representations of the Muslim woman is the Western narrative of the Muslim woman from about the eighteenth century on, the narrative that represents her as innately oppressed, veiled, secluded, and silenced. Yet this characterization is entirely absent from the medieval representations. Such an absence cannot be completely accounted for by the formal limitations of medieval literature.

This chapter is not meant to be a comprehensive catalogue of all the Muslim female characters in medieval literature—there are too many. It is an appraisal of certain common features in their representation and asks how this figure is produced in these texts, at this time.

## BRAMIMONDE AND HER HISTORICAL CONTEXT

One of the earliest portrayals of a Muslim woman in a European text is that of Bramimonde in *La Chanson de Roland*. The poem (its origins disputed by scholars who line up along a range from folk transmission to a single author-bard, Turold) recounts the death of Charlemagne's nephew Roland at Roncevaux in 778 C.E. at the hands of the Saracen King Marsile of Spain. Bramimonde is Marsile's wife and first appears in laisse (stanza) 50 of this founding text of French literature.[2] The scene is Ganelon's meeting with King Marsile. The two have just sealed their plot against Roland by swearing, Ganelon on holy relics, Marsile on a book containing "the law of Mahomet and Tervagan." Valdabrun is the first to present a gift to Ganelon in the courtly gift-giving that follows the oaths (laisse 48). After Valdabrun, another "pagan," Climborin, comes forth and presents Ganelon with his helmet. Queen Bramimonde, Marsile's consort, is the third gift-giver; she steps forward and gives Ganelon jewelry for his wife:

> *Atant i vint reïne Bramimunde:*
> *"Jo vos aim mult, sire" dist ele al cunte,*
> *"Car mult vos priset mi sire e tuit si hume.*
> *A vostre femme enveierai dous nusches:*
> *Ben i ad or, matice e jacunes,*

*E valent mielz que tut l'aveir de Rume.*
*Vostre emperere si bones n'en out unchesu*
*Il les prises, enn sa hoese les butetu.* (50³)

(Queen Bramimonde came up that very moment:
"I love you dearly, sir," she tells the count,
"my lord and all his men respect you so.
I'm sending these two brooches to your wife;
fine work of jacinths, amethysts, and gold,
they're worth far more than all the wealth of Rome.
Your emperor has none so beautiful."
Accepting them, he put them in his boots.)

The same phrase which brought in Valdabrun, "*Atant i vint*," is used to introduce Bramimonde. She is one more personage in the courtly receiving line—a high-ranking one, but there is nothing more striking about her entrance than that of the other characters. The speech she makes is similar to those of Valdabrun and Climborin; each says something to the effect that there was no better in the world of the item they were giving. Her more elaborate boast specifies that neither Rome nor the emperor has anything to compare to the pieces she gives Ganelon—more on this later. Why should Bramimonde signify anything more than a minor figure at the edges of this drama, which is, after all, about the activities of men in a very martial, male-dominated world? How does Bramimonde resonate with wider circles of meaning in historical context?

Commonly dated around 1100, *La Chanson de Roland* emerged after a century in which two closely related processes had been developing: first, the "notion of Christian unity and of a certain internationalism" had begun to take hold in that area we have come to know as western Europe (Brault, 17). Second, "the dim realization that Islam constituted a widespread and growing threat to Christendom" ushered in a new awareness, albeit mostly hostile, of the Islamic world (Southern 1953, 54). This may seem, today, to be stating the obvious. However, the disparate peoples of the former western half of the Roman Empire had not previously perceived Islam or its peoples as the major challenge on their horizon. For example, over a century after Islam had appeared on the world stage and even after Muslims had taken al-Andalus (as the Arabs called Spain), crossed the Pyrenees, and occupied a chunk of southern France,[4] the Carolingian chronicles (ca. 793)

regarded the Saracen[5] advance as just another attack on par with the pagan
Saxon threat in the north: "two terrible afflictions arose in two different
parts of the empire" (in Rodinson, 4). The Low Middle Ages are characterized by a general lack of curiosity and interest in the world of Islam. The
Carolingian Empire was oriented away from the Mediterranean Sea, inland
and northward. Neither Christendom nor Islam in the eighth century regarded the other as a discrete entity, much less as the arch-enemy. "We must
think in terms of gradually developing and changing cultures, not of abrupt
transitions, and not of absolute demarcation between Arabs and Europeans . . . ," Norman Daniels cautions (1975, 9).

In the tenth century, however, Otto I united what are today Germany
and northern Italy (with its ports and Mediterranean outlook) and earned
papal sponsorship to establish the Holy Roman Empire (962), which introduced pretensions to universal rule into the language of the times. "The
imperial Carolingian ideology centered on continental Europe gave way to
the ideology of Rome, which was founded essentially on the religious values of the papacy" (Rodinson, 6). The papacy was also active in the wars
against Arab raiders and occupiers of Italy throughout this period, and dis-
couraged the strategic alliances rival petty rulers had traditionally made
with the Muslims. In addition, by the eleventh century, many of the northern European tribes had joined the Franks in Christianity, while Islam and
its domains in Spain and elsewhere remained outside the fold. Residual
Christian hostility to Roman and local paganism fused with hostility to Islam. The Reconquista began in the 1000s, as small guerrilla assaults on
Muslim frontier posts in Spain. After 1050 it assumed the form of organized warfare, and by 1085, Christians had captured Toledo. Meanwhile, in
1060 Sicily had been wrenched from Muslim rule after 235 years.[6] Religious
homogeneity became the ascending rhetoric of the day in Europe: Muslim
communities could no longer be tolerated in its midst.

The language of holy warfare was in full swing after the mid-eleventh
century, as Cluniac monks, wanting a greater role for France, began to en-
courage Frankish knights to win glory for God and do penance for sins by
fighting in Spain. Meanwhile, the Seljuk Turks had converted to Islam and
were pressing on Europe from the East, finally pushing the Byzantine emperor to make the appeal to Latin Christendom that launched the Crusades. This increased the general sense that Europe was being squeezed between the pincers of a vast and powerful alien force. "This little portion of

the world which is ours is pressed upon by warlike Turks and Saracens: for three hundred years they have held Spain and the Balearic Islands, and they live in hope of devouring the rest," declared Pope Urban II at Clermont in 1095 (Southern 1953, 71). Urban's speech is signal not only because it inaugurated the First Crusade, but because it expresses a coming-to-consciousness of Europe as Europe, a discrete cultural entity distinct from Asia and Africa, and one which by right ought to be unified under Latin Christendom.

It matters little, in terms of relations with the Islamic world, whether *La Chanson de Roland* actually emerged in 1100 or, as disputed, a few years earlier, before the First Crusade. The "Latin Christian world's gradually developing ideological unity" had been producing a sharper image of the enemy before the Crusades commenced (Rodinson, 7). Crusading emotion had been building for decades, and with it, the image of Islam and its people as *the* paramount danger to the Christian world. When Bramimonde was produced, sometime between 1090 and the early years of 1100, this xenophobic emotion had risen to the highest pitch it would attain.

Thus if there is such a thing as a European outlook on the world, a sense of what is European as distinct from not-European, it began to develop and define itself in opposition to Islamic civilization. "Europe's notion of any foreign culture has been profoundly affected by its longer experience, up to the colonial age, of no other culture but Arabic" (Daniels 1975, 3), although when the Ottomans took the place of the Arabs, this was modified from "Arabic" to a vaguer, multi-ethnic "Islamic." China does not have a fourteen-hundred-year relationship of constant intimate commingling with Europe. Japanese did not cross-fertilize the languages of Europe with the vocabulary of astronomy, optics, mathematics, textiles, or of agricultural staples such as "rice" and "sugar," as Arabic did. India had no equivalents to the Mozarabs and Mudejars of Spain.[7] Buddhism, Hinduism, and Taoism were not perceived as such grave dangers as to generate thousands of Christian polemical treatises, as Islam did. Negative images of pagan civilizations that preceded the Islamic, including Roman and Old Testament pagans, were absorbed into the image of the new enemy. From approximately the beginning of the eleventh century, Islam began to acquire a special and negative meaning in European discourse. And what could the Muslim woman signify, as the Other within that powerful Other?

LIMITATIONS OF THE "ORIENTALISM" ARGUMENT:
GEOPOLITICAL LANDSCAPE AND GENDER FOOTINGS
OF MEDIEVAL TEXTS

15

*The Muslim
Woman in
Medieval
Texts*

This sea change in the direction of Europe and its relationship to the realm of Islam which evolved during the eleventh century created a boom market for images of the Muslim world. Thus it would be natural, if one were looking for the origins of that "way of coming to terms with the Orient that is based on the Orient's special place in European Western experience," to begin in this epoch (Said, 1). Nothing could be more misleading, however, than to subsume under the term "Orientalism" the production of texts about the Islamic world that began to thrive in the High Middle Ages. For Orientalism, as it has come to be defined after Edward Said's groundbreaking work, is not merely the distinction between "Orient" and "Occident" as a starting point for epistemology, a definition which could as easily apply to Homer as to Sir Richard Burton. Orientalism, in the specific sense that Said describes it, is a product of Western hegemony over the East, a discourse created from the relationship of Western power over the Orient to Western knowledge about the Orient. Said says:

> Orientalism depends for its strategy on this flexible *positional* superiority, which puts the Westerner in a whole series of possible relationships with the Orient without ever losing him the relative upper hand. And why should it have been otherwise, especially during the period of extraordinary European ascendancy from the late Renaissance to the present? The scientist, the scholar, the missionary, the trader, or the soldier was in, or thought about, the Orient because he *could be there*, or could think about it, with very little resistance on the Orient's part. (7)

It was very much otherwise in the Middle Ages; the European soldier, trader, or scholar ventured into the Islamic world at his greater or lesser peril, depending on the country and the circumstances. Christians made no serious sustained efforts to convert Muslims. They worked instead on the remaining northern pagans and contented themselves with fantasies of Prester John, a legendary Christian king supposed to live deep in Africa or Asia, who would one day conquer Islam from the East, convert everyone, and join his vast empire with Latin Christendom to form one universal world Church. Scientists as such are too few to speak of, although there are translators of scientific texts; these scholars usually approached the Islamic urban centers of learning only after the tide of Muslim political power had receded (Southern 1953, 66).

There is no question who had the upper hand from the eighth to roughly the fifteenth century. Nor is there any question that Europeans perceived an Islamic hegemony, despite myriad political divisions within the world of Islam, and even despite the Mongol invasions and the fluctuation at the boundaries of Muslim empires. From the point of view of Muslims, a sense of cultural identification with "Dar al-Islam," the Abode of Islam, extending from al-Andalus to Southeast Asia, existed simultaneously with political divisions and doctrinal differences. For example, although the fourteenth-century globetrotter Ibn Battuta "was introduced in the course of his travels to a great many Muslim peoples whose local languages, customs, and aesthetic values were unfamiliar in his own homeland at the far western edge of the hemisphere, he never strayed far from the social world of individuals who shared his tastes and sensibilities and among whom he could always find hospitality, security, and friendship" (Dunn, 7). "Security" is the most important word there,[8] as an indicator of political-military power and stability. It is easy to forget, when the lists of sultanates and emirates are dizzying to the eye, that long, stable periods are represented by words we read in a flash like "Ayyubid" or "Aghlabid." From a European perspective, too, the sun never seemed to set on the Abode of Islam. "To the South and the East of the Mediterranean as far as the mind could reach or report could verify, there were Moslems" (Southern 1953, 71). Even while Muslim dominion was receding in Spain, it was steadily advancing into eastern Europe under the Turks. There was never a break in the European sense of besiegement.

Thus European discourse about the world of Islam in the Middle Ages was not, strictly speaking, an imperialist project, nor did it accompany an imperialist project, as did nineteenth-century European discourse on the Orient. It is true that this discourse began at about the same time as the Crusades, but two factors differentiate that territorial aggression from imperialism. For one thing, it was, overall, a political and economic failure. A handful of tiny, disunited, short-lived outposts of European states may be an interesting experiment, or "heavily garrisoned trading post[s]," but they do not constitute imperialism (Daniels 1975, 201). For another, the Crusades were characterized by a lack of interest or competence in cultural

domination. Efforts at conversion of the Muslims were quickly abandoned,
if they were even tried. There was no attempt to impose European language, customs, or culture on the indigenous population. If anything, the
current flowed the other way: the Frankish settlers in "Outremer," as they
called Syria-Palestine, adopted some local customs within a generation, to
the shock of fresh arrivals from Europe (ref. Reinert). The object of the
Crusades "was primarily European, not missionary; not to extend religion
abroad, or even defend it from invasion, but to make its rule effective at
home" (Daniels 1975, 113).

Not even the Reconquista, although it was ultimately successful, quali-
fies as imperialism proper. Despite the fact that by the eleventh century,
Muslims had lived in al-Andalus as long as people of English stock have
lived in America today, and despite the fact that most of the Christians
involved had no actual hereditary claim to the regions taken, the Recon-
quistadores always maintained that they were only taking back what had
originally belonged to them. While the Reconquista may have shown glim-
mers that would later develop into Iberian imperialistic ambition, the
movement was too slow, too politically fragmented, and too piecemeal to
be termed imperialism. Moreover, the reality on the ground and its perception by people who write are two different things. The Christian advance and Muslim retreat was so gradual (lasting at least from 1085 to 1492),
and Christians were so used to seeing themselves as the underdog in this
struggle, that even when Muslim power was seriously depleted in Spain, it
took literary discourse on both sides some time to catch up. By no means
do these harried motions bear resemblance to the age of European imperialism and its "sovereign Western consciousness out of whose unchal-
lenged centrality an Oriental world emerged . . ." (Said, 8).

Said himself is careful to specify that Orientalism began as a discipline
only after the middle of the eighteenth century (42). His thesis exposing
the relationship between imperialism and Orientalism cannot be pinned
willy-nilly onto the very different medieval European discourse about Islam, although some have tried to do so. Were we studying how contemporary texts from the Islamic world discussed medieval Europe, Said's general
analytical approach might be applicable. Was there a tendency in classical
Islamic discourse to "occidentalize" the Europeans because of the material
relationship of this discourse to the realities of empire, particularly in those
areas where Muslims ruled European minorities or initial majorities, as in
Spain, former Byzantine territories, and the Mediterranean islands? (True,

the terms are not precisely reversed, since Islamic rulers never administered as colonies the heartlands of western Europe.) Such questions are outside the scope of this research. If it is medieval European discourse we want to study, we must take Said's starting point—the relationship of discursive knowledge to hegemonic power—and reformulate his questions to suit the study of a discourse produced by a vulnerable, overshadowed part of the world about a politically, militarily, economically, and culturally stronger one.

If they are not imperialistic energies, then, just what are the energies that went into the production of discourse about Islam and specifically the Muslim woman in medieval Europe? What are the material realities which pressed upon European writers and their audiences in this age and shaped the way they represented Islam and its peoples? How did the intensely perceived hegemonic dominance of Islamic civilization produce the European representations of the Muslim woman in high medieval texts?

To address these questions, approaches to Islam in medieval discourse need to be broken down and their connections to material realities examined. For example, at the same time that routine remote rivalry with the realm of Islam gradually metamorphosed into active focused hostility, the western European economy began to emerge from several centuries of subsistence-level stagnation. Trade with the Islamic territories was one factor in this slow economic growth. Islamic countries began importing raw materials, such as lead, silver, and copper, and also continued to import slaves from Europe (McEvedy, 58), while exporting luxury goods, which were nearly the only products cost-efficient enough to transport overland to the as-yet very small and out-of-the-way European market towns. Europe had only silver currency, while gold, with its obvious advantages for economic growth, was the currency of Islamic and Byzantine lands. The influx of money from Islamic lands to cash-poor Europe was needed for the economic development of market towns that would become urban centers and for the consolidation of the ruling aristocracy; it was the gold of renaissance. Reprehensible as every other aspect of Islamic civilization was to the orthodox clerical viewpoint, the material wealth of that civilization could not but be envied. Certain class or socioeconomic groupings thus had conflicting interests and ambivalent attitudes in representing Islam.

On one hand, ecclesiastical discourse needed Crusade propaganda from 1095 through the next century and a half and continued to emit Crusade-inspired material long after the Crusades were effectively over. This type of discourse needed to represent Islam as persecutor, as in Pope Urban's speech, often nostalgically building on the type of the pagan Roman ruler as persecutor in the tradition of the ancient Church Fathers. While the *chansons* are obviously not Church or religious literature, their preservation, "canonization," and survival depended on the involvement of churchmen and Church institutions. Although they may have been popular, many of the *chansons de geste* and certainly *La Chanson de Roland* also enjoyed official sanction, and their outlook is aligned, to some (not entirely stable) degree, with that official sanctifying power.

In this view, the superior power and wealth of Islamic civilization is an affirmation of its corruption and of the moral superiority of the Christian through virtuous poverty. At the same time, such wealth is cause for half-acknowledged envy, resentment, "the hatred of the unprivileged for the privileged" (Daniels 1975, 23). Speaking about the persecution complex of the Christians of al-Andalus, Daniels says:

> An approach to Islam which contributed to the common European tradition grew out of a seed-bed of resentment. The Christians were too many to forget that they had once been the masters. For some individuals the strain of living on the margins between different com-munities was intolerable. The difference could only draw attention to those aspects of Christian life which were flourishing in other parts of Europe, but which were not shared by the dominant Muslim commu-nity . . . These three factors gave Christians their vivid sense of being persecuted, even when nothing could be further from the facts. The Christian who did not attack Islam was sure of being left undisturbed, but he must always know that he was not free to attack. (1975, 31)

On the other hand, aristocratic or aristocratically sponsored texts, such as the cheerfully anticlerical *Aucassin et Nicolette*, might not toe the clerical line on Islam, just as aristocrats such as Frederic II Hoenstaufen flouted papal authority and sometimes made benign contact with real Muslims.

The aristocrats of the First Crusade shared ideological as well as terri-torial goals with the Church; they saw themselves as the instruments of God, who would act through them, his chosen people, to recover his land. Their religious motivations were no less genuine for being combined with a healthy attention to personal and dynastic profit. At the same time, rulers and local lords, both Muslim and Christian, often found it in their interest to make alliance with one another for economic or political gain, something which papal policy vehemently opposed. Such alliances might also open cultural avenues, if the parties involved happened, for example, to employ a Mozarab or Mudejar singer to entertain them while they were at it.

On the level of popular culture, melody, song, and folk stories poured into Europe from and through the Islamic world, carried by pilgrims, minstrels, merchants, and others who ventured in between. The extent and significance of their influence on European culture — or, more specifically, on the romance genre — still has not been adequately researched. The entry of romances from and through Islamic lands to medieval Europe was not a matter of Europeans finding "inspiration" in some remote Islamic fantasy realm of their own creation, as would happen later. Rather, textual materials from literature in Arabic, Persian, Turkish, and other languages of the region imposed and impressed themselves on a Europe that was in a position to receive such impressions without being entirely able to dictate the terms of the exchange. At a higher cultural level, there was grudging respect for the Islamic sciences, not just for their preservation of classical Greek scholarship, but for their obvious practical advances in technology and medicine. Translations from Arabic were a part of Islamic civilization that was valuable for Europe. This was acknowledged indirectly by the volume of translation in the twelfth century, whether sponsored by Church institutions or aristocrats.

On the gender horizon, as in the realm of cultural interaction, change was afoot. The eleventh- and twelfth-century Gregorian moral reform "marks a nadir in ideas of what women could and should be, setting ideals of womanhood which were both impractical and passive" (Stafford, 195). Such ideals co-developed with a curtailment of women's property rights and of opportunities for female regency. This must have been notable in contrast to the abundance of women regents in earlier centuries, especially the late tenth century, when great chunks of western Europe were ruled by female regents. "The tendency, as the Middle Ages progressed, was toward a lessening of the public activity of women, a lower place in ecclesiastical opinion . . ." (Stuard, 9). Coupled with the trend to consolidate aristocratic lines and preserve family property by primogeniture (which generated discontent and frustration among younger sons that was only partially released through the Crusades), such a social role change in Europe helps to explain the lurking menace of female power, represented as politically transgressive, in *Roland* and other texts.

All the different kinds of material Muslim—European relationships I have cited are neither comprehensive nor mutually exclusive; they overlap and mingle in many representations of Islam. Together with the broad outlines of the gender ideology of the times, they produce features in the representation of the Muslim woman that are unique to medieval texts.

## BRAMIMONDE THE TERMAGANT [9]

Roughly between 1100 and the 1400s, the new cognizance of Islam—this awakened curiosity, this kindled resentment—became manifest in the literatures of the area now known as western Europe. The Islamic hosts entered epic and romance, poetry and prose, aristocratic and popular literature; and the Muslim woman stepped into Western imagination.

Bramimonde is among the first, and the most prominent, examples of the figure, since the *chansons de geste* were the basis of much later literature. She is a character with a distinctive voice. It can be bitter: "*E! Sarraguce, cum ies oi desguarneie . . .*" (O Saragossa, today you've been despoiled . . .) (laisse 188). It can be stingingly caustic: "*Mar en irat itant!*" (He needn't go so far!) (196). It can be whining: "*Dolente, si mar fui!*" (I've been doomed to wretchedness!) (201). It can rise shrilly in desperation: "*Aiez nos, Mahume!*" (Give us aid, Mohammed!) (264). But it is ringing, emphatic, unmistakable. It is textually produced and acknowledged: "*A l'altre mot, mult haltement s'escriet . . .*" (She cries out in a piercing voice . . .) (188); "*A voiz s'escrie . . .*" (She screams out shrilly . . .) (264). Her speech has plot repercussions. Bramimonde's lament for Saragossa in laisse 188 is the first mention of the emir; she is the one to introduce, through speech, this important new element in the story. In the scene in which the emir's envoys arrive in Marsile's court to bring news of reinforcements, the overactivity of her voice twice interrupts the message being delivered. The envoys begin by asking the gods to "*[s]alvent le Rei e guardent la Reine!*" (protect the king and keep the queen from harm), at which:

> *Dist Bramimunde: "Or oi mult grant folie:*
> *Cist nostre deu sunt en recreantise:*
> *En Roncesvals malvaises vertuz firentu*
> *Noz chevaliers i unt laissiet cire;*
> *C'est mien seignur en bataille faillirent.*

*Le destre puign ad perdut, n'en ad mie,*
*Si li trenchat li quens Rollanz, li richesu*
*Trestute Espaigne avrat Carles en baillie.*
*Que deviendrai, duluruse, caitiveu*
*Lasse! qu n'ai un hume ki m'ociet!"* (195)

("Such silliness I hear!" says Bramimonde.
"These gods of ours behave like renegades.
At Roncesvals they worked malicious wonders;
they let our chevaliers be massacred,
forsook this lord of mine in the thick of battle.
His right hand's gone—he'll get no help from it—
that rich count Roland cut it off for him.
All Spain will be in Charles' keeping now;
forlorn, aggrieved, what will become of me?
Alas! Will no one here put me to death?")

Finally the envoys can take no more. *"Dame, ne parlez tant!"* (Don't talk so much, my lady) one of them tells her curtly (196). But as soon as the envoys state the message from the emir, Bramimonde butts in again sardonically:

*Dist Bramimunde: "Mar en irat itant!*
*Plus pres d'ici purrez truver les Francs:*
*En ceste tere ad estet ja set anz,*
*Li emperere est ber e cumbatant,*
*Meilz voelt murir que ja fuiet de camp;*
*Suz ciel n'ad rei qu'il prist a un enfant,*
*Carles ne creint home ki seit vivant."* (196)

(Says Bramimonde: "He needn't go so far,
for you can find the Franks much nearer here;
they've sojourned in this country seven years.
The emperor's a noble fighting man;
he'd rather die than flee the battlefield;
to him each king beneath the sky's a child:
King Charles does not fear any man alive.")

Her husband senses the not-so-subtle rebuke in her words: Charles would never flee the battlefield as Marsile did. Marsile, too, tries to silence her and reclaim center stage:

*"Laissez c'ester!" dist Marsilies li reis.*
*Dist as messages: "Seignurs, parlez a mei!"* (197)

("Have done with that!" the king Marsilla says.
He tells the messengers: "Address *me*, lords.")

The dying king struggles to assert his presence from behind his overbearing wife. Finally, Bramimonde is so insensitive in attending, or not attending, to her wounded husband, that she seems to accelerate his death of
grief—"*de doel*"—with her intense vocalization of despair. She is in the
sickroom, but she is watching and reporting the result of Baligant's fight
against Charles; when Marsile hears her shrieking the news of failure and
shame, he gasps his last. Bramimonde is more interested in the significant
action out on the battlefield than in the traditional female role of nurse-
maid to the wounded man in the bed behind her; in a sense, her shrieks
kill him.

Bramimonde is always pushing forward, beginning with *"Atant i vint reïne
Bramimunde . . . ,"* her first appearance. She is frequently "in front of "—
"*dedevant.*" When her husband flees the battlefield and dismounts in the
shade of an olive tree in Saragossa, there she is *"[d]edevant lui,"* in front of
him (187). When Emir Baligant arrives, Bramimonde *"vient curant cuntre lui"*
(went running toward him) (201). She is the first to rush out to speak to
the emir, not on behalf of her husband or his kingdom, but her own unhappy self: *"Dolente, si mar fui! / A hunte, sire, mon seignor ai perdut!"* (201) (I've
been doomed to wretchedness! / I've lost my lord, sire, so disgracefully!).
She is no object of the gaze in this state of forward presence; rather, she is
"*curant,*" running. Moreover, Bramimonde has a gaze of her own (264):
*"Quant ele vit Arrabiz si cunfundre . . ."* (On seeing the disorder of the
Arabs . . .) None of these qualities of Bramimonde is produced as good.
Bramimonde, by acting aggressively and loudly, almost usurping power
from her husband in the court scene with the envoys, fits the type of the
shrew. This is consistent with the view of women in general in the medieval
epic, in which assertive qualities are acceptable only in women who are
Christian saints or martyrs, and thus dissociated from ordinary womanhood. It is also consistent with the tenor of the Gregorian reforms which
span this period. Speaking of women in Anglo-Saxon epics, Jane Chance
says queens without religious sanctity who behaved unconventionally are
marked as immoral or diabolic (53).

One would expect the condemnation to be reversed in this case, since

Bramimonde's behavior is disruptive not to good Christian society, but to *"tort"* (wrong) Muslim society. And it is true that Bramimonde's interruptions contain material that is preparatory for her conversion, such as her increasing admiration for Charles. But does bad behavior in a *"tort"* society add up to ultimate good? Not quite. Pushy Bramimonde can be censured whichever way she is measured. This is due to the strange cohabitation of Christian values and knightly feudal values in the epic.

In the misogynistic quasi-clerical bent of the poem, the only good female is a passive one. We observe the behavior of an exemplary Christian woman in Aude, a completely inert figure whose only action is to die and whose only speech is to cancel her existence: *"Ne place Deu ne ses seinz ne ses angles / Aprés Rollant que jo vive remaigne!"* (268) (May God, his angels, and his saints forbid / that after Roland I remain alive.). *Roland* exegetes usually point to Aude's willed death as an "extension of her fiancé's" (Brault, 317), as a martyrdom "in witness to a principle" (Cooke, 177). However, Roland has a character and a life in the text before his sacrifice. Aude's physical presence is nothing but a negation of herself.

Meanwhile, in terms of values based on the feudal economy, such as shame, honor, vengeance, and loyal vassalage, Bramimonde's speech in front of the envoys is tinged with disloyalty to her lord and husband. It has often been pointed out how similar the Saracens in *La Chanson de Roland* are to the Franks. They have not only the same equipment, but also the same values, the same concepts of shame and honor, the same type of feudal hierarchy. They even speak the same language, French, and understand each other perfectly without interpreters. Marsile gives his glove to his vassal in the same way Charlemagne does; Marsile's nephew takes twelve peers to attack Roland and his twelve comrades; the Saracens worship a trinity just like the Christians', except that it is false. And Bramimonde's first appearance as gift-giver resembles that of many other European women in medieval epic. For example, in Anglo-Saxon literature, the aristocratic woman's "bond with her husband as well as with the warriors of her tribe was expressed symbolically through the giving of treasure" (Chance, 5). The fact that Bramimonde is a Saracen does not change the criteria by which she is measured as a woman from those which would be applied to any Christian European woman in similar circumstances. It is the wrongness, not the difference, of Bramimonde and the Saracens that has been emphasized in *Roland*. As Roland says, *"Paien unt tort e chrestïens un dreit"* (Pagans are wrong and Christians are right) (laisse 79). It doesn't matter if her lord is a *"tort"* Muslim; the feudal codes still hold. Even the other Muslims are better than Bramimonde on the level of feudal values: at least many of them are admired for their military prowess and loyal vassalage. "Turold," if fleetingly, wishes some of the finer knights were Christians.

Thus Bramimonde can be blamed by both overlapping value systems, the one based on Christian dogma and the one based on the late feudal economy. The amalgamation of those values produced not only *La Chanson de Roland* but the First Crusade. This is one point on which they agree.

While she is "forward" in other ways, Bramimonde is not explicitly sexualized. Although her first words are *"Jo vos aim mult, sire"* (I love you dearly, sir), this public sentiment is an extension of Valdabrun's ceremonious declaration of *amitie*, love or friendship, as well as of her husband's alliance with Ganelon, as she indicates: *"Car mult vos priset mi sire e tuit si hume"* (My lord and all his men respect you so). As many medievalists have pointed out, the verb *amer* indicates a diplomatic or political relationship and not an emotional one; it is frequently used in *Roland* in the sense of "to make peace with," "to cease hostilities," "to form alliance with" (Jones, 36). There is scholarly agreement that *Roland* contains almost none of what have come to be called "courtly love" conventions. In the context of Bramimonde's speech, *"aim,"* love, can be understood best as public esteem.

It is odd that Gerard Brault, who cautions that "one must not mistake *amistiez* in v. 622 for anything but a convenient and temporary alliance" (157), goes on to characterize Bramimonde's speech to Ganelon as one of "veiled eroticism," veiled because outright eroticism would tarnish too much a character Turold is reserving to illustrate the theme of conversion (158). This despite the fact that other works of the period—including the version of *Roland* in *The Pseudo-Turpin Chronicle*, "the clumsy handiwork of pious propagandists eager to turn to the Church's advantage the broad appeal of popular, poetic legend" (Short, 1)—find no difficulty in portraying sexually aggressive Muslim women who are later redeemed through conversion. Although Brault affirms the conventional and impersonal nature of Bramimonde's actual words, he continues, "Yet Bramimonde's words become bold and suggestive when situated in their true context, for the voluptuous and amoral Saracen lady is a stock character in epic literature" (157). Not yet. Bramimonde cannot be described in terms of this particular stock character because she is its prototype. Brault's assumptions about Bramimonde demonstrate the retroactive fallacy described at the beginning of this chapter, interpreting the medieval character through the grid of later accretions in the representation of the Muslim woman.

A person is hard put to find textual support for calling Bramimonde "voluptuous." In a text predominantly inhabited by men, Bramimonde's appearance does not stir up erotic desire in the way Aude's, for example, does. Aude's beauty and her death make her the point of intersection of two very strong emotive currents, both closely related to sexual desire.

However, there is contextual basis for attributing to Bramimonde some transgressive sexuality, although not of the scopophilically organized kind that focuses on appearance. In the poem's celebrated parallels between the Muslims and the Christians, Bramimonde is Aude's pagan mirror image. Just as Aude greets the emperor upon his arrival in the city, Bramimonde greets the emir; Aude seems to faint at Charles' feet, while Bramimonde before the emir theatrically parodies that faint. Given this, the emphasis on Aude's virginal quality would imply the opposite quality for Bramimonde. The original audience would likely have understood this hint at Bramimonde's transgressive sexuality; it could have come out in the unwritten parts of the poem's performance, such as tone of voice.[10] Another contextual factor is the medieval heritage of images of pagan women. Because Bramimonde is not Christian, the qualities of earlier not-Christian, *"tort"* women accrue to her. And nearly every *"tort"* woman in medieval texts, from Eve, Jezebel, and Delilah, to Semiramis and Cleopatra, is transgressively sexual.

Still, sexual aggressiveness is a relatively slender part of Bramimonde's character. There is a lack of eroticization of Bramimonde's body. Again, compare her to the inert Aude: Roland's fiancée comes in as *"une bele dame"* (a lovely girl) and dies in a faint at Charlemagne's feet as *"Alde la bel"* (Alde the Beautiful). These two phrases frame her brief appearance in the text like a halo or a mystique (268, 269). The few lines the poem spares to Aude formulaically describe her complexion, her posture, her anatomy, and so provide a scopophilic approach (i.e., an approach organized around visual pleasure):

> *Pert la culor, chet as piez Carlemagne,*
> *Sempres est morte; Deus ait mercit de l'anme!*
> *Franceis barons en plurent si la pleignent.* (268)

*Alde la bel' est a sa fin alee*
*Quidet li reis que el se seit pasmee;*
*Pitet en ad, si'n pluret l'emperere*
*Prent la as mains, si l'en ad relevee;*
*Desur l'espalle ad la teste clinee.* (269)

(Her color gone, she drops at Charles' feet,
is dead—may God have mercy on her soul!
The lords of France will weep and mourn for her.

The end has come for Alde the Beautiful,
although the king believes that she has fainted.
The emperor feels pity for her, weeps,
and takes her by the hands to lift her up;
her head has fallen down upon her shoulder.)

Aude is thus doubly an object of the male gaze, the gaze of Charlemagne and the barons, and that of the jongleur and his audience. But Bramimonde is not given scopophilic treatment, not even when she is baptized in the waters at Aix (laisse 290), a scene which could easily have lent itself to the pleasure of the look. Bramimonde is no Flaubertian Salammbo. Unfetishized, not the object of intense sexual attention, she moves briskly from action to action. There is no mysterious revealing or titillating unveiling when Bramimonde enters; the possibility for scopophilic pleasure is unexploited.

As a "forward" woman, the character of Bramimonde inserts into the poem a subtle challenge to its dominant feudal-Christian ideology. However, the text shunts her aside so much that many first-time readers cannot recall her, while many specialist studies of *Roland* barely mention her. Most *Roland* scholars consider her marginal to the central topics: the conflict between the outnumbered Christians and their pagan ambushers, the contrast between Roland and Oliver's characters, the betrayal and punishment of Ganelon, and the Abrahamic figure of Charlemagne. Some discuss her in terms of Turold's aesthetic talent, crediting Turold with skillfully developing Bramimonde to illustrate the "Theme of Conversion" in the poem, for example: "Thus the surrender of Saragossa by Bramimonde, which represents, at the level of the plot, the culmination of Charlemagne's expedition into Spain, succeeds at the same time in expressing, on a metaphorical level, the idea of spiritual conquest, a simple variation of the Theme of Conversion" (Brault, 313).

Yet Bramimonde is more deeply embedded in the central conflict than is apparent at first glance. She is an active participant in the intense competition between the Franks / Christians and the Saracens / "pagans." Her opening remarks in the gift-giving speech to Ganelon hurl defiance against the icons of Frankish power and indicate her will to participate in what Gilbert and Gubar call "significant action" rather than the idealized feminine role of "contemplative purity." While the other gift-givers merely say that the world in general has no better of the item they are giving, the queen names names:

> *Ben i ad or, matice e jacunes,*
> *E valent mielz que tut l'aveir de Rume.*
> *Vostre emperere si bones n'en out unches.*
> (50)

> (Fine work of jacinths, amethysts, and gold,
> they're worth far more than all the wealth of Rome.
> Your emperor has none so beautiful.)

With this barb, Bramimonde launches the first attack on the Franks in this martial epic. She strikes a blow at the prestige of the empire by disparaging its wealth, in a value system in which wealth and success are inseparable from moral superiority. "Rome" and "emperor" are icons not only of Carolingian power in the historical setting of the story, but more pointedly of Latin Christendom's power in the era spanning the First Crusade. Bramimonde carries the gold of Islam. The association of women and war loot is an old familiar one.[11] The *Roland* text accomplishes a metonymic substitution of Bramimonde for Saracen treasure. That is why not only must Saragossa be conquered, but Bramimonde must be carried back to France, specifically to Charlemagne's capital, Aix. On the way home, Charles stops at Bordeaux to place Roland's horn on the altar of the city's most ancient church, a horn he has filled to the brim with gold. Saragossa, Bramimonde, military victory, and gold are linked together in the same laisse:

> *Passet la noit, si apert li clers jurz.*
> *De Sarraguce Carles guarnist les turs,*
> *Mil chevaliers i laissat puigneürs;*
> *Guardent la vile ad oes l'Empereur.*

*Muntet li Reis e si hume trestuit,*
*E Bramimunde, qu'il meinet en sa prisun;*
*Mais n'ad talent li facet se bien nun.*
*Repairiet sunt a joie e a baldur.*
*Passent Nerbune par force e par vigur*
*Vient a Burdele la citet de valur:*
*Desur l'alter seint Sevrin le barun*
*Met l'olifant plein d'or e de manguns:*
*Li pelerin le veient ki la vunt.* (267)

(The night goes by, the light of day appears.
King Charles has manned the Saragossan towers.
He stationed there a thousand fighting knights;
they occupy the town for the emperor.
The king mounts up, along with all his men
and Bramimonde—he takes her as his captive.
He only plans to do what's good for her.
They head for home, rejoicing and triumphant.
With lively force they take Nerbonne in passing
and reach Bordeaux, the city of [renown].
On the altar of the noble Saint Seurin
he sets the horn, brimful of gold mangons:
the pilgrims going there can see it still.)

With this, Charles has parried Bramimonde's initial blow at his personal
and imperial wealth. Success, wealth, power, and *"dreit"* are zero-sum quantities in the outlook of *Roland.* The gold was on the Muslim side at the beginning of the conflict; at the end, it appears on the Christian side, Bramimonde having acted as the transferring agent. What is more, with this
touch the poet vouches for the authenticity and legitimate descent of the
poem. Anyone can go and see the gold and relics at Bordeaux, he claims.
The three centuries separating Charlemagne from the First Crusade thus
drop away, and the latter Franks can find support for their crusading enterprise in the example of the earlier Franks as perceived by their heirs.

For this descent of the poem to be legitimate, both the gold and Bramimonde must be cleaned of the taint of "paganism," or Islam, with which
they are initially associated. Before she can be incorporated into the heartland of Europe, Bramimonde must be emptied of her Saracen content. In
her case, this means not only changing her name for a Christian one, but

also erasing all the facets of her character that have been developed through the poem thus far. Bramimonde must be converted by the end of the poem, not only to Christianity, but to Christian, or Aldian, femininity. Her presumption in jumping into the fray of male action is rebuked by the forcing of feminine passivity on her.

This surrender is accomplished not only in the content but also in the form of the text. Her surrender of the towers in laisse 265 is also the surrendering of her character's voice in the poem; this is the first laisse in which Bramimonde is spoken of and does not speak. Up until this point, Bramimonde has spoken every single time her name has been mentioned in a laisse (50, 187, 188, 195, 196, 201, 264). She has also usually been the subject of the main clause of the sentence, as in 187: "*Devandat lui sa muiller Bramimunde / Pluret e criet . . .*" (In front of him his woman, Bramimonde, / is sobbing, wailing . . .); and 195: "*Dist Bramimunde . . .*" (Says Bramimonde . . .). By contrast, in the surrender verses, which approach the scene from the point of view of Charlemagne, Bramimonde is part of a conjunctive clause: "*Fiers est li reis a la barbe canue, / E Bramimunde les turs li ad rendues*" (The grizzle-bearded king is filled with pride, for Bramimonde has given him the towers) (265).

Making her surrender in laisse 265 more dramatic, the preceding laisse raises Bramimonde to the highest point possible in the narrative, physically, by placing her in the tower, and in terms of narrative, by allowing a rare, brief convergence of the narrative point of view with a woman's point of view. "The rout of Baligant's army is first narrated as if seen by a spectator on the battlefield itself (laisses 262–263), then, as the remnants of the Saracen horde, shrouded in a sinister cloud of dust (v. 3633), approach the gates of Saragossa, the point of view changes—this shift is marked by the phrase *d'ici qu'en Sarraguce* in v. 3635—to become that of Bramimonde" (Brault, 311).

The queen gives up her vantage point on the towers whence she had surveyed the battleground. Her uncharacteristic silence and passivity, which continue for the remainder of the poem, begin here: "*En France dulce iert menee caitive / Ço voelt li reis, par amur cunvertisset*" (She is to be led captive to sweet France. / The king desires that she recant through love) (266). Taken under guard to convert in France, Bramimonde, queen now only of passive grammatical constructions, makes no more speeches. (Again, it is difficult to accept the cognate-derived translation "love" for *amur* here; it is more likely that *amur* in this context is related to the political / diplomatic meaning of "peacefully") (Jones, 36).

The *Roland* lacks the sophistication to imagine an enemy that is truly different, let alone to exoticize that difference, to make alluring what is strange. In all the laisses that describe the Saracens—their physical appearances, their actions and deeds and world—there is not a single exotic object, prop, or phrase, not a single curved sword hilt, snowy white turban, or cry of "Amaun!" Perhaps the only sight in the poem that would qualify as exotic is the black army which enters the fray just after Roland has sounded his horn:

> *Quant Rollant veit la contredite gent*
> *Ki plus sunt neirs que n'en est arrement,*
> *Ne n'unt de blanc ne mais que sul les denz,*
> *Ço dist li quens: "Or sai jo veirement*
> *Que hoi murrum, par le mien escient."* (144)

(As soon as Roland sees this outlaw race,
whose members all are blacker than is ink
and have no white about them, save their teeth,
the count says: "Now I'm absolutely sure,
beyond a doubt, that we shall die today.")

Difference is monstrous; it brings death. The sight of real, unerasable difference, face to face, is unbearable. The idea that strangeness and unfamiliarity can exude an allure—the idea of the exotic—is unthinkable in this context.

Bramimonde is doubly strange, by creed and by gender, and doubly unbearable for the dominant ideology of the poem, more so because of the material advantage of "Islam" that was manifest in European political life and perceived in European writings. She has to be properly feminized for the story to be closed. Only when Bramimonde has been converted to Christianity and to femininity is the battle really over. Christened and quieted, she is renamed Julienne.[12] Yet even after she has been "julienned," she materializes as Bramimonde once again, in the last laisse. After the whole course of the poem, Charles is disturbed to realize that yet more unconverted pagans plague the borders of his world.

> *Quant l'emperere ad faite sa justise,*
> *E esclargiee est la sue grant ire,*
> *En Bramimunde ad chrestientet mise,*
> *Passet li jurz, la noit est aserie,*

*Li Reis se culchet en sa cambre voltice.*
*Seinz Gabriel de part Deu li vint dire;*
*"Carles, sumun les oz de tun emperie,*
*par force iras en la tere de Bire,*
*Rei Vivïen si succrras en Imphe*
*A la citet que paien unt asise.*
*Li chrestïen te recleiment e creint."*
*Li Emperere n'i volsist aler mie:*
*"Deus!" dist li Reis, "si penuse est ma vie!"*
*Pluret des oilz, sa barbe blanch tiret.*
*Ci falt la Geste que Turoldus declinet.* (291)

(The emperor, on meting out his justice
and satisfying his enormous rage,
led Bramimonde to Christianity.
The day goes by, and night comes quietly:
the king has lain down in his vaulted chamber.
Saint Gabriel came down from God to say:
"Call up the armies of your empire, Charles,
for you are to invade the land of Bire
and there assist King Vivien at Imphe,
the city which the pagans have besieged;
the Christians there call out and cry for you."
The emperor had no desire to go:
the king cries "God, how tiring is my life!"
His eyes shed tears, he tugs at his white beard.
The story that Turoldus tells ends here.)

The Frankish emperor occupies a telling space in Bramimonde's opening speech: she has mentioned him in five of her seven speeches. Now, on
the opposite side, Bramimonde occupies the penultimate spot in the emperor's closing thoughts. This laisse is often cited as an indication of "Turold's" ingenuity (e.g., Brault, 336–337) because with it he brings the story
back to its beginning; he produces the metaphysical cause of Charles'
egress, thus making the narrative circle perfect and circumscribing Bramimonde within it.

　　Yet after the reverberations from the last laisse have died down and the
poem is over, the old Saracen Bramimonde overshadows her pale Christian
successor. It was a sudden silencing that wrenched out the old Brami-

monde, cut her vocal cords mid-shriek, and substituted for her a flat, un-developed Julienne. This woman's conversion, her being Julienne, is crucial to "Turold's" meaning—yet in the very last laisse, just before Charles' divine dream, she is referred to again as Bramimonde. The poet is not in full possession of Bramimonde's meaning; he has difficulty making her "Julien-nicity" stick. The "Theme of Conversion" backfires. It is the bad Brami-monde, the "*tort*" Bramimonde, whom the poem has convincingly brought to life and cannot seem to kill. Bramimonde is simply a more successful cre-ation than Julienne. Termagant Bramimonde's vituperations echo in the ear afterward. This jarring quality of Bramimonde remains to bother the edges of *La Chanson de Roland* and undermine the perfect circularity of its logic.

## THE LIKES OF BRAMIMONDE

The overbearing Muslim noblewoman who converts and leaves her coun-try to enter a Christian European society appears over and over in medieval texts. The Anglo-Norman cleric Orderic Vital invents a Saracen princess when he tells the story of Bohemond's Eastern imprisonment in his *Histo-ria Ecclesiastica* (1130–1135); she falls in love with the prisoner, converts, and follows him to France. Orderic is the first to introduce what F. W. Warren calls "the story of the enamoured Moslem princess," whose essential ele-ments are "the release of a prisoner by the daughter of his captor; her con-version to his faith; her return with him to his native land" (346). To which we may add, the woman's active pursuit or wooing of the man and the conflict with her father which this precipitates. This character type, called a "wanton queen" in some romances, has great rank and power in her own country, but leaves it for a lower ranking, less powerful position as a Chris-tian wife. Despite that, the lasting contribution, the collective impact, of these representations is the initial character of the termagant.

Orderic's story is this: the Frankish crusader Bohemond is captured by the Turkish Emir and imprisoned with other Frenchmen. The Emir's daughter, Melaz, visits them in the dungeon, avidly discusses compara-tive religion, and befriends them. Two years later, the Emir is at war with his brother. Melaz lets the prisoners out to help her father on the battle-field. When they return to their prison as promised, she incites them to seize the citadel, which "held an immense treasure" (Warren, 341). Her father returns and upbraids Melaz, who announces her Christianity. Melaz proceeds to "arrest all the Moslems in the palace, garrison it with the

French and usurp the power" (342). The Emir gives in, promises safe passage to Antioch for the Franks, gives Melaz permission to marry Bohemond, and even joins his daughter in Christianity. After the Christians have been escorted to Antioch by its king, Bohemond convinces Melaz to accept his cousin Roger as husband in his stead. Thus with peace and harmony all around, "in the midst of universal plaudits the wedding took place" (343).

Warren traces some elements of this story, minus conversion, all the way back to Seneca, but maintains that Orderic knew nothing of this source. Orderic's source, via pilgrim or knight, is the *Thousand and One Nights*, which contains several stories that have all these elements—except, of course, the conversion is to Islam (Warren, 348; Metlitzki, 165). Melaz is Orderic's invention (her name comes from a Greek word meaning "swarthy"), whereas the other characters, as well as the bare facts of Bohemond's imprisonment and his captor's skirmish with a neighboring Muslim ruler, are historical (Warren, 348–349; Metlitzki, 162). Orderic, as a churchman, involves Tancred in Bohemond's rescue "to convey the impression of Christian unity," when actually the king of Antioch did not even contribute to Bohemond's ransom (Metlitzki, 165). Nor did the historical Bohemond keep his promise of peace; upon release he promptly attacked Aleppo.

Josian is another Saracen princess who converts for love of a Christian knight and follows him to England as his wife in the Middle English *Sir Bevis of Hampton* (1300), a romance so popular it "acquired a circulation from Ireland to the Urals" (Bolton, 78). Once again the Muslim princess "characteristically pursues her own ends with cool deliberation" (Metlitzki, 168). The beautiful Josian, white as "snow on red blood," enters unbidden into Bevis' chamber, cures him with her medical arts "so well taught" (Ellis, 243), throws her arms around his neck, and otherwise makes her desire obvious. It is Josian who dresses him for battle and gives him the magnificent sword named Morglay and the famous steed named Arundel. After the battle, she brings him into her own chamber, wines and dines him, and announces to him that she wants "Thy body in thy shirt all naked" more than "all the good that Mahoun maked" (251). Her promise of conversion is a desperate last attempt to overcome Bevis' virtuous objections to her wanton proposition, and it works. Markedly contrasted to this is her utter passivity in the conversion scene, in which she speaks no words and submits "white as any swan" to the submerging by the bishop, who is Bevis' paternal uncle (264).

In *The Romance of the Sowdone of Babylon*[13] *and of Ferumbras his Sone who con-querede Rome* (early 1400s), the Sultan's daughter Floripas converts, heaps abuse on her father and his religion (besides murdering several Muslims), then marries a Christian knight who had been her father's prisoner, and de-fects to his land. In this popular second-rate romance, the Sultan dotes on Floripas ("My doghtir dere, that arte so free"), listens to her counsel, for-gives her for smashing the jailer's skull with a key-clog, and entrusts her with his valuable Christian prisoners (l. 1615). The rather fierce Floripas pushes her hapless old duenna, who would not let her feed the prisoners, out a window to be dashed against the rocks, preaching "who so wole not helpe a man at nede / On evel deth mote he dye!" (ll. 1581–1582). Floripas keeps the prisoners in her bedchamber, where she forces a proposal of mar-riage (mitigated by her promise to convert) on Sir Guy, whose options are understandably limited. Having extracted Guy's promise, celebrated by kissing and merrymaking among all the prisoners in her chamber, Floripas unleashes the Christians against the well-stocked palace; they seize it and throw her father out. Before the battle is pitched the next morning, wanton Floripas bids all the Christian knights "take your sporte" (l. 2087) that eve-ning with her fair maidens, who, even in "Babylone," are "white as swan" (l. 2749). During the blockade of the castle, Floripas relieves the Christian knights' hunger with her magic girdle. When they run out of projectiles, she gives them her father's silver and gold to throw, upon which the Sultan, afraid for his treasure, stops the attack.

After many tedious plot twists, Charlemagne arrives and saves the day. Floripas presents him with holy relics from Rome, won by the Saracens in previous battles. The Sultan is given an opportunity to convert—although his daughter hollers for his immediate execution—but he spits in the bap-tismal font and gets the axe. Floripas is then baptized. Not surprisingly, all direct speech by Floripas stops at this point; the baptism of this erstwhile very busy and outspoken woman is conducted in one short phrase in the passive: "Dame Florip was Baptysed than" (l. 3191), and that is her last men-tion. Just rewards are distributed all around by Charles:

Thus Charles conquered Laban
The Soedone of Babyloyne
That riche Rome stroyed and wan
And alle the brode londe of Spayn.
(ll. 3259–3262; p. 93)

and the story is closed with Charles-come-lately in the spotlight and Floripas nowhere to be seen.

Unlike Bramimonde, Josian and Floripas are sexy minxes, no mistake. So are numerous other "wanton" Muslim queens and princesses in the *chansons* and romances. The transgressive quality which is expressed as shrewish loquaciousness in Bramimonde manifests itself in sexual looseness with later Muslim heroines. But they are not merely passively seductive; they are active seducers. These Muslim princesses initiate much action in numerous *chansons de geste* and romances (Daniels 1984, 79; Warren, 357). They are often knowledgeable in the medical arts, with a hint of magic. Thus their sexual confidence is often linked to superior scientific, technical, and supernatural knowledge. It is an active sexual quality rather than one which would render them objects of the gaze.

In medieval texts, the sexuality of Muslim women is not a state of objectification for male pleasure to which they are condemned by a severe, prohibitive religion, as eighteenth-century views of Islam will represent. Here the Muslim woman's sexuality is an indication of her outrageous liberty and a part of the permissive, orgiastic morality which medieval Church polemicists saw in Islam[14] and fussed about as a cause of much Christian renegadism (Daniels 1984, 70). Meanwhile the loose sexual mores of these Muslim women are not all that different from those of courtly European women: the preoccupations of the religious line of thought do not make the whole picture. But as far as the secular voice in medieval literature is concerned, there is little attempt to represent the actual manners and customs of other peoples; all the dalliances are based on high medieval European conventions of amour, *fin* and not so *fin*. "The great knights and ladies, both Saracen and Christian, behave according to the poet's fancy, but behave alike" (Daniels 1984, 78).

There is one remarkable footnote to Floripas in *The Sowdone*: the giantess "Barrok, the bolde," is the only other named Muslim woman in the story. This superhuman "dame" appears and is dispatched within all of sixteen lines, but not before she takes her toll. She is the wife of the tollman Alagolfre, who is killed for refusing to let the Christian knights across the bridge. Barrok then rages forth, smiting all whom she strikes with her scythe "like a develle of helle" (l. 2948) and doing much damage to the Christians until King Charles bashes her brains out of her head and the "cursed fende fille down dede" (l. 2952). "Many a man hade she there slayn, / Might she never aftyr ete more brede!" the next lines exclaim. She

is mentioned again briefly after the Saracens have been vanquished, when
her two giant infants are found by a Christian knight. Charles is delighted
and christens them Roland and Oliver, anticipating the accrual of their
fighting strength to his cause—they are already a strapping four feet tall at
seven months. But they refuse all food, wanting only their "dame's" milk;
this adds, in retrospect, a kind of desperate pathos to Barrok's earlier vi-
ciousness. Finally, "Thay deyden for defaute of here dam" (l. 3036). Here is
one of the few Muslim women in medieval texts who is not noble or royal.
She shares, however, Floripas' iron gut for murder and mayhem and a certain fierce quality. Other Muslim women tower above the Christians in
aristocratic stature; deprived of that type of power, this lower class Muslim woman is still represented as a formidable challenge. She is a kind of
Grendl's mother who, despite the inevitability of her destruction, manages
to leave behind a striking picture of the enemy superpower of Islam in female form.[15]

One issue in the "converts, marries, and defects" theme—though not
the only one, and maybe not the one that explains the most—is obviously
the traffic in women as a function of the power struggle between men. The
sultans and emirs, fathers and husbands of the women who convert are typically portrayed as inept rulers, warriors, and strategists despite their authority over vast realms. That their daughters or wives betray them and get
into bed with Christians expresses a will to challenge Islamic power, using
women as accoutrements. This is a variation on the "master-plan" of a medieval usurper: "murder the king, get the gold-hoard, marry the widow.
Since the widow usually sat on the gold the two went together" (Stafford,
50). That the commodity value of Muslim women is so great, usually
greater than that of whatever Christian women are in the texts, and that
they are so prized as ornaments, is in striking contrast to the representation
of Muslim women in the eighteenth and nineteenth centuries, when they
are more pathetic than prized.

Melaz, Josian, and Floripas do not just marry, but physically change
countries. They will live and reproduce in Europe, will gift their commodity value to Europe, like women who "passed from court to court as formal gifts to seal peace" (Stafford, 46). As the vessels through which king-
ship, property, and inheritance are passed, these royal princesses transfer the wealth of Islam into European hands through their marriages. It is

reasonable to predict that even though no mention is made of marrying Bramimonde, Charles will probably soon gift her to a baron he wishes to reward, as in fact happens in other versions or continuations of the *geste*. Such a royal widow could not possibly stay on the shelf for long (Stafford, 50).

Such cross-civilizational transfer is perhaps the ultimate expression of the roles of the noble lady as gift-giver and the royal foreign bride as peacemaker, and it points to the ambivalence of those roles. "Women were less rooted in the soil than men; they brought new influences from distant parts and established bonds between men . . . ," but these multiculturalism workshops were not quite welcomed with open arms (Southern 1953, 76). A foreign bride was a constant reminder of the war and tensions she had been married to settle; if it was her family that had suffered defeat, she could become an agent of vengeance (Stafford, 45). The romances (especially *Bevis*) stress the complete elimination of their Muslim princess's filial feelings toward her defeated father, as if to stave off any possible future disturbances from her presence in the bosom of Europe.

The rebellion against the father led by the daughter in each of these stories might also be a "way of talking about developments in Christian society and concomitant discontents in the Christian West, and especially in its overcrowded privileged class" (Daniels 1984, 92). From this angle, the main accomplishment of the motif of the "enamoured Muslim princess"—or better, the "transformed termagant"—is the disintegration of a ruling family and the encroachment of a new family on its ancient privileges. Perhaps the theme is a reflection of inchoate social transformations and economic developments in high medieval Europe.

All of these representations insist that the women are not forced, but come of their own accord—"*par amur*"—to the Christian side. These heroines do not act for personal liberation. (In fact, they give up a great deal of personal status and liberty by defecting.) They do not even change sides because of the greater power of the Christians: they usually express the desire to convert while the Christians are still underdogs and the odds against them seem great. That the women simply see the innate truth, "*dreit*-ness," of the Christian side indicates how powerful was the appeal of the ideal of world harmony and universal order under the homogenizing leadership of Western Christendom.

Orderic's *Historia* is dated at 1130–1135. The preserved *chansons* about the legend of William of Orange were composed in the 1130s and 1140s (Passage, 281). *La Prise d'Orange*, completed before 1200, modifies the "enamoured Moslem princess" theme by bringing the hero to her land, Orange,[16] not as captive but in disguise. The Christian this time is already in love from afar with the Muslim queen Orable and comes seeking her, but is then discovered and captured. Orable, who is wife of the Saracen king of Orange, visits him in jail and promises to free him and his friends if he will marry her: she will also convert (thus rendering her marriage to Tibalt null). Orable further urges William to seize the tower and depose her husband. He agrees; the plan is carried out; when they marry, she gives William Orange as her dowry.

Orable "possesses Melaz's prudence and wise determination" (Warren, 350); Wolfram von Eschenbach expands on this trait in *Willehalm*, his contribution to the William material (ca. 1221), where Arabel-Gyburc becomes ideal woman. This unfinished story tells how Gyburc's father, King Terramer, and her ex-husband, King Tibalt, pursue her and William to Orange and wage costly war to get her back. All William's kin and the king of France besides are enlisted against the monumental Saracen host. Gyburc dons armor and sword to fend off her father's attack on her husband's estate, provides the proper sexual comforts to her returned husband, and advises her maidens on the best feminine comportment. She graciously entertains her husband's people and even preaches to his war council on the finer points of Christian chivalric behavior, urging mercy toward the Saracens should they be captured. Her love of Willehalm leads her to divine love, the supreme goal of all Wolfram's characters, and so sanctifies her that Wolfram invokes her in prayer as a saint.

By Wolfram's day, the crusaders' black-and-white division of the world into Christians versus Saracens had been modified. The Mongol invasions in the thirteenth century made Europeans realize that there was a pagan world beyond Islam. In Wolfram's *Parzival* (1197–1210), the hero's father Gahmuret can earn his fame fighting for the Caliph of Baghdad and keep the sympathy of the poem's audience; this could never have happened in the world of *The Song of Roland*.

The twelfth century saw a flood of translations from Arabic into Latin, translations which expanded the field of European vision. Wolfram's own fanciful claim that he got the Grail story from "Kyot," who had translated it from the "heathen writing" of a half-heathen scholar "Flegetanis" (possibly al-Farghani) of Toledo (stanza 453), has inspired much unresolved speculation. At least it points to an awareness that much popular romance material came from Eastern sources. In any case, crusading hostility against the Islamic "infidel" had crested and calmed since Urban's galvanizing appeal at Clermont in 1095. Christians and Muslims had settled into a more nuanced range of relationships.

This is reflected in Wolfram's work. Instead of a dogmatic division of the world into *"tort"* and *"dreit,"* Wolfram, however muddled his information may be about the world outside Europe, maintains that certain concepts, such as *"triuwe,"* steadfast devotion (Gibbs, 65), operate on a basic human level common to all peoples. Certainly these concepts are derived and universalized from European court culture and from Christianity, but they soften the rigidity of the Christian-Muslim divide. In *Willehalm*, for instance, the poet always maintains that Gyburc's former husband, King Tibalt, is acting out of grief and love when he pursues her, even when he attacks Provence. The Saracen's motives are perfectly understandable on a basic human level.

It is true that in *Parzival* the blackness of the Zazamancians initially makes Gahmuret "ill at ease" (11), and that when the governor's wife kisses him he little relishes it (13). However, Gahmuret's uneasiness pales in comparison to Roland's horror at the sight of the army of black men with nothing white about them but their teeth, an omnivorous, monstrous image. Gahmuret is no provincial paladin but a world traveler in an era when to be cosmopolitan meant knowing the great Muslim centers; times had changed since *La Chanson de Roland*.

Belakane is another Muslim queen whom Wolfram adds to the medieval repertory in *Parzival*. She is "in the midst of a brave defense" of her kingdom when she first appears in the story (stanza 16; Passage, 11). Queen of Zazamanc, she enlists the service of the gallant French knight Gahmuret, with whom she has fallen in love at first sight, and promises marriage and her throne in return. Queen Belakane is both a Moor and black, and Wolfram enjoys joking about her complexion: "If there is anything brighter than daylight—the queen in no way resembled it." But quickly he establishes

that "a woman's manner she did have, and was on other counts worthy of
a knight" (stanza 25; Passage, 14). It is "as though Wolfram wishes to stress
the difference in color from the beginning, precisely to make it clear that it
is not important to Gahmuret" (Gibbs, 88). What is stressed about Belakane is that she has the qualities "universally" admired in a lady: purity,
love, loyalty, suffering; this is what makes Gahmuret fall in love with her.
Belakane's essential qualities make her as worthy of love, and as capable of
suffering for it, as a Christian woman. "Never was there a woman more en-
dowed with charms, and that lady's heart never failed to include in its ret-
inue a worthy company of womanly virtues and true modesty" (stanza 54;
Passage, 31).

There is still the matter of her faith, but her inner qualities are enough
to overcome even that: "Gahmuret reflected how she was a heathen, and yet
never did more womanly loyalty glide into a woman's heart. Her innocence
was a pure baptism . . ." (stanza 29; Passage, 17). This, in a medieval text, is
a remarkable treatment of an unconverted woman. Consider that Belakane
could have been portrayed as sexually aggressive in her pursuit of Gahmuret, since she is the one who falls in love with him and offers herself to
him if he vanquishes her enemies — certainly a forward if not wanton lady.
She is a woman ruler under no male authority, nominal or otherwise. A
woman in such an unconventional position, unsanctified by Christian values, is usually represented in medieval texts as transgressive, immoral, dia-
bolical (Chance, 53). Instead, Wolfram gives her dignity and treats her wooing of Gahmuret with delicacy.

Gyburc's sexuality, too, is an explicit part of her idealized womanhood.
In one remarkable scene that proves Wolfram was one medieval romance
poet who diverged from the "courtly love" tradition of portraying love as
foreign to marriage and sex as outside the bounds of the sacred, Gyburc has
sex with her "*ami*" Willehalm and then, lying naked with him against her
breast, addresses a solemn prayer to God (stanzas 100–102; Passage, 71–
72). An Orderic or a "Turold" could never have pulled that off. Nor is it
likely that they would have found her open mantle before a hall filled with
dinner guests as benign as Wolfram does: "From time to time she allowed
the mantle to sway open a bit, and any eye that glanced beneath it then
caught a glimpse of paradise" (stanza 249; Passage, 145). This, by the way,
is the only reference to Gyburc which is organized to produce scopophilic
pleasure; even the sex scene is not scopophilic; rather, it represents Gyburc

in terms of touch ("In softness the Queen herself was like a very gosling"). At any rate, as much as Charles Passage insists that Wolfram was a devout Christian with "no tinge of heterodoxy" (6) because of approving references to him in clerical texts, this is a decidedly unvirginal "holy lady." Surely from an orthodox point of view there is something not quite kosher, so to speak, about Wolfram's unequivocally laudatory treatment of a woman whose character, in less forgiving hands, could have had many aspersions cast upon it. As a foreign bride who brought war upon her husband's people she could have become resented and suspected, but Wolfram executes a stalwart defense.

Wolfram is equally forgiving toward Belakane's unbaptized state and considers Gahmuret's abandoning her the one blot on his record (Christoph, 42). His departure causes Belakane, with whom we are clearly meant to sympathize—she is compared to a turtle dove on a withered bough, bereaved of her mate—suffering unto death. Although Gahmuret claims in his letter that he left Belakane because she was not a Christian, it is clear that he would not return if she were to become one. In fact, when she reads Gahmuret's parting letter, Belakane indicates her willingness to receive baptism for his sake. "In this, Belakane anticipates Gyburc, who comes to a knowledge of God through Willehalm, and so, by perfect human love . . . comes to know divine Love" (Gibbs, 89). The real reason for Gahmuret's departure is his love of adventure, the same reason for which he hesitates to marry Herzeloyde, Parzival's mother. He cautions her: "If you do not allow me to go jousting, I still know the old trick that I used when I left my wife . . . . When she applied the checkrein to keep me from battle, I forsook a people and a country" (stanzas 96–97; Passage, 55).

Belakane and Herzeloyde have in common "the perfection of their womanhood" (Gibbs, 92), their love of Gahmuret, and also the suffering he has caused them. As women, queens, and wives, then, Wolfram's Christians and Muslims share qualities and experiences which blur differences in race and religion. Moreover, the Muslim is a greater queen, as a ruler in her own right; she has the power to endow Gahmuret with a domain. Gahmuret returns to Europe as the king of Zazamanc, having acquired from a Moorish queen the title, land, and name with which to re-enter the courtly society he had left as a landless younger son. At the end, Belakane is a passive, suffering woman, who only realizes her heart's desire—love, ultimately divine love—through her son Feirfiz (who converts and marries into the Grail family). The initial image of Belakane, that of an independent queen undertaking the military defense of her land with dignity and pursuing the man she desires, has clear affinities with the termagant model but offers a variation on it.

The female focus of *Willehalm* does not easily stay passive. The story begins after Arabel has become Gyburc, whose conversion and perfection of character make her an honorary European, pushing her "Saracenicity" into the background—but not entirely. Although Gyburc has not only converted, but left the native lands over which she was queen to become the wife of a petty local chieftain, Wolfram frequently calls her by her former title, "queen." But "Giburc the Queen" (stanza 108; Passage, 76) is a contradiction in terms, since each half of the name undoes the other. Arabel was a queen; Gyburc is a margrave's wife. Arabel no longer exists, or does she? This resurfacing of her old identity subtly underlines the higher rank and greater power of the Saracen world she has brought into their midst. She may be, then, "Wolfram's most complete demonstration of his ideal, womanhood realized to its utmost limits" (Gibbs, 74), but some of her "ideal" features can be read waywardly rather than simply as evidence of Wolfram's consummate artistry.

For example, Gyburc's much-vaunted quality of Christian poverty may be disguised disgruntlement with the conditions of her present life. She says, "I was a queen, however poor I may now be. In Arabie and at Arabi I walked with a crown upon my head in the presence of princes, until one prince embraced me. For his sake I determined to practice poverty . . ." (stanza 216; Passage, 128). When her husband's father arrives at her doorstep with a host of warriors to be fed, and this just after the castle has been besieged and depleted thanks to their lateness, Gyburc offers to serve them personally—but not without reminding them of her former wealth in the same breath: "And if all Todjerne, Arabie and Arabi were free of heathen and in my service, I would still entrust everything to you. I surrendered those for this poverty of ours" (stanza 262; Passage, 151). Gyburc may be a termagant in disguise.

The *Willehalm* narrative shies away from dogmatism in developing Muslim characters, considering them in terms of chivalric virtues rather than true or false creed, as when Gahmuret speculates on Belakane's heathenness and deliberately turns from it to more important criteria for her worth. This attitude toward interfaith marriage seems to emerge from Wolfram's moves toward cosmopolitanism and universalism, an impulse more typical of early Renaissance than of medieval texts.

A century and a half after Wolfram, the fact of one such marriage was causing major discomfort. In 1346 the Ottoman Sultan Orkhan married the Byzantine Princess Theodora; she went to live with him in the Turkish capital. Their wedding was celebrated with enormous pomp on the European side of the Bosporus, which was still under Byzantine rule. Neither of them changed their religion. The papacy had always been opposed to matches with infidels, but the realities of Ottoman invasions and the need for good economic relations overcame the finer theological scruples; the official hope was that Christendom would benefit and its followers eventually increased by this tactic. Still, the event was hard to digest for the rest of Europe, which did not have the unique relationship that Italy enjoyed with the Ottoman Empire in the fourteenth century. The anxieties about Christian-Muslim miscegenation that underlay medieval culture are expressed in one of Chaucer's narratives.

In *The Canterbury Tales*, the Man of Law tells how the Sultan of Syria falls in love with Constance, daughter of the Emperor of Rome. The Emperor accepts the Sultan's proposal of marriage to Constance because of the Sultan's conversion and promise to convert his subjects. This prospect angers the Sultan's mother, a "welle of vices," who plots with her courtiers to feign Christianity until she can kill the Sultan at his wedding-day feast:

> "Lordes," she said, "ye knowen everichon,
> How that my sone in point is for to lete
> The hooly lawes of oure Alkaron,
> Yeven by Goddes message Makomete.
> But oon avow to grete God I heete:
> The lyf shall rather out of my body sterte
> Than Makometes lawe out of my herte.
> "What sholde us tyden of this newe lawe
> But thraldom to oure bodies and penance,
> And afterward in helle to be drawe
> For we reneyed Mahoun oure creance?
> But, lordes, wol ye maken assurance,
> As I shal seyn, asstentynge to my loore,
> And I shal make us sauf for everemoore?"
> (ll. 330–343)

The Man of Law, whose priggish self-righteousness has already surfaced
among the company of pilgrims, is inspired at this juncture to tirade, first
against the Sultaness, then against all women:

> O Sowdanesse, roote of iniquitee!
> Virago, thou Semyrame the secounde!
> O serpent under femynynytee,
> Lik to the serpent depe in helle ybounde!
> O feyned womman, al that may confounde
> Vertu and innocence, thurgh thy malice,
> Is bred in thee, as nest of every vice.
> O Sathan, envious syn thilke day
> That thou were chaced from oure heritage,
> Wel knowestow to wommen the olde way.
> Thou madest Eva brynge us in servage;
> Thou wolt fordoon this Cristen mariage.
> Thyn instrument so—weylawey the while—
> Makestow of wommen, whan thou wolt begile.
> (ll. 358–371)

The lineage of the Muslim woman wends through Semiramis, founder of
sensual Babylon, to Eve in her most misogynistic formulation. Like women
in general, she is the preferred instrument of Satan; being Muslim, she has
even more reason to perform his work against Christians. The Sultaness
leads the nobles of Syria into a bloody plot to oust the Christian presence
from the land, the success of which reflects the final failure of the Crusades
(the final political vestiges of the crusader states were a hundred years gone
by Chaucer's day). She has the Sultan and all the Christians, immigrants
and converts, hacked to pieces at the feast, and achieves her ambition to
rule, "For she hirself wolde al the contree lede" (l. 434). However, she
spares the innocent Constance, who is put to sea with food and wealth and
told to wend her way back home alone.

The Sultaness is not mentioned again. When the Emperor of Rome
later hears of the terrible end to his daughter's first marriage, he sends
troops to take revenge on the Syrians; "They brennen, sleen, and brynge
hem to mischance," but the Sultaness does not appear to be touched personally by this general vengeance. Not only does she undergo no conversion, which would transform her Bramimondian shrewishness into accep-

table femininity, but by faking conversion, the Sultaness mocks the whole baptism-into-world-harmony fantasy, the naiveté of which was completely apparent by Chaucer's time. This she does to uphold the "law" of Islam, a word which implies the temporal sway of Islam as much as its spiritual realm. In defending the faith and leading the Muslims, she becomes, by implication, a caliph of sorts.

The Sultaness does not convert and is not recuperated by her meritorious qualities, like Belakane. Given that, the most notable thing about the Sultaness is that she stays: she lives. Chaucer's Man of Law finds the Sultaness of Syria very disturbing and yet cannot finish her off in the narrative, although the English mother-in-law is punished for her similar persecution of Constance. Thus the Sultaness remains a loose end in a tale in which every other end is tightly wrapped up in a moral, in which everyone else gets their just desserts. For all we know, the Sultaness survives this raid to continue "leding" "al the contree."

The Man of Law was anxious about consequences, but a lighter contemplation of love across faiths began even before Wolfram conceived his cosmopolitan ideal. *Floire et Blancheflor*, a French romance ca. 1155–1170, itself of Arabo-Persian origins (Bolton, 78), tells of a Muslim prince and his Christian beloved. Floire's mother figures as a wise queen in the story, and several lesser Muslim women help Floire in his search for Blancheflor, the lovely Christian maiden of noble origins who was raised in his parents' home as a servant, then sent away when Floire's interest in her became apparent. The king to whom Blancheflor is sent does mew her in isolated women's quarters with his other concubines-to-be, in possibly the first prototype of the seraglio or harem in Western material on Islam. Yet this is presented as an exceptional kingly custom, reminiscent of the Tower of Maidens in the biblical story of Esther, rather than associated with a specifically Islamic tradition—after all, Floire's father is a Muslim king too, and he does not enclose his women in such quarters. Moreover, most of the Muslim women in the story are outside this enclosure and appear to lead lives indistinguishable from the lives of ordinary European women. Since the story deals entirely with Muslim characters except for Blancheflor, the terms of self/other are reversed: Muslim is the norm and Christian is the foreign element. At least it is so until the last moment of the denouement, when the fluid terms of this playful romance are aligned with the Church-dominated ideological superstructure of the medieval world, by hook or by crook. And so our erstwhile gentle hero Floire, at the cost of verisimilitude, not only embraces the faith of his bride but, as the new king, beheads, burns, or flays anyone who does not follow suit.

In *Aucassin et Nicolette* (ca. 1200), which has roots similar to those of *Floire et Blancheflor*, the boy is Christian and the girl, with whom he is finally reunited, is Saracen. Aucassin and Nicolette find the pleasures of interreligious love great enough to risk censure from any authority. The boy's love of the Saracen girl makes him an intransigent son who does not fulfill the duties of his social and economic class, *"rien faire de tout ce qu'il aurait du"* (does nothing of all that he should be doing) (Michaut, 123). Here the anticlerical sentiment is voiced explicitly and by the hero himself. When he is told that he risks hellfire by loving Nicolette, a Saracen girl who was bought, baptized, and raised by his father's vassal, and thus triply forbidden by the class barrier, the (residual) Saracen taint, and filial loyalty, he says:

> *En paradis? Qu'ai-je a y faire? Je ne cherche pas a y entrer: mais que j'aie Nicolette, ma très douce amie, que j'aime tant! Car en paradis vont seulement ces espèces de gens que je vais vous dire. Ils y vont, ces vieux prêtres et ces vieux "éclopés et ces manchots," qui, tout le jour et tout la nuit, restent à croppeton devant les autels et dans les vieilles cryptes . . . . C'est en enfer que je veux aller! Car en enfer vont les beaux clércs et les beaux chevaliers . . . . Et la vont les belles dames courtoises, qui ont deux amis ou trois outre leur mari; et la vont l'or et l'argent et les fourrures, le vair et le gris; et la vont harpeurs et jongleurs et ceux qui sont les rois de ce monde . . . .* (Michaut, 125–126)

(In Paradise what have I to do? I care not to enter, but only to have Nicolette, my very sweet friend, whom I love so dearly well. For into Paradise go none but such people as I will tell you of. There go those aged priests, and those old cripples, and the maimed, who all day long and all night cough before the altars, and in the crypts . . . But in Hell I will go. For to Hell go the fair clerks and the fair knights . . . And there go the fair and courteous ladies, who have friends, two or three, together with their wedded lords. And there pass the gold and the silver, the ermine and all rich furs, harpers and minstrels, and the happy of the world. [Mason, 6])

One can see from this that authority figures do not come off well in this romance. The father gives a false promise to allow Aucassin one kiss with Nicolette if he fights for the patrimonial estate. When the father breaks his word, Aucassin flouts feudal convention by releasing his father's archenemy and begging him to attack and bother his father. Aucassin is loyal only to Love, *"qui vainc tout chose"* (which conquers all) (Michaut, 123). This nose-thumbing at the old feudal order is in the rebellious-young-man tradition of courtly love poetry.

We know we are not at Ronceveaux when the hero *"était beau et gracieux et grand et bien fait de jambes, de pieds, de corps et de bras; il avait des cheveux blonds et boucles menu et les yeux vifs et riants . . ."* (Michaut, 123). (Fair he was, and pleasant to look upon, tall and shapely of body in every whit of him. His hair was golden, and curled in little rings about his head; he had grey and dancing eyes . . . [Mason, 2]). He looks exactly like his *ami*, who is the same age and has the golden ringlets, blue laughing eyes, and shapely figure. That we have totally left behind the world of the *chansons de geste* with its knightly ethos is clear when Aucassin rides listlessly into his father's battle, his arms limp by his sides, striking no blow, paying no mind when his lance is taken, intent on neither spoils nor honor but daydreaming about Nicolette. Only when he is captured does he wake up and defend himself, for the sake of seeing her again. When his father imprisons him, the boy moans for Nicolette or death but makes no move to escape. All the heroism in the story is Nicolette's.

The invention of an imagery of feminine heroism is one of the remarkable achievements of this little work. Take the scene in which Nicolette escapes from the cell in which she, meanwhile, has also been imprisoned, and about which she sings (in contrast to Aucassin's passive hopelessness):

> Lack, great pity 'tis to place
> Maid in such an evil place. . . .
> Men have done me foul despite,
> Sealed me in this vaulted room,
> Thrust me to this bitter doom,
> But by God, Our Lady's Son,
> Soon I will from here begone,
> So it be won. (Mason, 5)

She lies one night looking at the moon and listening to a nightingale's plaint—quite traditional images so far (although at this point in history maybe they still have some freshness). Then this enterprising teenager gets up, puts on her best silk mantle, and slips out the window on a rope of tied bedsheets, landing in the garden. She delicately and purposefully "took her skirt in both hands, the one before, and the other behind, and kilted her

lightly against the dew which lay thickly upon the grass, and so passed
through the garden" (Mason, 13) (*Elle relèva ses vetements d'une main par devant et*
*de l'autre par derrière, à cause de la rosee qu'elle voyait abondante sur l'herbe, et descendit a*
*travers le jardin* [Michaut, 127]). What a perfect medieval version of "how to
succeed in a man's world without smudging your makeup!" If ever Anonymous was a woman, surely it must be so here.

Nicolette visits the tower where Aucassin languishes, gives him a lock of
hair through a crevice, and bids him farewell. When guards approach, she
draws the folds of her cloak about her and crouches in between the pillars
until the dangerous moment passes. She climbs a fence and then has to walk
across the moat and scale the side of the castle. No problem: our heroine
carves footholds in its walls with a sharpened stake. (This is the girl against
whose translucent insteps daisies make black bruises.) Undaunted, Nicolette enters the woods—

> Since I die, ah, better then
> Trust the boar than trust to men
> (Mason, 18)

—and engineers a house: "very pretty it was, and very dainty, and well furnished, both outside and in, with a tapestry of flowers and of leaves" (20).
She tests Aucassin's gumption there in the woods, after which she performs
quick surgery on his dislocated shoulder.

Finally, the two of them, reunited, set out to sea to escape Aucassin's father. The lovers are tossed up by a storm in the land of Torelore, where the
king is confined to childbed:

> "I'm a mother," quoth the King
> "When my month is gone at length,
> And I come to health and strength,
> Then shall I hear Mass once more
> As my fathers did before."
> (Mason, 30)

Meantime, the queen is waging war—by pelting the enemy troops with
baked apples and fresh cheese. The lovers live blithely in Torelore for three
years. A Saracen pirate invasion separates them again, but begins their restoration to their rightful places. Aucassin is welcomed as ruler to his country, his father having died during the Torelore sojourn. Nicolette is restored
to her father, who turns out to be the king of Carthage. When he plans a

royal match for her, she flees in disguise and returns to her adoptive land as a minstrel. Conveniently, her master has died; she confides in his (heretofore unmentioned) wife, a sympathetic and loving mother figure. This woman helps Nicolette restore herself to Aucassin. They are married with much song and joy and Nicolette is crowned Countess of Beaucaire.

Nicolette is Saracen, yet she is Christian too. She has been baptized and has known no other religion since early childhood. Yet she is always the girl from a far country, *"de terre étrangère,"* the girl from Carthage, the girl bought from the Saracens (Michaut, 124). Although she is Christian, the joy of her father when she is returned to him is sympathetically related, and religion is not a problem for anyone. She does not need to hurl invectives at his religion, dispossess him of his treasure, or turn him or his kingdom over to Christian lords. It does not matter that he wants her to marry a Saracen; the problem is that he wants her to marry anyone at all, while she loves Aucassin. The Saracen invasion of Torelore is not a cataclysmic devastation but what makes possible the eventual restoration of the lovers to bliss. Orthodox religious dogma matters very little ("Preach me no preachings—" Aucassin to his father [Mason, 10]); those are not the sensibilities this story satisfies.

Nicolette is different but the same. She is *"étrangère,"* but there is no attempt to make an exotic spectacle of her. Physically, she and Aucassin are identical, with matching blond ringlets and blue eyes. So then why does her Saracenicity keep popping up? Is Nicolette simply a European lady with a "Saracen" tag stuck on her? Is Bramimonde based on a Basque queen? Are any of the medieval Saracen characters based on "true models?"

Labeling a character "Saracen" has significance, however transparent or cosmetic the label may seem. Realism is not a formal goal in medieval romance. Somehow it is important that Nicolette is foreign and that she comes from the enemy—and, not just any enemy, but The Enemy. The fact that she is called "Saracen" inserts her into the conventions used for representing Muslims. If Nicolette deviates from those conventions, that too is significant. At the same time, she is deliberately represented as wholesome, normal, quite the girl next door . . . next castle, that is. Perhaps this defiant assertion of two seemingly contradictory conditions is the whole point. Perhaps Nicolette is "Saracen" for the sake of that very same flouting of religious authority that makes Aucassin snub paradise, for the delight of creating a successful quasi-interfaith couple whose triumph is the vanquishing of parental authority and official dogma.

Few of the familiar medieval motifs regarding Muslim women appear in the characterization of Nicolette. Technically, she is certainly a "Forth-Putting Lady," but this element is not developed in the way it is for Josian or Floripas, as a somewhat crude, shocking sexuality. The text makes it appear as the most natural thing in the world for Nicolette to behave in ways which would earn her censure by dominant moral standards. The three years Aucassin and Nicolette lived in the castle of Torelore in "ease and great delight," what were they doing? The question is gracefully dodged. She can climb towers like Bramimonde and throw her arms around her lover like Josian in her bedchamber and still get to keep the halo of Aude.

We cannot get much further from *La Chanson de Roland* in style and substance than *Aucassin et Nicolette* at the other end of the century. *Roland* is a carefully crafted epic poem which has premiere place in the canon of French literature, and on it distinguished scholars have hung their careers. *Aucassin et Nicolette* is a light-hearted "cantefable" mixing together prose and poetry, "which betrays its Arab inspiration in the name of the hero, al-Qasim, as well as in its prosimetric form, characteristic of Arab narrative style" (Metlitzki, 245), and which is not considered a major work in surveys of the period. *Roland* ties up all loose ends under the banner of Charlemagne's empire in the spirit of the First Crusade's aggrandizing mission. *Aucassin et Nicolette* blithely asserts several contradictory things at once. For example, in a poetic section, Aucassin's prison is first described as an underground vault, but later, in prose, it is a castle tower to which Nicolette perilously climbs. The wife of Nicolette's godfather suddenly appears at the end of the story without explanation. These might be considered defects, sloppiness in aesthetic standards. Or they may indicate that the story is being contested by editors between tellings and has been caught in unfinished process—or simply that its pleasures lie elsewhere than in narrative logic, proper form, and aesthetic perfection. In *Roland*, the character of Bramimonde resists the either/or, good/evil determinism which binary logic requires and forms a knot in the text that can help us read against the grain of the poem's dominant discourse. Nicolette, in an entirely different genre, is not a resistant character because there is no binary stratification in the text to resist. The text tosses around binary terms like apple pies, and Nicolette is one factor in its zigzagging treatment of man and woman, Saracen and Christian, enemy and friend.

Christine de Pisan's *Le livre de la cité des dames* (1405) merits brief mention here, although it contains not a single Muslim man or woman. Christine's

is a work of moral didacticism, part of her "ardent campaign to rehabili-
tate her sex in her contemporaries' eyes" (as Warner says in her foreword
to Pisan, xiii). This is an enormous enough task, given the barriers she
faced. Including a Muslim woman, a representative of the most powerful
enemy faced by medieval Christian Europe, in the Who's Who she com-
piles would have undermined its legitimacy.[17] It is enough that the first
woman she lists is not a European but Nicaula, empress of Ethiopia, and
that she includes the Arab queen Zenobia of Palmyra; enough that she re-
deems Semiramis, Circe, and Dido, all pagan prototypes which influence
the representation of the Muslim woman in medieval literature. It is
enough that the Amazons, women at the borders of Europe whose con-
quests straddled Europe and Asia, draw her praise. Christine's unwilling-
ness to add to the Western narrative of the Muslim woman is, at least, a
meaningful abstinence.

RESURFACINGS

Nicolette and Bramimonde show the range and the common features of
medieval European representations of the Muslim woman. The Muslim
woman generated in these texts is higher ranking than the Europeans, men
as well as women. Bramimonde, despite her silencing, remains the highest
ranking woman in *La Chanson de Roland*; the Franks are not portrayed as having any woman of her stature in their lands. Gyburc is the only queen in
sight in Orange, and is represented as certainly a better one than King
Louis' wife. Belakane gives Gahmuret the rank without which he might not
have been able to return to Europe. The "enamoured Moslem princesses"
in Orderic, *Sir Bevis*, and *The Sowdone of Babylone* all rank higher than the
Christians with whom they dally. This holds true for the Sultaness of Syria
and even Nicolette. Her rank is not an empty title, moreover; it generates
a problematic that is not directly acknowledged but simmers underneath
the text. How to explain the "masterful nature" (Warren, 357) of these
women? How to account for the way these characters, once introduced,
lunge forward into the narrative fray? There is something "too much"
about the Muslim women characters produced in these medieval texts, as
if a giantess were lurking or a genie bubbling inside them. The task of these
texts, having created this representation and this problematic, is to reduce
this raw "too-muchness" to manageable proportions.

Since medieval European texts were not in a position to "orientalize" the Orient, to create a system of knowledge about it, to delimit and differentiate it, their tendency is to do just the opposite: to make it the same. If nineteenth-century French and English literature will tend to feminize the entire Orient in relationship to a dominant Europe, representing even its men as effeminate, these texts seem to masculinize even the women of Islam. Instead of distancing, othering, making Oriental, these texts are "same-ing." For one thing, they assume that the Muslims are at least the equals of Europeans. (Some, like Wolfram, go further, as when he daringly calls the Saracen king Terramer "the mightiest man who wore a crown in those times," while King Louis of France is shown as an inept ruler [*Willehalm*, stanza 302, Passage, 172].)

These texts do not produce the Saracens as an entirely different, inferior, exotic species, nor as subhumans[18] who can be dissected, fragmented, and possessed through scopophilic representation. That project is for the literature of Orientalism to undertake in the eighteenth and nineteenth centuries. It is as superpowered superhumans that Muslims must be accounted for in a discourse that does not have the prerogative of scrutiny, the tools of classification and representation, to encompass them. Thus the Muslims are confusedly "normal" (like-European, like-male) people who, however, do all the "*tort*" (wrong) things (e.g., the woman acts "*tort*-ly": she is unfeminine, assertive, belligerent). The logic in epic and romance is either to eradicate the Saracens or to finish their normalization, to "same" them, although this ideological imperative often fails to cohere. Most often, the Saracen men are eradicated and the woman—for there is usually only one Muslim woman in the story—is "samed."

This disquieting female is remade into a Christian and into a woman who fits a dominant medieval conceptualization of the normative feminine. Her excessive speech, her direct discourse are silenced in the narrative; her excessive motion and "forwardness" in the plot are rendered inert. At the same time her character is fitted smoothly into the patriarchal economy by becoming the vessel through which desirable wealth passes into Europe. These texts move steadily toward homogenization, until at the end the Muslim woman can be absorbed into Europe in a way which is simply impossible in nineteenth-century texts. She can be "as one" with her Christian husband, can blend in and be accepted as if she had never been "Saracen" at all.

Except of course that the Saracen residue is never totally erased. The way the Saracen residue resurfaces is the way the figure of the termagant disrupts the smoothness of the text. I have now charted such resurfacings in a generous cross-section of medieval literature.

The need for homogenizing difference is understandable in the *chansons de geste*, which presume a state of cataclysmic conflict between Europeans and a Muslim enemy. But if a regenerative homogeneity is the goal of the romance, then why make the lady-love initially Saracen at all? Why not simply present a "home-grown" medieval romance? One must ask whether exogamy is the root of romance generally, and whether the local roots of medieval romance are inextricable from its foreign sources. Does the romance, a development of the later Middle Ages, have something to do with the quest for marriage partners further and further afield, after the early medieval fluidity of tribes and families had solidified and the Church's broad classification of relationships prohibiting marriage had increased its sway? Was the oriental romance material so popularly absorbed during this period, and did the romance genre flower so quickly, in part because of a readiness and need to explain the presence of the foreign element at the hearth?

That the aristocratic foreign bride could be a destabilizing element in noble households was recognized. And Islamic elements, though they had abided in the heart of Europe since 711, were rediscovered as devastatingly alien when the concept of a European/Christian identity boiled toward the First Crusade mark, and beyond. That romance narratives over and over process a foreign bride to the point at which she can be accommodated in the ancestral home parallels the process by which Islamic cultural material, disturbingly reminiscent of economic, military, even colonial-settler domination, is made admissible in the European imagination. The two processes merge when the foreign female is a Muslim woman.

## Chapter Three

# THE MUSLIM WOMAN
# IN RENAISSANCE TEXTS
## *"Una mujer a la morisca vestida"*

SYCORAX AND ZANTHIA AT THE THRESHOLD

From about the middle of the fourteenth century, the Italian city-states began to flourish. The preceding century of commercial prosperity had increased urbanization, improved travel between cities and communication in general, accelerated social change, and stimulated intellectual growth in ways that produced a new consciousness. What became known as Renaissance soon spread to the rest of Europe. Salient features of this new era most relevant to Western relations with the Islamic world are the beginnings of European exploration and expansion overseas; the start of the Slave Trade;[1] the development of modern nation-states in Europe; and the end of religious ideological unity in Christendom, along with a general decline in the power of the Church. Features most relevant to gender issues in Europe are changes in prescriptive male views of women through the trends of secularization, Reformation, and Counter-Reformation; the embryonic growth of the middle ranks of society with their new sexual division of labor; and the birth of new concepts of individualism and domesticity. Obviously the two sets are not neatly separable.

It is even more difficult to speak of the West as a unit in this era than it was in the Middle Ages. Written discourse about Islam now comes from a

wider variety of sources. There is greater variation in the concrete experiences of European nations vis-à-vis the Muslim world—or that part of the
Muslim world which touched them. However, the primary broad historical trend is the increased power and resources of European nations, concurrent with a very gradual, imperceptible decrease in the power and resources of the Islamic world. Islamic empires in and close to Europe begin
to decline and European states begin to build overseas empires, creating a
shift in the distribution of power between the West and Islam.

The years 1492 and 1699 make a convenient and meaningful frame for
this period. The first, the fall of Grenada to the King and Queen of Castile,
marks the end of independent political existence for Muslims in Spain. The
second, the year of the Treaty of Karlowitz (in which the Ottoman Empire
was forced to relinquish Hungary, Croatia, and Slovenia to the Austrians),
marks the effective end of Ottoman domination in eastern Europe. Between them is another milestone—the 1571 Battle of Lepanto, at which the
Ottoman navy was unexpectedly crushed by a combined European fleet.
However, the era between Grenada and Karlowitz also saw the Battle of Alcazar (1578), at which Turkish viceroy Abdul-Malek defeated troops drawn
from all over Europe. It was not Europe's world yet. Thus the other broad
feature that characterizes these centuries is the uncertainty of the result in
the contest for world resources and power, the fluctuation of the pendulum
between Lepanto and Alcazar, and between a hundred smaller Lepantos
and Alcazars.

Historians, even those who are critical of European hegemony, tend to
exaggerate European ascendancy during this period, looking for the earliest traces of factors that became the foundations of colonialism in the eighteenth and nineteenth centuries. While it is easy to see with the advantage
of hindsight that this period did witness a shift in world power in favor of
Europe, that shift only subtly and gradually registered in the discourse of
Western self-perception, let alone in the rest of the world's appraisal. European nations were just beginning to assert themselves as equals among
the great empires of the world, although ideological superstructures would
never permit them to admit explicitly that they had not perceived themselves as equals before. And if their contact with so-called "primitive" societies in the New World and Australasia generated a sense of European superiority, their increased contacts with the Islamic behemoth certainly did
not yet do so. The Ottoman Empire, the Moghuls in India, the Safavids in
Persia, and others were to varying degrees still vigorous, powerful states,

still regarded themselves as such, and for the most part were still so re- garded by others. The nascent European empires had to use negotiation, compromise, ingenuity, diplomatic bargaining, and ingratiating ambas- sadors (often bearing comically unwieldy gifts as tribute), in addition to military force, to gain their first foothold on the ladder of world power.

For example, the Portuguese, in setting up their string of trading posts along the African and Indian coasts, were too few to impose their author- ity or culture on the populations they encountered. They faced mostly Muslim rulers, hostile and protective of their trade monopolies. "Recog- nizing, where need was, native kings, treating, trading, settling, mingling, and marrying among the native races . . . ," it is difficult to say if they mas- tered or were mastered by their experiences abroad (Abbott, 1:158). The little-mentioned return portion of da Gama's voyage is revealing: having roused the enmity of the Moghul ruler of Calicut, who assembled forces to destroy these upstart intruders into Arabo-Indian trade routes, da Gama and his crew beat a fast retreat "[w]ith the pumps in their hands and the Virgin Mary in their mouths" (Abbott, 1:104), barely making it to the Azores Islands with a loss of two-thirds of their number, including da Gama's brother. Portugal spent the next several years fighting Muslim al- liances for control of the seas.

In the 1530s and 1540s France was a fast ally of Turkey, and at one point submitted to the sojourn of the colorful privateer Khayr al-Din Khidr (known in the West as Barbarossa) with his fleet at Toulon, where he not only required that church bells temporarily suspend their ringing but openly sold Christian slaves recently captured in his victory over Italy's Charles V (Durant, 515, 697). England obsequiously solicited Ottoman fa- vor, perhaps outdoing itself with the 1599 offering of an elaborate organ complete with artificial chirping birds and wooden angels that blew trum- pets at clock-work intervals (Chew, 164). These are not isolated incidents but representative illustrations of the fact that in this phase of expansion Europe was still compelled to acknowledge the sovereignty and integrity of Islamic countries. Perhaps one of the most characteristic and revealing fea- tures of this era is that while Europeans had begun to take slaves systemat- ically to build their own empires, they knew they themselves could still be randomly enslaved by Islamic powers.

So it is difficult to maintain that "the idea of European identity as a superior one in comparison with all the non-European peoples and cul- tures" (Said, 7) is the foremost shaping factor in Western representations of Islam at this early date. For while "with the emergence of colonialist exploits came also the insistence upon the otherness of the other, upon the absolute difference between the dominating and the dominated culture" (Bartels, 2), neither the domination nor the insistence sprang up overnight. Even after European states had in fact, by the end of this period, superseded most of the above-mentioned empires in the race for world resources and power—not to mention in sheer ambition—the non-European world (at least the Islamic parts of it) still had some power and authority to resist. The West did not yet have the power to completely subdue that world, even in its own cultural discourse. An enterprise which requires acknowledgment of other forces in the arena has discursive practices different from those of an enterprise which affects the absolute subjugation of all others.

It is true, as Abena Busia points out, reading Shakespeare's *The Tempest* as colonial metaphor in discussing the representation of the black African woman, that Caliban's mother, Sycorax of Algiers, is deliberately silenced, unvoiced, "constructed as being essentially absent from any locus of dramatic action or power" (86). It is also true that in two other English plays, *The Knight of Malta* (staged 1619) and *The White Devil* (1612), a very vocal black ("blackamoore") woman, named Zanthia in one play and Zanche in the other, picks up a pistol onstage and shoots a European man at the center of the dramatic action. Busia is correct in unearthing prototypes for what was *later* to become the dominant way of representing the African woman. However, at the time, a variety of modes of representing her overlapped and coexisted and mingled. Some of these reflected the new will to conquest in its crudest form, while others reflected a lively awareness of the obstacles to such conquest. At the time, who but a few visionaries would have known that Sycorax, and not Zanthia, was the shape of things to come?

How is the Muslim woman represented in Western literature from the Renaissance to the end of the seventeenth century? What in Western approaches to Islam, as well as Western understanding of gender, now shape the representation of the Muslim woman? This chapter will profile a range of variations rather than make assertions about one unified Western image, for representations of the Muslim woman in this period defy linear charting.

The era contains a Renaissance humanist discursive practice which approaches the Muslim woman without the distancing and displacing mechanisms of imperialist/Orientalist domination—that is, it displays a genuine indiscriminacy between Muslim and Christian women, rather than an artificial dichotomy between the good "us" and bad "them." Second, it contains the seeds of the prototype of the Muslim woman in later colonial literature. A representative example appears in a text from Spain, whose overseas empire had expanded earliest and whose subjugation of its Mus- lim population approximates later efforts by European colonial powers to control Muslim societies: this is Zoraida of the Captive's Tale episode in *Don Quixote*. Muslim women on the Jacobean stage form another cluster; their portrayals combine several tangential traditions, such as that of witch lore, misogynistic discourse, and the discourse on Africa, to produce curi- ous twists on the stock material of the Muslim woman in the context of an expanding, naval-based commercial empire. Finally, the late seventeenth century French stage provides a representation of the Muslim woman that reflects the rigidity of a consolidated absolute monarchy and the moral severity of the Counter-Reformation. However, before addressing this complexity, I will discuss a transitional precursor to Renaissance modes of representing the Muslim woman.

## THE PLATEAU OF INDIFFERENCE

In terms of the Western encounter with the world of Islam, as in much else, the Italian Renaissance opens a rich vein of experiences. Italy, standing be- tween the mountain passes into northern Europe and the trade routes to points East, had always had strong associations with the Byzantine Empire (northern Italy had been part of Byzantium). When that empire was over- come by the Turks and the affiliation of the area turned from Christian to Islamic, political allegiances may have become more complicated, negotia- tions more delicate, but the routes of exchange on the ground (and the sea) remained, despite official ideological animosity. "In Italy . . . every state of any importance sought, at one time or another, the assistance of the Turks in fending off their rivals. . . . the Ottoman Turks may therefore have been accepted as Europeans of a sort . . ." (Rodinson, 35).

This Italian intimacy with the Islamic Other—traditional foe of France, far-off enemy of England, overbearing nemesis of Christian Spain—lends a unique cosmopolitan feeling to Italian Renaissance explorations of iden- tity. It never occurs to Giovanni Boccaccio's Florentine storytellers in *Il De- cameron* (1348–1353) to reflect on the religious or racial difference of Mus- lim characters who crop up in their tales. Pico Della Mirandola in his *De Hominis Dignitate* (1486) has no problem drawing from Arabic ("Chaldean") philosophy to articulate his notion of humanism. Even when the sources of extraction are not that explicit, even when a more orthodox Christian attitude toward Islam is consciously adhered to,[2] the influence of Islamic structures of thought, the experience of Islamic modes of reference, even of fabric, food, music, military technology, and aesthetic objects of Islamic production, permeate Italian consciousness in this era.[3] For example, gold coins, traditionally associated in medieval Western texts with the Islamic world (and commonly used there and in Byzantium), had been introduced to Europe via Florence and Venice in the 1200s, and revolutionized finance.

Italy remained the middleman between Europe and the East until Portugal began importing gold, ivory, and slaves from the west coast of Africa after 1415. A healthy awareness that Italian prosperity depended in some part upon mutually respected trade relations with the Islamic world produced a new conceptualization of the relationship between "Islam" and "the West." And "the West" here is specifically Italy; this new conceptualization fleetingly infiltrates Western discourse in general inasmuch as Italian texts form part of a Western tradition; its residue occasionally turns up in the texts of other European nations.

The striking feature of this new approach to Islam is its sense of confraternity and equality with the Ottomans. Here it must be made clear that the Ottoman Empire remained during most of this period, for Italy as for the rest of Europe, a dominant world power.[4] Beside the seemingly inexorable Ottoman march into eastern Europe, the wars and invasions between various European kingdoms seemed petty scufflings. However, the commercial success of Italy's city-states made them at least the economic partners of the Turks (who nevertheless required tributes and elaborate diplomatic overtures to deign to enter mutually beneficial agreements with the Italians—from the Ottoman point of view, there was no question of equality).

From the Italian perspective, a novel sense of equality was enabled by both material and ideological factors. First, in their prosperity, the Italian city-states did in fact narrow the quality-of-living gap that existed between Europe and Islamic lands, and their financial clout gave them respected positions at the world trade table dominated by Turks, Persians, Moghuls. This equilibrium allowed for an ebb in the traditional European resentment of Islamic power. Second, the rejection of the idea that persons are to be defined solely by communal boundaries in favor of a philosophy of individualism enabled a genuine curiosity about Muslims, who could now be considered as people like any others. It was a short-lived attitude, but one which deserves mention here because it produced a certain plateau in the Western representation of the Muslim woman. Her treatment, in this unique context, fits into neither the medieval nor the seventeenth-century modes.

Just as Italy, in this period, is the middleman between the West and Islam, so Boccaccio is a kind of bridge between the medieval and Renaissance worlds. The seventh story on *The Decameron*'s second day, on the theme "Of those who after being baffled by divers chances have won at last to a joyful issue beyond their hope," relates the adventures of Alatiel, beautiful daughter of the Sultan of Babylon. Sent by ship to her bridegroom, the King of Algarve, she is stranded in Italy and, because of her beauty, is involuntarily recruited as the mistress of one man after another for a total of nine men in four years, all the while managing to hide her identity. She finally gets to return home and marry her intended after all, and make him think she's a virgin, to boot. Pamfilo tells this that the ladies might not desire beauty so much, seeing how many trials Alatiel's superlative beauty caused her.

Elisa tells how the daughter of the King of Tunis falls in love, by reputation, with the Christian Prince Gerbino of Sicily, and he with her (fourth day, fourth story). They exchange tokens. She is promised to the King of Granada; Gerbino pursues the ship on which she sails to her betrothed. His grandfather, King Guglielmo, has promised the King of Tunis safe passage for the ship. When the Saracens guarding the Princess are overtaken by Gerbino, they kill the Princess before his eyes and dump her body overboard. Guglielmo executes Gerbino, "choosing rather to abide without posterity than to be held a faithless king," in a conclusion which abundantly satisfies the day's theme, "Those whose loves have had unhappy ending" (250).

No one converts. No one discusses theology. No one insults their own gods, or anyone else's. Interfaith marriages are not the key to world unification under the banner of Christianity; neither do they have to precipitate or follow cataclysmic struggle between good and evil. One is assumed to be able to identify the geography and the Muslim and Christian identities of the various characters, without its having that much relevance for the story. When the Sultan of Babylon bids his daughter farewell, he commends her to God, "*l'accomando a Dio*" (sentence 9). The word is simply

"*Dio*," the same "*Dio*" that Emily, Pamfilo, and the rest of the company would naturally name—not Tervagent, Mahound, or any foreign-sounding idols.

The values of Muslim and Christian kings are mutually supportive, as King Guglielmo's execution of his grandson shows. Pamfilo assumes the ladies will be able to empathize with Alatiel without Alatiel being required to betray her father or renounce her creed. In the story of the Tunisian princess, in which young lovers rebel against parental figures, the listeners' sympathies are directed toward both lovers, even though the man betrays a king of Europe, a Christian, his grandfather, for the sake of a Muslim woman. She is not made into a seductress for this. There is no sense of Europeans versus non-Europeans, but a nonchalant worldliness which takes for granted the motley of languages, creeds, and races that criss-cross the Mediterranean, having arrived because of common interest at a pragmatic *modus vivendi*. The interest that binds them all together is mercantile.

The second day's ninth story tells of a Genoese woman falsely accused by her husband and sentenced to die. She escapes and, disguised as a man, serves the Sultan of Alexandria until she exposes the man who framed her, recovers her husband, reappropriates her female identity, and returns home rich. The happy denouement is put into motion by a great trading exposition sponsored by the Sultan: a "great assemblage" of "merchants, both Christian and Saracen . . . to which, in order that the merchants and their merchandise might rest secure," the Sultan dispatches his guard, headed by the disguised Genoese woman, "who was by this time well versed in the language of the country." This great assemblage of merchants is precisely the field from which Boccaccio's text, his Italy, his Florentines, and his Muslim characters emerge.

Alatiel is shrewd enough to know her market value. If her beauty causes her problems, she knows that revealing her royal status would make her an even more valuable commodity and rule out hope of a safe homecoming. Although privately strategizing with her ladies, she makes public silence her defensive weapon and manipulates what resources she has until the Mediterranean waters return her home. Even after she returns home and can speak again, her clear sight of women's commodity value is not blurred by sentiment. With cool deliberation, she preserves the life and status she wants for herself and out-maneuvers male commodification of her body by making her husband believe her a virgin. The character delineated resists definition as passive object of male desire. The Princess of Tunisia is not so clear-sighted, but she belongs to a different type, the type of the star-crossed lover. She retains elements of the forward princess, since it is she who first falls in love with Gerbino. The plot is forwarded because she is represented as having spoken her desire for him; word reaches him, and he reciprocates.

The point is, neither Alatiel nor the Tunisian Princess are seen as exotic, foreign, *different* creatures. No assertion of European superiority, a feature of colonialist literature, is apparent. There is a certain indiscriminacy, a lack of proper distinctions, in Boccaccio's representation of Western and Islamic women. Alatiel is beautiful in the same way any of the Florentine ladies could be beautiful, not (looking ahead toward Romanticism, for example) in some dark-eyed "Oriental" way. Even this beauty, which could have lent itself easily to a mode of visual pleasure that highlights and fetishizes her difference, passes quickly as a plot element rather than a scopophilic image. Moreover, it is not necessary to erase the Muslim nature of Alatiel and the Tunisian Princess and have that nature persistently resurface, as in medieval texts. Thus there is no need to change her from an active to a passive woman, or to associate her being Muslim with a transgressive female personality in the first place.

These Muslim ladies are rather less "masterful" than earlier medieval examples. They seem no more exemplars of difference than Lisabetta, Simona, or any of the European women in *The Decameron*'s other stories. Like these, their lives are circumscribed by the gender constraints of a uniformly and interreligiously patriarchal Mediterranean world. Boccaccio's Muslim women do not convey a double Othering—the difference of being Islamic plus the difference of being women. Only sexual difference, which they have in common with his representations of European women, remains. Being a Muslim woman is here a matter of *in*difference. Textually no preference is shown for Muslim or European. Yet these characters remain, simply as women, always within the category of difference—and this inevitably has a subliminal connection to the world of other Others without, and thus to their Muslim-ness, hovering in the background.

In *The Decameron* it is accepted that the Islamic world routinely rubs elbows with the European world. This is not a bad thing or a good thing, it is just *there*, an indifferent matter—for after all the jostling, the two worlds (at least as they meet in the Mediterranean) are not so alien after all. It is not necessary to expend tremendous narrative energy to homogenize Islamic elements or Muslim women because they are already homocentric, having as their common center that great assemblage of goods and people, the Mediterranean marketplace. Patriarchal modes of control are as agreed upon throughout it as are weights and measures; throughout it, women's bodies are as exchangeable as other commodities.

Marguerite D'Angouleme represents no Muslim women in *The Heptam-eron* (1558), a collection modeled on *The Decameron* and concerned with the corruption of the clergy, the jealousy of husbands, and women's strategies for circumventing these and other injustices. She has the occasional soldier returned from war with the Turks or captivity in Tunis (see story 10). She pointedly declares that the truth came from a foreigner, a Turk, about an incident in story 13. The closest she gets to empire or Muslim lands is Candia (off Greece), in a story which begins with a botched colonial-settler enterprise and centers on the resourcefulness of a woman stranded on a desert island, a sort of female Crusoe but without the will to conquest and profit (story 67). Marguerite, like Christine de Pisane, is silent on the matter of the Muslim woman.

MOMENTS OF EQUILIBRIUM: ZENOCRATE
AND THE GLORIOUS ENTERPRISE

Traditional medieval myths of Islam waned or went into latency in this period because the forces producing them (e.g., the Church) had stalled. And the engines (e.g., of modern European colonization) which were to churn out the great Orientalist modes of knowing Islam had not yet begun to rumble; indeed only the first pegs and rivets of this machinery had been soldered. This is a curious lull, then, in which older Western myths of Islam, cut off from their sources, mutate, transform, and seem to float randomly, while emerging new myths are still vague and unsteady.

As for the old hostility, three factors caused it to lose momentum. First, whereas the medieval West seemed to have no other anvil but Islam against which to hammer out its perceptions of itself in the world, the introduction of further elements into the arena mitigated this confrontation. In the thirteenth century, the Mongols arrived on the scene, mowing down Muslim and Christian alike. At first the West believed that these were the long-awaited pro-Christian powers coming to eclipse Islam and unify the world, but that bubble burst quickly. Beside the ferocious Mongols, the erstwhile "pagan" Muslims seemed positively brotherly, and "the original division of the world between Christianity and Islam must have yielded to . . . a greater relativism in ideological vision" (Rodinson, 28). European rulers' realization that the Persians, too, were bitter enemies of the Ottomans added to this relativism.

The second factor which diminished traditional enmity toward the Islamic world was the passing of ideological unity within western Christianity. The third was the waning of Church power in favor of secular protonational rulers. Islam had long been considered a schism, a heresy broken off from Christianity. When such schisms multiplied in the sixteenth century, the Islamic schism no longer seemed such an atrocity; Christian sects were busy accusing each other of many of the offenses that used to be attributed to Islam. Moreover, some humanists injected a current of skepticism in religion altogether. At the same time, stepping into the power vacuum left by the Church, national monarchies, "well on the way toward absolutism," had by the end of the fifteenth century replaced the medieval organization of political life in Europe (Abbott, 1:110). These new polities had a more pragmatic than religious approach to relations with Islamic states.

As for newer attitudes toward Islam, these were beginning to form against the backdrop of European maritime exploration, new-found commercial prosperity, and the growth of several European states into transoceanic empires that could compete with Islamic empires. First Portugal and Spain, then England, the Netherlands, and France, inched their ways along the coasts of other continents in a bid to establish trading outposts and colonies abroad. Most portentously, Europe's detection of a hemisphere hitherto unknown to it meant that the search for gold and glory could circumvent the entrenched Islamic powers; at long last, another source of wealth, another outlet for surplus populations, another focus for reserve energies, ambitions, and desires, and one more vulnerable to them, was available. A quick sketch of the inaugural era of European imperialism will provide some historical context for the changing representation of the Muslim woman.

If Italy negotiated mutually profitable relations with the Ottoman Empire, the Iberian kingdoms attacked their own Muslim frontiers with a fierce will to eradicate the Moors by military "re-"conquest. The final blow was the defeat of the last Muslim kingdom, Grenada, in 1492, the year of the trans-Atlantic voyage that would forever alter the balance of world power. Meanwhile, Portugal had actually captured Ceuta, a Muslim city just across the Strait of Gibraltar (1415). The capture of Ceuta marks a threshold, "a turning-point in human affairs. . . . it was the connecting link between the older crusading movement which sought to win back Jerusalem and the Holy Sepulcher from the infidel, and the modern conception of winning the world for commerce and for Christianity" (Abbott, 1:85).

Under the driving energy of Prince Henry "the Navigator," Portuguese ships pushed down the west coast of Africa, setting up stations to import gold and ivory. By 1446 the first thousand black Africans were brought to Europe as slaves; the systematic import of black Africans for slavery in Europe and the Americas had begun. When da Gama rounded the southernmost point of Africa in 1497, his Portuguese king wasted no time in styling himself "Lord of the Conquest, Navigation, and Commerce of Ethiopia, Arabia, Persia, and China" (Abbott, 1:105). This would have been laughable had it been known to the inhabitants of those lands, but no one laughed when the Portuguese reached the west, or Malabar, the coast of India, and later Indonesia, at last circumventing the resented Turks. Spain conquered great chunks of the newly "discovered" territories and, through forced labor of the indigenous population and imported slave labor from Africa, overshadowed Portugal in the New World enterprise during the sixteenth century. In the meantime, Ferdinand Magellan circumnavigated the globe (1519–1521), allowing Spain to invade the Asian routes thus far monopolized by Portugal among European states. The upper hand in world trade began to circulate from one aspiring European empire to another.

Francis Drake's 1572 plunder of a Spanish New World island made him a hero in England and was hailed as a harbinger of English imperial ascendancy; this was realized in England's defeat of the Spanish Armada in 1588. Queen Elizabeth founded the Levant Company for trade with the Ottoman Empire, followed by the East India Company, establishing the economic backbone of the empire. (It was at this point that the queen rather disingenuously suggested to the Turks that fellow monotheists such as themselves join hands against idolatrous Spanish papists, showing how far ideological relativism had come.) England made overtures to Persia as well, and when in 1596 the cape of Africa was once again rounded, this time in England's name, the English too achieved the coveted back way to the East. Barrier after barrier that had delimited the old world fell away before European enterprise, and the horizons of human endeavor seemed boundless.

Christopher Marlowe's interminable drama *Tamburlaine* (1587–1590) appeared in the context of both the Renaissance humanist straining against the traditional limits on thought and Europe's widening arm of empire. The historical Timur (d. 1405), a Mongol conqueror who swept through Asia, had been "praised in a long series of humanistic histories as a successful ruler whose own cruelty had been a visitation of punishment upon sinners" (Ribner, xxv). The English considered his humbling of the Ottoman Sultan Bayezid, who had reduced much of eastern Europe to vassalage, to be particularly expressive of divine retribution at work. While Marlowe uses the "Scourge of God" idea, the play is a youthful exaltation of a human prowess that in its glorious enterprise defies all boundaries, including those of conventional religion, be it Christian or Islamic. By presenting a drama in which almost all the major characters, both heroes and villains, are Muslim, this text leaves behind medieval literary conventions of the Muslim as the infidel arch-enemy bearing the diametric opposite of every quality found in the Christian heroes.

Marlowe's Tamburlaine is nominally a Muslim, but in spirit a classical pagan in the mold of Ulysses and Achilles—or a Renaissance man in the mold of Faustus. In his burning the "Alcoran" and defying "Mahomet" there is a protest against orthodox religion generally, and Christianity most pointedly. To religious superstition he contrasts "[t]he God that sits in heaven, if any god, / For He is God alone, and none but He" (pt. 2, V.ii.199–200), without specifying this God as Christian in any way (there is no mention of Jesus, cross, Trinity, or any identifiably Christian association). Marlowe uses the freedom to criticize "Mahometan" religion as a cover for criticizing Christianity, and any belief in a personal God who guides the daily lives of people (Ellis-Fermor, 142). If there is any divine spirit, Marlowe strongly implies, it is manifest in the human ambition to rise to sublime heights (Ellis-Fermor, 140). The embrace of a pagan spirit of *virtu* over orthodox Christian pietism places this text in a line of humanistic discourse, starting with Machiavelli, which has a relativist, pragmatic, even realpolitik approach to the relationship between the West and Islam—a discourse which identifies with the party of the devil.

Naturally, the exaltation of human *virtu* is mostly an exaltation of male *virtu*, and the glorious human enterprise leaves women in their traditional social berths. Whether wives, mothers, maids, or concubines, the women in *Tamburlaine* are trophies and accessories to men and rarely budge from rather wooden roles. Zenocrate, daughter of the Sultan of Egypt, is waylaid by Tamburlaine on the way to her intended husband. He decides she must be his empress, and she, absorbed by the indomitable will he exudes, agrees.

Zabina is the empress of the Turkish Sultan Bajazeth, and like him, is completely crushed by the fall from glory they experience at the hands of Tamburlaine. When her husband bashes out his brains rather than suffer ignominious captivity, she, with some delirious ranting, follows him.

Zenocrate and Zabina seem but shadows of their husbands. They even catfight while their husbands take the field (III.iii), parroting the men's rhetoric of conquest and glory. Only after Zenocrate has witnessed some of the human cost of this rhetoric—her husband's slaughter of the Virgins of Damascus; his ravage of that city, her hometown; the suicide of the noble couple Bajazeth and Zabina—does she begin to question it. She says, in one of the few vibrant passages given a woman character:

> Those that are proud of fickle empery
> And place their chiefest good in earthly pomp,
> Behold the Turk and his great emperess!
> Ah, Tamburlaine my love, sweet Tamburlaine,
> That fights for scepters and for slippery crowns,
> Behold the Turk and his great emperess!
> . . . . . . . . . . . . . . . . . . . . . . . . . . . . . .
> Ah, mighty Jove and holy Mahomet,
> Pardon my love! Oh, pardon his contempt
> Of earthly fortune and respect of pity,
> And let not conquest, ruthlessly pursued,
> Be equally against his life incensed
> In this great Turk and hapless emperess!
> And pardon me that was not moved with ruth
> To see them live so long in misery!
> Ah, what may chance to thee, Zenocrate?
> (V.ii.291–308)

But since the overall movement of the play valorizes Tamburlaine's magnificence of spirit even in its amazing cruelty, and since she reverts to passive endorsement of Tamburlaine's ideals, Zenocrate's critique remains a faint remonstrance. It is a piece of conventional piety movingly expressed, rather than a foreshadowing of the truth or a powerful indictment. Olympia (in Part 2) is another loyal wife, whose heroic mettle in executing a family suicide pact (she kills her son, burns his body with that of her soldier husband who has died of war wounds, and prepares to kill herself) is called worthy of Tamburlaine's admiration (III.iv.40). The fortitude with which she tricks her captor into fulfilling her resolve to die is a female reflection of that will to mastery embodied in Tamburlaine; self-annihilation rather than conquest is apparently the only direction it can lead in a woman.

In the context of the great "discoveries" and the imperial enterprises upon which Europeans had embarked in the sixteenth century, *Tamburlaine* is at once a paean to man's will to power and a howl in protest of its limits. As such, Marlowe's play, which enjoyed a popular reception, goads its audience to see Tamburlaine as European man at the threshold of glory, daring the things that had never been dared before. "Give me a map," Tamburlaine declares, "then let me see how much / Is left for me to conquer all the world" (pt. 2, V.iii.123–124). At Damascus, "he boasts that with his sword for pen, he will anew reduce the countries to a map, of which the meridian-line will pass through that city" (Seaton, 164). This is no random metaphor for conquest in the midst of intense controversy among European nations about the Line of Demarcation. Neither is the imagery which clusters around Tamburlaine unrooted in historical conditions, an imagery "brilliant, with the hard, blatant lustre of gold and jewels" (Ellis-Fermor, 153). This is the specific, concentrated form of wealth of sixteenth-century empires, which relied on the transport of precious metals over long routes.

By expressing the condition of modern man through a hero who is Muslim (but also an enemy of Muslims), Marlowe's text signals an absorption into European identity of all that had heretofore been admired in the powerful Islamic nemesis—admired, envied, and cast in negative terms because of ideological inhibitions which the Renaissance lifted. The worldliness, the virility, the Machiavellian qualities of the lion and the fox, for which Islam had earlier been castigated by chroniclers and popes, were now provocatively suggested as the desirable ideals. Those disturbing qualities which had once and would again be projected onto an alien and unequal Islam could be momentarily incorporated into the self. If Europe was preparing to step into the position that until then had belonged to Islamic empires straddling the world, Nemesis could briefly be Mentor. Who better to embody that glorious human endeavor than a Muslim conqueror, since Islam had already soared to where Europe hoped to soar? Marlowe's text is a clapping on the shoulder of the Muslim—brother, peer, colleague in the glorious endeavor.

The Muslim woman, in such a scenario, is not represented as a function of civilizational or Islamic difference. Just as Tamburlaine is represented in human terms rather than in terms of the literary conventions of the Muslim/pagan Other, Zenocrate, Zabina, their maids, Olympia, the Virgins of Damascus, and the Turkish concubines are represented as a function of the simple difference of female gender, and not the complex difference of Islamic Other/female gender. The representation of the Muslim woman here bears traces of what I have termed Boccaccio's "indifference" to the Christian–Muslim divide, in that it does not use that divide as the ultimate marker of meaning. The portrayal of Zenocrate, for instance, employs conventions of the noble maiden in distress, the loyal wife, the good mother, the decorous queen, but no conventional Muslim woman material. "As far as Zenocrate is anything at all she is a virtuous, god-fearing Elizabethan matron . . ." (Ellis-Fermor, 149). Perhaps the most that can be said is that Tamburlaine's acquisition of Zenocrate as she treks across the Islamic heartland in the rather confused geography of the play may parallel the ardent European ambition to intercept coveted Islamic trade routes. In this frame, it comes as no surprise that Zenocrate's beauty is described in terms of commodities that were at the core of global rivalries between empires: "silver tresses," showers of pearls and sapphires, and, specifically, an "ivory" complexion (pt. 1, V.ii). This is in line with the increase of precious mineral imagery in the blazon of the female body in Elizabethan love sonnets. The way patriarchy at home uses the female body parallels the way empire abroad appropriates valuable commodities. What is notable here is that this commodification is entirely a function of the gender differentiation at home; it is very difficult to substantiate any textual use of "Islam" material to complicate the differentiation. This textual practice assumes an equality and interchangeability between Muslim and Western women.

There is virtually no trace of the stock medieval material of the "enamoured Moslem princess" in *Tamburlaine*, the use of which would entail activating Islamic difference as a force. There is no aggressive or errant femininity posited as Muslim which needs to be transformed into seemly Christian femininity. Except for scattered petitions to "sacred Mahomet," a novel form of Islamic invocation, there is precious little in their speeches to differentiate these women as Muslim. Nor is there yet a sign of the Muslim woman, still an emperor's wife more than a slave or concubine, being pushed into an entirely inferior, voiceless difference through the insidious knotting together of colonialist narratives on Islam and femininity. An exhilarated strand of Renaissance humanism in the text of *Tamburlaine* has caused the absorption, the evaporation, of her Islamic Otherness, and has postponed that extreme differentiation which the beginning of European imperialism would accelerate.

BLOND PAGANS AND THE EQUIVOCAL ENTERPRISE

The Muslim woman in medieval texts is represented not as a function of European supremacy over all others, but as a function of Christian resentment of superior Islamic power; she is differentiated as the intimidating and powerful female factor of an intimidating and powerful enemy. When that power differential begins to level off, as it does in fits and starts between the fifteenth and the seventeenth centuries, two things happen to the representation of the Muslim woman in the moments of equilibrium.

In some texts, the level of differentiation itself slides to the point of indiscriminacy between the representation of Muslim women and Western women, and the Muslim woman's textual presence declines or wavers significantly in relation to what it was before. (In late eighteenth- and nineteenth-century texts, the decline will continue further, until the Muslim woman is far inferior to the Western woman in textual presence.) Elsewhere, texts which do activate the Muslim–Christian binary by manipulating the Muslim woman material simultaneously deconstruct that binary and the ideology which produces it. Subversive textual elements, as well as historical contexts, prevent any smooth reading of European supremacy versus Islamic inferiority or evil.

The first case is clear in the example of Zenocrate. Torquato Tasso's *Gerusalemme Liberata*, as we shall see, provides more equivocal examples of the second. While Tasso's epic poem, the expression of a Renaissance humanism more religious than that of Marlowe, reactivates Islamic difference and does not represent the Muslim woman in terms of gender alone, it undermines its own distinctions between Christian and Muslim. It well illustrates how wider changes in notions of gender also yield changes in the representation of the Islamic difference.

Copious discourse on the role of women "blossomed forth about 1500," showing how central a redefinition of gender was in the transition to early modern Europe (Bange, Dresen, and Noel, in Dresen-Coenders, 12). The Renaissance generated a new set of attitudes toward sexuality and gender which generally improved upon the old view of women as dangerous sexual beings, thus opening novel social spaces.

"For the first time in Western history," for example, "men stressed the fact that females should be educated. The Platonic orientation in humanist thought may have spurred them to do so" (Bell, 182). Education was not meant to overturn woman's subordinate domestic role, for its primary purpose was to make her a worthier wife and an abler mother. However, it served to enlarge her influence, at least within the household. Of course, it was mainly aristocratic women who benefited by this trend; the witchhunts can be read in part as an indicator of the extreme fear of the power of poor women in a turbulent century of peasant revolts, religious wars, and plagues. Yet the expectation that upper- and middle-class women be book-learned and eloquent is noteworthy in comparison to medieval ideals which equate women's book-learning with black magic and loquacity with unchastity. Many medieval representations of Muslim women associate them with a learning and loquacity that is suspect; changing Renaissance ideals subdue that suspicion.

The Reform movement, the religious arm of the Renaissance, also ushered in a revision of religious positions on marriage, even among those who did not split from the Church. The misogamy which had typified the Church's approach to family life was now contested by a new philogamy. Reformers' rejection of celibacy as an ideal and their valorization of the marital state enhanced the position of women in the family (at least on the level of ideology). So did the fact that a greater number of texts were being written by married laymen and by women themselves. A pivotal related change was the revaluation of sexuality as a good in itself, separate from procreation. This is obviously a striking departure from medieval Church thought and is connected to Neoplatonism. The novel proliferation of nudes in painting, especially religious painting, shows how sexuality, the senses, and the body were given new value and even sacralized. That such nudity "creates a tension between erotic attraction and religious meaning" and contests Church doctrine is evident from the Church's response: the Council of Trent in 1563 tried to ban nudes in religious paintings, with uneven success (Miles, 203).

The status of courtesans, a new class of refined, educated, and very influential prostitutes openly patronized by aristocrats and monarchs, is another indicator of the revaluation of sexuality. So is the striking new element of sexual display in aristocratic clothing. Loose medieval robes disappeared. The naked leg became acceptable for men—and who could overlook the codpiece, that "phallic exhibition padded into permanent erection" (de Marly, 35)? For women, the beribboned petticoat was suddenly exposed, "bringing glamour and sex appeal to underwear" (Ewing, 26), and hair, previously cowled, capped, or wimpled, could fall long and loose in sensuous disarray on court occasions.

The relative sexual hedonism of aristocrats was not a paradise for women, however. It also allowed the female body, still the locus of what is now a celebrated rather than a condemned eroticism, to be reappropriated in new ways for male sexual pleasure, as in the blazon conceit of the Renaissance love sonnet. Sexual freedom in practical terms meant more (although not absolute) sexual freedom for men. This ethos was partly a response, after all, to the exigencies of aristocratic marriages, which were always political alliances or property exchanges more than romantic attachments, and it offered no alternative to the commodification of women implicit in such arrangements. Further, after the early phase of the Renaissance, a conservative reaction retrenched against some of the general opening toward sexuality.[5] Yet if sexuality gained some positive value in itself, then women, having always been seen from a male perspective as the locus of sexuality in the universe, were bound to improve appreciably in standing. Any reevaluation of sexuality also served to soften the traditional indictment of Islam as sensual and Muslim women as sexually overbearing.

To review, the essential elements of the "enamoured Moslem princess," as I have sketched her in the medieval section, are her high social rank and aggressive, forward personality, frequently manifested as loquacity or "wanton" sexuality and sometimes aided by magical knowledge; her active pursuit of a Christian man held captive by her father or husband; her release of him from captivity and aid to him against her father and the Muslim forces; her conversion to his faith and transformation to a passive femininity; and her journeying with him to his native land, transferring to him her father's wealth and property.

*Gerusalemme Liberata* takes this "enamoured Moslem princess," one of whose stock qualities was being the only major female Muslim character in the story, and splinters her into three Muslim princesses involved in three variations on the conventional plot. The three subplots end with different ambiguous messages rather than with the single homogenous one of medieval treatment. Although Boccaccio's blithe indifference to the Christian-Muslim divide is gone, this text undermines any absolute demarcation of that divide. Several Muslim women in the *Liberata* are drawn, like *Tamburlaine*'s women, in terms of conventional Western gender categories, a representation which minimizes their "Islamic" evil but deflates their textual presence. For example, Altomoro's absent loyal wife has been likened by critics to Andromache, Hector's wife in *The Iliad* (Stephens, 176). Yet there remains one Muslim female who has as subversive a textual presence as the medieval Muslim woman, and who needs to be overthrown, redeemed, and integrated for the epic plot to reach fulfillment and the allegory to achieve wholeness.

Of Tasso's three Muslim princesses, Erminia superficially approximates the conventional type. She has high rank as the daughter of the King of Antioch; this is literalized in her elevated physical position on the ramparts overlooking the battle (reminiscent of Bramimonde) when she identifies Christian combatants for the Muslim leader. She takes the initiative in pursuing the Christian knight Tancred. Her leaving the embattled city in disguise to seek the object of her unrequited love is something of a betrayal of Muslim forces, since she intends to use her medical skill to heal a prominent foe. However, a major shift in the balance of power has taken place: Instead of having fallen in love with Tancred while he was the prisoner of her father, Erminia fell in love with him when he took her captive after defeating and killing her father:

And when her city and her state was lost,
Then was her person lov'd and honor'd most.
(6.56)[6]

It is her captivity, not his, that is the springboard for transformation. Since her father's kingdom has already fallen, she is not needed to transfer wealth and land through union with the Christian. Nor is she key in helping the Christians take Jerusalem—she cannot even govern her horse, which carries her off into a pastoral interlude tangential to the battle (canto 7).

The woman is thus removed a degree from the center of the dramatic action and assigned a secondary feminine sphere, while the primary struggle—the struggle for Jerusalem—takes place in a masculine world. Her femininity is not portrayed as errant and in need of transformation; she is already a seemly, virtuous woman as a Muslim. She is not a wanton like *The Sowdone of Babylon*'s Floripas or *Bevis of Hampton*'s Josian, but a blushing virgin; "The heav'nly beauty of her angel's face," no less, shines forth from this (pagan!) damsel (7.18), who dresses in saintly blue and sports "locks of shining gold" (6.90 and 6.92). Since her action of seeking out her knight's chamber is not all that different from theirs, and since she practices the medical arts as they do, this shows how notions of acceptable feminine behavior expanded during the Renaissance.

Significantly, Erminia's stock conversion is entirely missing. Because her Islamic-ness has been so underemphasized, because she has been so blond and so angelic and so *good*, it is as if, on a covert level, the text is indicating that she needs no conversion. Most readers find her conversion implied, but the fact that it is not actualized leaves an indeterminacy to the plot and an ambiguity about the Christian-Muslim divide which ideological imperatives in this post-Tridentine text by a devout Catholic would not be expected to allow.

The aggressive quality absent in Erminia can be found in another natural blond, Clorinda, the warrior woman who "hated chambers, closets, secret mews, / And in broad fields preserved her maidenhead" (2.39). She obviously takes direct part in the male world of significant action, the battle for Jerusalem. Despite this transgression of traditional female behavior, Tasso protects her from any charge of wantonness by insisting on the chastity of the "warlike maid," as in the above lines from Fairfax's translation, thus restricting her potential danger—and reducing her potential power, if Tasso's claims are taken as effective. She also has a Christian counterpart in the chaste wife Gildippe, which serves to remove any Islamic specificity from her martial activities and further reduces their disruptive power. This reflects a new appreciation and appropriation of the "heroic" woman which some scholars consider characteristic of the Italian Renaissance; it is an outlook in which "virago" becomes a word of praise instead of censure (see Jacob Burckhardt, in Bell, 200–205). Yet Clorinda, far from being a wanton lady, is the unknowing object of Tancred's love and gaze and pursuit, from when he spies her face under her lifted visor (1.47). First he penetrates her shiny armor with his gaze; later, "His sword into her bosom deep he drives" (12.64): she dies at his hand.[7]

All this is further complicated by the mid-story revelation that Clorinda is actually a Christian by birth, daughter of the black queen and king of Ethiopia. Her mother, unable to explain the birth of the white child and fearing the wrath of her very jealous husband, switched her with a more suitably tinted infant, and Clorinda was mistakenly raised in "Macon" lore. Even after she discovers her origin, she prefers to remain loyal to the people among whom she was raised; only when mortally wounded by Tancred does she request baptism. Is this a last-minute saving of Tancred from the censure of having loved a "paynim?" For by the moral standards of heavenly Jerusalem, the Christian knight must virtuously refuse to fall for any "pagan" maidens. Aucassin loved Saracen Nicolette only in open defiance of father, religion, and country, and she was even baptized; Tancred is the Christian hero of a holy Crusade and no such open defiance of dogma is tolerable in him—but an equivocal resistance may be obliquely conveyed by delaying her conversion to the last minute.

In any case, the revelation of Clorinda's origin undermines the demarcation between Christian and Muslim that is crucial to the overt ideology of the text. Ostensibly, the poem is supposed to inspire its contemporaneous readers

> [t]o win fair Greece out of the tyrant's hands
> And those usurping Ismaelites deprive
> Of woful Thrace, which now captived stands,
> You must from realms and seas the Turks forth drive,
> As Godfrey chased them from Judah's lands,
> And in this legend, all that glorious deed
> Read, whilst arm you: arm you, whilst you read. (1.5)

Yet if a white infant can be born to black parents, if Christians can be black and non-European, if staunch defenders of Islam can turn out to be secret Christians unbeknownst even to themselves, if in killing what he thinks is his male Muslim foe Tancred unknowingly kills his female Christian beloved, how can Tasso's contemporary Christian reader raise his hand and smite? The best he can do is read the poem as an allegory of the soul (which it is) and smite the evil within himself, embrace the blond pagan struggling toward grace within himself. The stability of the line dividing one group from the other is shaken, no matter how much the official ideology of the poem insists otherwise.

Tasso scholars have previously pointed out the ideological inconsistency of the *Liberata*, in which overtly declared doctrines are undermined by the covert effects of the text (Stephens, 169–174). A deconstructive critic calls the poem "the first manifest example in Italian literature of a conscious identification (although repudiated at the level of ideology) with the forces of evil, the first great example of solidarity with the 'pagan enemy'" (Sergio Zatti, in Stephens, 170). Feminist critics have suggested that the text does not differentiate substantively between Christian and Muslim female characters, subordinating both to patriarchal order (see Stephens, 172)—which is not inconsistent with the notion that the text identifies with the

(male) pagan Other. Other critics maintain that Tasso's devoutly Catholic
intentions and his own explication of the *Liberata* in other writings ought to
be the primary criteria for reading the text (Roche, 49–50). Yet no matter
how anxious Tasso was to prove the orthodoxy of his epic, the richness,
depth, and empathy with which he portrays the Muslim side exceed the
ideological necessities for such description.

Armida, the very blond and lovely enchantress and princess of Damascus, is the woman whose presence most infuses the text of *Gerusalemme Liberata*. In canto 4 she enters the Christian camp and, following her magician
father's instructions, plays damsel in distress so persuasively that the cream
of the Christian knights follow her out. These fifty she lures to her castle
on the Dead Sea. There she, with a hundred virgins serving, wines and dines
them, tries to make them convert, then turns them into fishes for refusing
(except one apostate). Rinaldo appears and rescues them, and they hurry
back to camp, contrite at having been tempted by Armida's wiles. Meanwhile Armida falls for Rinaldo and he is enchanted by her. She flies him
off to her Atlantic island, where she reigns as queen and he is willing to live
in "bondage" in her "empire" of sensual delights (16.21).

Godfrey, the Christian commander, told in a vision from heaven that
Rinaldo's return is critical for the Christian cause, sends two knights to re-
trieve him. As they advance through the Strait of Gibraltar, the knights ask
the mysterious woman who navigates the ship if anyone has ever passed this
point, and what lies beyond it. Only Ulysses has crossed before, she an-
swers, and he never returned; as for the lands beyond,

> As divers be their nations (answer'd she)
> Their tongues, their rites, their laws so different are.
> (15.28)

The Christians, bent on obliterating the one different law that has absorbed their energies for so long, are thus made aware of a vast panorama
of differences still awaiting subjugation. This point will be crossed again,
she foretells, by a "knight of Genoa," when the unknown sites will be
named and their profane people converted to the true faith. Tasso thereby
links the explorations of his own times to both the classical Greek heritage
and the Crusades, loading territorial expansion with ideological value for
the very cultural identity of Europe.

The knights' task, upon which the fate of the Crusading army awaits,
is to rescue Rinaldo from what is described as Armida's "*Impero / imperio*

(*imperium*), the military and political term for the power to command" (Stephens, 194). This term is also used in the original text (according to Stephens, 194) to describe the authority of Godfrey, the supreme Christian commander (1.33). The empire ruled by the Muslim witch-princess undermines European *imperium* and must be broken before Jerusalem can be won in the battle proper.

What seemed obvious by Tasso's time but of course never occurred to his medieval sources was that the path to Christian (now better called European) victory over the *imperium* of the Islamic East lay due west. It was America that ended Europe's obsession with Islam as its ultimate nemesis and alter ego. By sailing beyond the Gates of Hercules to sneak a furtive back entry to the East, and stumbling upon another enormous source of wealth along the path, Europeans ensured the eclipse of Islamic hegemony, which had stymied their every other effort. The "position of the Ottoman Empire in the world trading network had altered substantially" by the end of the sixteenth century; gone was its "stranglehold" on trade routes (Lee, 86). Gone also was Islam's stranglehold on the Western imagination of the Other, although it retained a unique footing in that imagination.

Yet Italy's peculiar position in the new age of imperial expansion was ambiguous. The "knight of Genoa" would find no support in Italy, and no wonder: The movement west, the waning of Muslim power, meant that Italy's importance as middleman would also fade. Italy's prosperity was in many ways dependent on Ottoman prosperity. On the other hand, Italy was the seat of the papacy, with its strident views on the necessity of Christian supremacy over Islam. The challenges of the Reformation had given impetus for a revitalization of the Church Militant, in the forms of the Inquisition, the Council of Trent, the Jesuits, and other orders. Tasso's text evinces a peculiar Italian ambivalence toward the Muslim world.

The *Liberata* posits this ambivalence in the form of a Muslim woman. Armida is declared a "wanton" and a "virgin" in the same breath (4.31–34). She is called a Circe (4.86) and yet described in the very vocabulary of Petrarch's Laura and even the Virgin Mary (Stephens, 174). She is overtly condemned as a witch who seduces the soldiers of the Lord, and yet the stanzas blazoning her beauty and describing her real anguish at Rinaldo's rejection work the conceits of Renaissance love poetry quite earnestly to evoke attraction and empathy. Most remarkably, she is recouped at the end, and this without a baptism scene or even an explicit conversion (although her conversion is implied).

As Stephens asks, "Why should the vain and willful Armida be salvaged at the cost of Gildippe, who is both a Christian and a faithful wife?" (175). Why, if not to recuperate her sensuality and redeem the Islamic materialism she represents? For all its moralism, the text conveys a sensitivity to the real beauty of Armida's world, its waters clear and fresh, its snow and greenery, its golden light—not to mention "[t]hese naked wantons, tender, fair and white," who

> [m]oved so far the warriors' stubborn hearts,
> That on their shapes they gazed with delight;
> The nymphs applied their sweet alluring arts,
> And one of them above the waters quite
> Lift up her head, her breasts, and higher parts,
> And all that might weak eyes subdue and take;
> Her lower beauties veil'd the gentle lake. (15.59)

Now, the knights resist, as they must, and liberate Rinaldo from all this exquisite lust. Yet, in the context of the greater acceptability of nudity in sublime Italian Renaissance painting, in the context of a more open integration of sexuality in daily life, are these delights really to be as sternly eradicated as the morality of the poem insists? Pagan Armida is a witch, it is true. Yet the ugly aspects of witch-hood are relegated to Alecto, the Fury in the enchanted forest, who takes the shape of an enormous hundred-armed giantess who goes out in a blaze of glory, vanquished by the repentant Rinaldo in canto 18. This leaves Armida the glamour of flying through the air and other winsome witch activities. Falling for her charms is really rather delightful—and the tempted men, while not exactly excused, elicit sympathetic understanding and classical parallels:

> What wonder if Achilles were misled,
> Or great Alcides, at their ladies' sights,
> Since these true champions of the Lord Above
> Were thralls to beauty, yielden slaves to love?
> (4.96)

The relationship of Armida and Rinaldo, founded on lust, remarkably survives. He finds genuine value in her which he wishes might be won over to Christianity. He could have left her to kill herself, if the moral schema of the poem were strictly condemnatory of her values. Instead he wants to make her queen (of her rightful kingdom)—if only she would remove the

"veil" of paganism from her heart. These are the lines in which her conversion is strongly implied (but not explicitly proclaimed):

*"Ecco l'ancilla tua: d'essa a tuo senno
dispon," gli disse "e le fia legge il cenno."*

(Behold [she says] your handmaid and your thrall,
My life, my crown, my wealth, use at your pleasure. —
Thus death her life became, loss prov'd her treasure. [20.136])

This turn reverses the terms of power that governed their relationship on
the island, giving the *imperium* to its rightful owner in a Pauline model of
marriage (Stephens, 194). Not only does Rinaldo redeem Armida, but
Tasso puts in her mouth the words of the Virgin Mary, *"Ecco l'ancilla tua"*
(Behold your handmaid) (Luke 1:38), causing a prominent Tasso critic to
"wince" (Giamatti, 209).

Ambivalence toward the still somewhat powerful, still magical, still seducing Muslim woman is a product of both the flux in social appraisal of
gender roles and the ambiguity in Western, especially Italian, relations with
Islam. Tasso's intense anxieties about orthodoxy—he was afraid the poem
had too much love and magic, submitted it to numerous critics, and only
authorized publication of a sternly edited version (Nelson's introduction to
Fairfax, xv–xix)—may indicate that, on some level, he was aware of this
ambivalence.

SHE IS WHAT WE HOPE SHE IS NOT:
ERASING ZORAIDA

Spain's relationship with the Islamic world was from the beginning mediated almost wholly by its Moors. It was unlike Italy's relationship with the
Ottomans in that the Moors had been an organic part of Iberian society.
Clearly and unambiguously by the sixteenth century, they had become a
powerless minority in their own land, targeted for total eradication by the
imperatives of a consolidated, absolutist state and a repressive, militant
Church. While the Renaissance (at least the early Renaissance) elsewhere
in Europe produced transitional moments of supple equivocality, of subdued differentiation between Christian and Muslim, in Spain Islamic difference became the site of intense ideological anxiety. Church and state in
Spain worked assiduously to scrub out every residue of Islamic presence in

the interest of national unity. Only among the large landowners, who valued their numerous Morisco farmers and tenants, were there pockets of resistance to the general policy, and the power of these aristocrats diminished steadily in this age of absolute monarchy.

Initially the terms of Granada's capitulation guaranteed Muslim rights, but the conversion rate was too slow for the Catholic kings, who decided to apply harsher methods of persuasion. This tactic provoked the Revolt of Albaicín in 1500; after suppressing it, the monarchs punished all the Moors of Castile with a choice between baptism or exile (Chejne, 7). In 1524, the Moriscos[8] of Valencia and Aragon were given the same ultimatum and prohibited from using the Arabic language or maintaining Moorish customs. A revolt there produced a compromise guaranteeing Morisco rights, which was rescinded shortly thereafter because of charges that the Moriscos were supporting enemies of Spain. Suppression led to revolts, which produced further suppression. The Revolt of the Alpujarras, as late as 1568, protested a 1566 edict

> prohibiting the Moriscos the use of the Arabic language, annulling of
> all contracts written in Arabic, surrendering all Arabic books within
> thirty days, and prohibiting any Moorish rite, Moorish clothing,
> and the use of Arabic names and customs. The edict also called for
> destroying all public baths, requiring Moriscos to leave the doors
> of their houses open, unveiling women and requiring Castilian dress,
> and ceasing to dance the zambra and sing. (Chejne, 10)

The Moors were always suspected of links with the powerful Turks, with the Mediterranean pirates who plagued Spanish shipping, even with Lutherans—and, after 1588, with agents of the anti-Spanish coalition comprising England, Holland, and France. As early as 1582, expulsion was one of the options on Philip II's table; other solutions for the Morisco problem, besides sporadic suggestions of re-education, charity, and patience, were ghettoization, a ban on intermarriage, and castration (Chejne, 13). In 1609, Spain finally decreed the expulsion of Moriscos "so that," as the Duke of Lerma put it, "all the kingdoms of Spain will remain pure and clean from this people" (Chejne, 13). The goals of the self-exorcism were so extreme that "[e]ven the word *Morisco* was decreed to be forgotten, for its use would constitute bad taste" (Chejne, 13).

Under these conditions, the representation of the Muslim woman is suddenly more highly charged than ever before. The Muslim woman gains importance as the object of ideological contest, even while her textual presence is muffled and her power circumscribed. It is the Moorish taint in the very appearance of the Captive and his lady companion at the inn in *Don Quixote* (pt. 2, chap. 37) which disrupts the conversation of the Spanish gentlemen (even though she herself, it later appears, is enveloped in a new and strange silence):

> *Muchas palabras de comedimiento y muchos ofrecimientos pasaron entre Don Quijote y Don Fernando; pero a todo puso silencio un pasajero que en aquella sazín entro en la venta, el cual en su traje mostraba ser cristiano recien venido de tierra de moros, porque venía vestido con una casaca de paño azul. . . . Entró luego tras él, encima de un jumento, una mujer a la morisca vestida, cubierto el rostro con una toca en la cabeza; traia un bonetillo de brocado y vestida una almalafa, que desde los hombros a los pies la cubría. . . . (660–663)*

(Many compliments and offers of service passed between Don Quixote and Don Fernando, but they were all silenced by a traveler who at that moment entered the inn. By his dress he appeared to be a Christian newly arrived from the land of the Moors. He wore a short blue-cloth tunic. . . . Behind him on an ass came a woman dressed in Moorish fashion, with her face covered and a veil on her head; she was wearing a little cap of gold brocade and was swathed in a cloak that enveloped her from her shoulder to her feet. [384])

On the surface, the Moorish presence, marked sartorially, momentarily disrupts the very civilized discourse between two men, at least one of whom represents the landed nobility of Spain. The underside is that this only appears to be very civilized discourse; in fact, one man is crazy and the other is humoring him. The binary between order and disorder, seemingly figured as Christian Spanish versus Moorish or Morisco, is already cleverly displaced in Cervantes' text by Don Quixote's craziness, the disorder within the Spanish side of the binary.

Its publication in 1605 meant that the first part of *Don Quixote* preceded the "abrupt muffling of the 'Morisco problem' in official discourse" which happened after the expulsion was completed in 1614 (Burshatin, 113). Nevertheless, the highly charged meanings dress conveys immediately alert us to the irreducible difference of the Morisco or Moorish element; not only do Moors dress distinctively, but apparently even a visit to a Moorish land is enough to mark a Christian with telltale taints of Moorishness. These require storytelling, explanation, to defuse their danger. As for the woman, *"a la morisca vestida"* (translated "dressed in Moorish fashion," although "dressed in Morisco fashion" may be more accurate), she is already in direct violation of the law of the land.

We have never before encountered such a thing as Muslim or Islamic dress in any European representation of the Muslim woman. Twice again the narrator refers to the strangeness of her dress in the paragraph describing her entrance to the inn, even naming her as *"la que en el traje parecía mora"* (663) (she who seemed from her dress to be Moorish [384]). Her attire is referred to two more times in conversation before the Captive's Tale even begins. Even the name of the garment she wears, *"una almalafa,"* points to an irreducible Islamic difference, *al malafa* being Arabic for "the cloak" or "the wrapper." *Una* redundantly adds the Spanish (indefinite) article to the Arabic (definite) article, making a hard, indigestible unit out of the two Arabic components, and *almalafa* underlines the impossibility of describing a Moorish woman without using the outlawed Arabic language. Cervantes' choice of language undermines official ideological insistence on the "purity" of Spanish and its separability from Moorish elements, even while showing the effects of this ideology at work—for without it, *"a la morisca vestida"* would not exist.

Zoraida, the woman dressed in Morisco fashion, is a turning point in the representation of the Muslim woman. Conditions which had produced the earlier, more powerful Muslim female image stubbornly lingered past their prime in the larger European scene, manifested especially in European-Ottoman relations. Spain was part of this larger scene, but its unique domestic situation simultaneously created another set of representational conditions.

Spanish state policies for the administration, control, and subjection of Muslim communities had already advanced to a point that England and France would achieve only in the nineteenth century (and not in quite the same way). What Said calls the *"positional superiority"* (7) of the West over the Muslim world is in place at this point—but only inside Spain itself. Outside, Spain could exercise dominance over Muslims only equivocally.[9] Outside played havoc with inside; the possibility that the powerful Turks would come to the aid of their Moorish co-religionists worried Spanish rulers constantly. Even after Philip III ordered the expulsion of all

Moriscos in 1609, "there remained the preoccupation of cleansing the land of the remaining infidels and those who managed to return from exile" (Chejne, 13).

Dorotea asks the Captive, "*esta señora es cristiana o mora? Porque el traje y el silencio nos hace pensar que es lo que no querríamos que fuese*" (664) (is this lady a Christian or a Moor? Her dress and her silence make us think she is what we hope she is not [385]). "[W]hat we hope she is not" . . . we are insecure, but we hope. Residual Moriscos in Spain were always suspected of being what authorities hoped they were not. Further elision suggests that "she is . . . what she is not." The Moriscos (being Morisco) are what they officially are not, since the sixteenth-century edicts no longer allowed such a thing as Morisco ethnocultural identity.

What accomplishes such erasure? What can simultaneously signify presence and absence? The text itself tells us: "her dress and her silence." Dress and silence are the marked components of a new version of the Muslim woman. Together they make up the meaning of her veil. It is this veil, and the fabrication of her veil in the Western narrative, which absents the Muslim woman from the scene.

Cervantes' text (actually his Moorish narrator, whom I will discuss shortly) refers to Zoraida as *la embozada*, the muffled or veiled one; her *almalafa* completely covers her, *la cubría*, so that she is there and not there at the same time. This veil is a sign of erasure which leaves telltale traces, a narrative repetition of the process which preoccupied Spain throughout the sixteenth century, the erasure of the Moorish presence. So there is a great difference in meaning between Zoraida's veiling and Dorotea's or Luscinda's. For Dorotea too veils her face upon hearing of the arrival at the inn of Luscinda's party, consisting of Luscinda and four masked men; Luscinda herself arrives with her face veiled.[10] But only Zoraida's veiledness becomes a metaphor for her identity and embodies this quality of absence in presence.

"[I]f the Arab woman's introduction at Juan Palomeque's inn is characterized by the '*embozo*' which hides her features, her presence in the 'Captive's Tale' is similarly obscured, remaining 'muffled' behind the metaphor of the veil which personifies her in the story" (Garces, 70). As a Moor in Spain at this juncture in history, Zoraida can only be represented as nullified. Nullification is evident even in her announcement of her name: "*Sí, sí, María: Zoraida macange!—que quiere decir no*" (665) (Yes, yes, Maria—Zoraida *macange*, that is to say, not Zoraida at all [386]). Now the Aquilar edition (eds. Soriano and Morales) glosses *macange* thus: "*Macange, del arabe ma kan chey.*" But *ma kan chey* in Arabic means more than simply "no" or "not Zoraida at all;" it suggests that Zoraida *never* existed, that Zoraida has never been anything: it is a denial of history, echoing the Spanish state policies that strove mightily to make it seem as if the Moors had never existed, had never been in Spain at all. Yet Cervantes' text contains fissures that deliberately undermine the ideological edifice that walls Zoraida into the void.

The figure of Zoraida thus heralds a new type of representation—a type that will become well entrenched under Western colonialism—while retaining features which destabilize and delay that entrenchment. Elements of the "enamoured Moslem princess" still inform Zoraida, yet we find an increasing emphasis on elements of what I term the "rescued Muslim maiden," a latecomer to the gallery of the Muslim woman in Western literature.

Thus Zoraida's high rank is indeed literalized in the elevated position of her window overlooking the courtyard of the Christian Captive's prison, but instead of having authority and influence, she is as much a captive as he is in this place. While the Christian man is indeed a prisoner in Muslim territory, he is no longer directly a captive of her father. She does initiate contact with him and propose marriage, but this time in so laborious, so coded a manner as to emphasize the impediments to her speech instead of her loquacity or eloquence. She does assist the Christians against the Muslims, but waits for them to develop and initiate the plan of escape, rather than aggressively and directly initiating the central action herself. Conversion, betrayal, and abandonment of the father, transferal of his wealth and jewels, and the voyage to Christian land are retained without much change because they are compatible with the new narrative of the rescued Muslim maiden. No longer is she evil, even in her pre-Christian state; instead, she is romanticized and idealized—and silenced—as an object of pity and compassion, and of the gaze. The central change in the Muslim woman from active to passive is indicated by the fact that the enamoredness of the enamored Moslem princess springs from herself, whereas the rescued Muslim maiden needs to be rescued by another.

Yet all this story is narrated in Cervantes' text by a Moor, or ostensibly by a Spaniard who had to translate from the romance Arabic of the Moorish/Morisco Cide Hamete Benengeli, "*autor arabigo y manchego*" (424) (the Arabian and Manchegan author [209]). With this device, this reminder of the inextricability of Spanish and Moorish identities, the text slyly sabotages its own structuring of Islamic difference. Specifically, it subverts the Spanish man's, the Captive's, narrative of Zoraida—for he is actually the first one representing the Muslim woman. And he whose narrative is subverted, lest it be forgotten, is a soldier whose formative experiences involved fighting Muslims, especially in a Lepanto-like naval defeat of the Turks. Although the autobiographical similarities between Cervantes and the Captive, Ruy Perez de Viedma, are often noted, there is obviously an ironic distancing between them, through the double device of the Moorish narrator and his Arabic-speaking Spanish translator. Also, the story of the arrival of the Captive and Zoraida is interrupted by Don Quixote's discourse on the relative glories of arms and letters, which he decides in favor of arms. The endorsement of conquest by a man living in a fantasy is obviously a double-edged authorial statement on such an enterprise.

Not only Zoraida's Islamic identity but also her sexuality is transformed by the metaphor of her veil. The sexuality of Moors in general was the center of great anxiety in sixteenth century and even later Spanish culture, insinuating the repopulation of Spain with the dirty element from which it needed cleansing, as the proposed castration "solution" to the Morisco question makes abundantly clear. Spanish society had inherited the medieval European view that Islam was a sexually licentious religion, without, apparently, later inheriting the mitigating effects of Renaissance Neoplatonism on that view (Garces, 74). At the same time, the notion that women in general always pose a sexual danger remained powerful in Spain. The Moorish woman's sexuality is therefore doubly dangerous, and so Cervantes portrays her in other works (e.g., *Persiles*). In order for Zoraida to be the rescued Muslim maiden in the Captive's narration instead of the wanton, threatening, enamored Moslem princess, her sexuality must be constrained into a tolerable form. That form, for the Captive, is the impossible, repressed, paradoxical sexuality of the Virgin Mary, which is implied by her motherhood and yet never existed. "Lela Marien" who infuses the Captive's narration of Zoraida's story, who appears in Zoraida's dreams to guide her, whose name Zoraida adopts in Christianity, is the mold into which Ruy Perez forces Zoraida to make her sexuality acceptable.[11]

When, after having seen only her hand from behind the window screen, Ruy Perez describes his first sight of Zoraida, he declares that her beauty is too much to tell: "*Demasiada cosa sería decir yo agora la mucha hermosura, la gentileza, el gallardo y rico adorno con que mi querida Zoraida se mostro a mis ojos . . .*" (705) (It would be beyond my power now to describe Zoraida's great beauty, her gentleness, and the rich, brilliant attire in which she appeared before me [415]). His sense of being overwhelmed is similar to the feelings of the knights upon sighting Armida; it is a trace of the "too-muchness" of the older model of the Muslim woman. He goes on to describe the quantities of pearls and jewels that ornament her, pearls which he links to the wealth of the Moors and specifically to the wealth of her father. Finally, he arrives at a way of reducing her too-muchness to fit his symbolic order: he makes her an object in his economy, saying triumphantly, "*[D]e todo lo cual era señora está que ahora lo es mía*" (706) (She, who was once mistress of all this, is now mine only [415]). Evading the sensuality and the economic power of the Islamic Other suggested by her pearls, he makes her his own personal divinity:

> *Digo, en fin, que entonces llegó en todo extremo aderezada y en todo extremo hermosa, o a lo menos a mí me pareció serlo la mas que hasta entonces había visto, y . . . me parecía que tenía delante de mí una deidad del cielo, venida a la tierra para mi gusto y para mi remidio.* (706)

> (All I can say is that Zoraida then appeared so exquisitely attired and surpassingly lovely that, to me at least, she seemed the perfection of all I had ever beheld. . . . I felt that some goddess from Heaven had descended on earth to bring me happiness and relief. [416])

He can then idealize her loveliness as a manifestation of spiritual purity and perfection dedicated to aiding and succoring him, rather than a manifestation of sensuality. The Captive verbalizes the mental process with which he has performed this disengagement of Zoraida's sexuality when, to Dorotea's crucial question, "is this lady a Christian or a Moor? Her dress and her silence make us think she is what we hope she is not," he responds, "*Mora es en el traje y en el cuerpo; pero en el alma es muy grande cristiana*" (664) (Moorish she is in body and dress, but in her soul she is a very devout Christian [385]).

The idealization and objectification of Zoraida continue at the inn. When Zoraida unveils, all present are dazzled by her beauty. When she fervently discloses her new name, "Maria, Maria," the company is moved to compassion. Instead of being an affirmation of Zoraida's own presence, however, such idealization reaffirms the overarching Christian Spanish presence, with its prerogative of both owning her as property and making her an object of pity as romanticized Other. Her passivity in this idealization is reinforced by her passive body language, but most of all by her silence, that distinct silence to which Dorotea refers when she says "her dress *and her silence* make us think she is what we hope she is not" (emphasis added).

The din made by this silence is deafening. Suddenly there is a need for translators at every juncture between Christians and Muslims. Bramimonde, Belakane, and Floripas needed no translators; neither did Erminia, Clorinda, and Armida. The Captive's Tale posits communication between Christian and Moor as a formidable difficulty at a time in history when chairs in Arabic were being established in the European universities, when scores of people still moved, voluntarily or involuntarily, between Spain and North Africa, depositing reams of words in each other's languages. The representation of the language barrier in this text is therefore as much a function of the official ban on Arabic as of realism. The effects of ideology can be seen, for example, in the phrase *"no sabía hablar cristiano"* (663) (she did not know the Christian tongue [385]). "The Christian tongue" is a completely meaningless term except in the context of the dominant, Golden Age Spanish ideology's equation of Arabic with Islam, and its obsession with erasing it.

Zoraida is not uncommunicative. She speaks with her body, as when she makes a deep bow in response to Dorotea's overture. She signals with her hand, communicating through her window with the Captive in the prison courtyard below. Notably, she is, as Garces puts it, "a writer, who writes the corpus of her own story in the three letters dedicated to the Spaniard" (67). Most important of all, in the beginning she literally speaks, and fluently: "let us recall the Moorish woman's voluble conversation with the Captive, in her father's presence, where her discursive abilities are enhanced by the subtle double-entendres with which she questions the Spaniard about his plans to leave Barbary" (Garces, 72). In fact, in addition to Arabic she speaks a pidgin tongue *"que ni es morisca, ni castellana, ni de otra nación alguna, sino una mezcla de todas las lenguas con la cual todos nos entendemos"* (705) (which is neither Morisco, nor Castilian, nor of any nation, but a medley of all languages, by means of which we can all understand one another [415]). If she has such an ability and knows a language with such remarkable scope, by what criteria can she possibly be characterized as silent?

Zoraida's silence is similar to the silence of other African women characters in European literature, which Busia describes as "a deliberate *unvoicing*, rather than any intrinsic absence of speech on the part of the woman"

(87). Her silence is produced not by incapacity or disinterest, but by the hardening of the Christian-Muslim binary. It is the result of "the insistence upon the otherness of the other, upon the absolute difference between the dominating and the dominated culture" (Bartels, 2), of the increasing irreducibility, in this case, of Moorish difference. It is a "voicelessness in a discourse in which sexuality and access to language together form part of the discourse of access to power" (Busia, 87). It is a disguise and a denial of her actual loquacity, her intrinsic ability to speak, and her subjectivity. That is what her veil, knotting together "her dress and her silence," signifies.

Yet there is a slipping apart of that knot because of the very nature of Cervantes' text—a loose, playful, vernacular composition that audaciously ridicules the idea of truth itself, undermining its own authority to impose meaning. Cervantes, or his narrating persona, facetiously prefixes the manuscript with sonnets by imaginary people, thumbing his nose at the whole idea of authenticity. He goes on to say that his ostensible narrator, the Arab Cide Hamete Benengeli, is from a *"nación ser mentirosos"* (280) (a nation much inclined to lying [109]), and yet later he calls him a *"historiador muy curioso y muy puntual en todas las cosas"* (348) (a very careful historian and exact in details [156]), leaving the baffled reader to wonder whether he is joking one time or the other, or both. Garces points out the intriguing parallel between the playful authorial hand and Zoraida's "enigmatic female hand" (68) and notes that Cervantes' problematizing of the truth-falsehood binary is repeated at the level of the letters Zoraida writes to the Captive when she cautions *"no te fíes de ningun moro, porque son todos marfuces"* (trust no Moor, for they are all perfidious tricksters [408]). This crafty sleight of hand collapses the entire text of the Captive's Story, as well as the whole text of *Don Quixote* itself, around an unsolvable riddle:

> If Zoraida is a Moor who belongs to the world of the *"marfuces,"* her use of this originally Arabic word, now adopted by the Spanish language, redoubles the linguistic ambiguities of her letter, conveying an exotic and indeterminate quality to her text. The word *"marfuces"* functions here as a "trace," an imprint which links Zoraida's text with the pre-text of her ancestors, at the same time that it subverts her identity as speaking subject, reinforcing the undecidability of her position, concerning the question: is this woman a (true) Christian or (a deceitful) Moor? (71)

This riddle, Garces continues, "points at a crisis in signification and a collapse in the signifying function of Zoraida/Maria as text." Such a collapse is no less than a deconstruction of the whole edifice of Spanish ideology regarding the Moors. The Aguilar edition glosses "*marfuce,*" also spelled "*marfuz,*" as "*felaz, engañoso, o astuto*" (false, deceptive, cunning). Tracing it back to Arabic, *marfuz* means "rejected." The Moors/Moriscos comprise the rejected element in Spain, which is what the collective "we" of Spanish society "hope" it is not. The idealized, romanticized Moorish woman bears the traces of those other, *marfuz*, Moors, "whose presence . . . in the conqueror's universe of discourse is illusory" (Burshatin, 101). She discredits her own idealization and obscures her own presence with cryptic uncertainty.

The multiplicity of meanings in Cervantes' text filibusters my chances of claiming that Zoraida is the completely passive, veiled, and silenced Muslim woman of later Romantic literature. Nevertheless, we can already see in her the effects of a metamorphosis from an older representation to a newer one. In later centuries, when European imperialism stabilized into an entrenched system with distinct discursive practices, little Zoraidas could be fashioned in deadly earnest; all Cervantes' playfulness would drop away, replaced by a grand Promethean claim to the Truth.

## MOOR OR LESS: BLACK JILLS AND WHITE DEVILS

In *The Merchant of Venice* there is an off-stage Muslim woman, apparently a girlfriend of the clownish Launcelot, Shylock's servant. When Launcelot wisecracks to Lorenzo that the latter's conversion of Jews, specifically the angelic Jessica, will raise the price of pork in the commonwealth, Lorenzo replies, "I shall answer that better to the commonwealth than you can the getting up of the negro's belly: the Moor is with child by you, Launcelot." Launcelot quips, "It is much that the Moor should be more than reason: but if she be less than an honest woman, she is indeed more than I took her for" (III.v). The Muslim woman on the English stage in the seventeenth century splits into two divergent types, both reflecting general developments in gender discourse but also reflecting the specific sociopolitical moment of England in the domestic and international scene. On the one hand are women such as Launcelot's Moor: vulgar, libidinous, and too much to handle. The true descendants of the forward Muslim woman of medieval epic despite their demotion from upper to lower economic class, they are more and more marginalized as the Muslim woman becomes less and less.

For she who replaces them is a reduced Muslim woman, reduced in agency,
subjectivity, force of character. We have seen intimations of her face in
Tasso, in Cervantes. She is angelic, submissive to male authority, the type
of woman always cited as the exception in the numerous misogynistic dia-
tribes of the age; she is, in a sense, a reincarnation of Alde.

This bawd/virgin or witch/angel binary is obviously not limited to the
representation of the Muslim woman. Patriarchal discourse in the West always contrasts a "good" woman who is a paragon of the authorized notion
of femininity with a "bad" woman who epitomizes all that is considered
unfeminine. What is intriguing is the specific ways this patriarchal narrative of woman overlaps and criss-crosses with the narrative of Islam to produce a Muslim woman who can collect these contradictions into her Othered body.

Western culture begins its encounter with Islam by representing the
Muslim woman primarily as a "bad" woman, although there is always a
complexity about her negative qualities, reflecting the appeal of the pros-
perous Islamic world, that makes her recuperation desirable. A short but
rich interval of neutrality intervenes, when the value of the Muslim woman,
*qua* Muslim, is indeterminate or equivocal. Then the spectacle of the
Muslim woman in Jacobean theater provides two divergent models, at a
crossroads of sorts. The "badness" of the original subversive and more
powerful Muslim woman is isolated and left irredeemable, reflecting an increasing contempt for her world. A transfer of association occurs whereby
intensely negative qualities in her are linked more and more to sub-Saharan
Africa and the truly "pagan," that "third term outside the binarism," and
less and less to Asia (Turkey) and Islam (Bartels, 3). Shakespeare's Moorish whore in the above scene is suddenly "negro," while the "Muslim
woman" proper becomes more often "milk-white"; (in Romantic literature
darkness returns to her hair and eyes only). Recall how Ruy Perez stressed
Zoraida's exceeding whiteness of hand. One might say that at this point the
Muslim woman splits (although not conclusively) into a "black" Muslim
woman and a "white" Muslim woman.

Black-complexioned Africans had been on the European scene ever
since the explorations of the west African coast. Although the Slave Trade
in black Africans was well established by this time, blacks still appeared in
Europe in other capacities as well, capacities which bespoke the still-viable
energies of non-European cultures.[12] In seventeenth-century English texts

black-skinned Africans are called "black Moors," which indicates that they were associated with a predominantly Islamic milieu. Even so, their difference was doubled by their concurrent association with a pagan Africa which was considered truly outlandish and physically grotesque. The black African element becomes an extremely negative quantity during the seventeenth century, associated with devilry and monstrosity. Although precedents exist for the regard of horror directed at the Negro (e.g., when Roland sees the Negro army as sure harbingers of death in the *Chanson de Roland*) and for the equation between physical blackness and moral evil, this was not the only way blackness had been represented in earlier European literature (recall Belakane in *Parzival*, for example, and Clorinda's Ethiopian parents).

Yet in the seventeenth century, a "bad," "black," dangerous Muslim woman is on her way out of the gallery, passing a "good," "white," passive Muslim maiden on her way in. A prescient insight led Shakespeare to push Launcelot's whorish Moor, a vestige of the "bad" Muslim woman, off stage, as he similarly marginalized the Algerian witch Sycorax in *The Tempest*,[13] but he was premature; the "bad" Muslim woman is a stubborn termagant and wrests a last performance out of the lesser geniuses who followed him.

*The Knight of Malta* (by John Fletcher, Nathan Field, and Philip Massinger; staged 1619, published 1647) offers an opportunity to see the "bad" and "good" elements of the Muslim woman fully externalized into two separate characters. Zanthia, black Moorish servant to the virtuous lady Oriana, is an assistant to the villain of the play, while Luscinda, "milk-white" captured Turkish virgin of noble origin, is a foil for the play's hero. Luscinda, despite her lowly status as chattel, upholds the values of the established order in regard to both the Christian/Muslim and male/female hierarchies. The "metaphysical emptiness" her purity signifies, to paraphrase Gilbert and Gubar (21), makes her an ideal vessel for the ideology of the Knights of Malta, which is an ideology of Christian European (and male) supremacy.[14] Zanthia militates vigorously against the established order, using her blackness to assert a defiant alternative morality. Although the men of Malta abuse her as a monster, a demon, and a savage, her ingenuity and expressiveness declare her a creative, active woman and belie their jeers as manifestations of the same insecurity that makes them banish her in the end.

All this occurs against the background of Malta, a key Mediterranean island that had always been part of a disputed intermediate zone between the Islamic world and the non-Muslims to the north. In the early years of Islamic expansion, Malta was quickly taken and quickly lost by the Muslims. The Order of the Knights Hospitalers, founded during the early crusading period, had conquered Rhodes and made it their base (1310), only to be driven from it by the Ottomans in 1522. Charles V gave the Order Malta in 1530 and they became known as the Knights of Malta. Unsuccessfully besieged by the Turks (1565) and harassed by North African pirates, Malta at the time of this play still connoted a sense of precarious, recently-won stability at the very edge of Christian Europe. Its situation was complicated by the fact that in addition to focusing the struggle between the Knights of Malta and the Turks, it was also the object of Spanish territorial claims, against the objections of England, which had its own interest in the island. Still, in the play, an international Christian European solidarity coalesces around the Order of Malta as an embodiment of both Christian and humanist virtue, with a Frenchman being the only corrupt knight. Malta slightly resembles Spain as a frontier zone battling Islam and unable to come to terms with the Islamic Other that is integral to its history and identity.

The part of Luscinda's story that precedes her entry onstage bears some resemblance to Zoraida's, so that Luscinda could be considered a continuation of Zoraida. The "beautiful Turkish woman" first appears as loot taken in the recent battle against the Turks; quarreling soldiers ask their general to award her to one of them (II.i). At first the Danish Norandine dismisses her with misogynistic bile (intensified by the pain from his wounds), but then allows her to speak. "Victorious sir," she reproaches,

Tis seldome seen in men so valiant,
Minds so devoyd of vertue: he than can conquer
Should ever know how to preserve his conquest,
Tis but a base theft else. Valour's a vertue . . .
(II.i)

By upholding a distinction between legitimate conquest and "base theft," Luscinda helps preserve the rationalizing structure for imperial domination. She pleads for a kinder, gentler domination which would not include the violent "wronging of weake woman"; she is not interested in her "liberty" or in challenging the established system of masters and slaves, but only in her "honour" within that system. Impressed by her speech, as he should be since it reaffirms his value as a soldier, he gives her to her gentle-manly captor Miranda, the play's hero, which satisfies her.

Toward the end of the play, Luscinda's counterpart to Ruy Perez (Angelo, disguised as Collonna) tells his own "Captive's tale" before the male authorities of Malta. He was a Christian prisoner in Turkey when he met her, and "doubly won her," first to the true faith, then to himself (V.ii). They were "contracted," fled Constantinople before consummating the marriage, and were captured first by Turkish galleys, then by the Knights of Malta, who seized the vessels. When she appears before Norandine, then, she is in a position similar to Zoraida's at sea, when "Moorish clothes bespeak not her origins so much as the kindness of French pirates," because they politely refrain from raping her (Burshatin, 115). Luscinda, too, is already Christian at heart, and her beauty is not so much a reflection of her Islamic origins as a test which will reaffirm the virtue of the Order of Malta.

Luscinda is allowed two moments of effective speaking, one in the above scene with the general, and a similar one with Miranda, the play's hero, in which she recalls him to the true meaning of the cross he wears, evades ravishment, and mitigates the misogynistic apprehensions of her disguised husband, who watches the whole unsuccessful seduction from hiding. For we are prepared by Collonna's misgivings to believe that if Miranda had been successful with this "virgin of fourteen," it would have been her fault because

> they are all born Sophisters, to maintain
> That lust is lawfull, and the end and use
> of their creation. (III.iii)

It is not clear whether by "they" Collonna means women or Turks; the ambiguity is rich because both are applicable in a play which rails against women as much as it boasts against Turks. There is also some blurring in the quotation between Turks and Muslims in general, including Moors and black Moors, in a linguistic context in which to "turn Turk" means to profess Islam and the Moor was "a corporate Moslem personality" (L. Johnson, 35) (not to mention a political context in which Turks and North Africans alternately ruled northern African kingdoms). Certainly Angelo's accusation that "they" would consider lust lawful applies equally to any of "them." As early as the opening scene, the legality of lust in Islam is vividly (and approvingly, since the speaker is the lustful villain) described:

> Great Solyman that wearies his hot eyes,
> But to peruse his deck'd Ceraglio,
> When from the number of his Concubines
> He chooseth one for that night, in his pride
> Of them, wives, wealth, is not so rich as I
> In this one smile from Oriana sent. (I.i)

And so we come at last to the issue of the seraglio. Its central position in the later Western narrative of Islam is curious, since the institution is not of Islamic origin, having been a prominent feature of the social organization of gender in ancient Greece and Rome (as well as Persia and India), and later, medieval Byzantium (Ahmed, 17 and 27). When the Arabs migrated to the former lands, and when the Turks replaced the Byzantines, the upper class among them, and especially the rulers, readily adopted the idea of secluded quarters for women from their predecessors. The multiple genealogy of the concept is reflected in the etymology of the word "seraglio." From Latin *serraculum*, "enclosure, place of confinement" comes Italian *serrare* (with French and Spanish cognates), "to lock up, close." The Italian form seems to have merged with the meaning of the Turkish word *serai* (lodging, palace), and the resulting English "seraglio" and French "*sérail*," meaning both women's quarters and the women inhabiting them, as well as retaining for a while the general meaning of palace, seem to have been used solely in relation to Turkey and the Islamic world (OED).

Presumably, falling heir to a remnant of the ancient Western gyneceum, Ottoman sultans maintained seraglios for several hundred years, ever since they replaced the Byzantine emperors. Yet it is only in the very late sixteenth and mostly in the seventeenth century that the term or the image springs into European discourse; the first citation is 1581. The first English citation for "harem," whose etymological origins are entirely Arabic but whose meaning comes more from European usage than from its Arabic roots, is 1634 (OED). Across the channel, too, the "first descriptions of the harem in France appear in seventeenth-century travelogues," two of the earliest being J. B. Tavernier's *La nouvelle relation de l'intérieur du sérrail du Grand Seigneur* (1675) and Jean Chardin's *Voyage en Perse* (1686) (Behdad, 111).

In those and subsequent decades, the references multiply quickly. Obviously, this has something to do with the increase in Western travel litera-

ture about Turkey in particular, which is a direct result of European governments courting Ottoman alliances.[15] Yet significant levels of travel,
trade, and intermixture between Christian Europeans and Muslims had
taken place for centuries. Muslim and Christian communities had lived side
by side in Spain, in eastern Europe, and on Mediterranean islands and
coasts. Why did the seraglio just now capture the European imagination?

Since the appearance of the seraglio/harem in Western discourse on Islam does not correspond to its development in the Islamic world, it is likely
that developments within the West caused the topic to suddenly become
fascinating and meaningful. Political, socioeconomic, and cultural developments prepared the ground for reception of the idea of the harem.[16] Politically, the centralization of government concentrated power in the Crown,
so that by the beginning of the seventeenth century in England (after mid-
century in France), absolute monarchy prevailed. Hierarchy and despotism
on the political level was reflected in the authority of the patriarch in the
family and in the rigidity of primogeniture. The era's obsession with genealogy and heraldry tracing the male line of descent demonstrates the
acute emphasis on patriarchal authority (Vickers, 210). At the same time,
as England moved from an agrarian to a more urbanized mercantile economy, the reorganization and specialization of labor increasingly pushed
women out of the site of production, which was no longer primarily the
home or farm. This sexual redivision of labor eroded the economic position of women and began to create and to idealize a separate sphere for
women in the home.

Needless to say, this happened very gradually and unevenly. In general,
though, the "confinement of women in the interior world of the family left
bourgeois man 'free' to accumulate capital" (Rowbotham, 3). Economic
prosperity affected the physical features of the home:

> In the sixteenth and seventeenth centuries the homes of people who
> were neither very rich nor very poor grew bigger, became more impor-
> tant, and began to be subdivided. The houses started to have two
> floors, there was some differentiation of function, new among the
> peasantry. It became common for yeomen farmers, for example, to
> have bedrooms, an important move towards the notion of individual-
> ity and sexual privacy. (Rowbotham, 3)

The middling townspeople began to generate a family unit suitable to capitalist production, and with it generated a morality which consecrated do-

mesticity and the domestic woman. This ideological development preceded and prepared for the full-fledged economic establishment and political empowerment of a middle-class culture which would not see fruition for another hundred-odd years.

It was the towns and the guilds which to some degree took over the Church's role as guarantors of morality, enforcing the line between honorable and immoral conduct (Pigaud in Dresen-Coenders, 40). Since rulers depended increasingly on middle-class wealth to control the nobility, the influence of bourgeois morality began to seep up into the highest levels of society. For example, it became the vogue for aristocrats to have their portraits done in familial or domestic settings. From another angle, as mentioned, both the Church and the dissenting sects placed a new emphasis on marriage and family life.

Yet after the early Renaissance opening toward women, the "original humanist stress on feminine learning and the development of the intellect for virtue's sake was lost in the Reformers' insistence on the 'word,' which in the case of women returns full cycle to Paul of Tarsus' narrow view" (Bell, 200). Mainstream Puritan thought did assert the spiritual equality of women and their rights of conscience; the insistence upon a single sexual standard and companionate marriage ameliorated the wife's position. However, woman's place on earth remained subordinate to man, and after a brief exhilarating period of spiritual leveling which saw the rise of women prophetesses among dissenting sects, there was renewed emphasis on women's submission. "Reformation preachers thunderously addressed themselves to erring wives, and a great part of their sermons dealing with women is not much more than advice to husbands on how to keep wives in their place" (Bell, 200), their place increasingly being in the newly isolated and separated private sphere. All these developments together began to push toward a more rigidly hierarchical separation of male and female worlds and toward the enclosure of women in an idealized private realm.

The great advantage of the harem or seraglio as a discursive concept, entering the Western narrative of Islam at precisely this moment, was its basic similarity in structure to the emerging gender paradigm in European societies. Because of this inherent similarity, the concept of the harem could serve from this point onward as a negative foreign counterpart to the ideal household. It was useful for exploring an intricate network of issues facing early modern European societies, including the problem of "natural" individual liberty, the organization of sexuality, and the proper role of women.

Alain Grosrichard concurs in *Structure du serail: La fiction du despotisme asiatique dans l'Occident classique* that "*la 'relation du serail' trahit son appartenance profondu a un Occident qui commence a interroger les principes de ses institutions politiques, les fins de l'éducation, le rôle de la famille, l'énigme du rapport entre les sexes*" (The "story of the seraglio" betrays its profound belonging to a West which had begun to question the principles of its political institution, the goals of education, the role of the family, and the enigma of the relationship between the sexes [cited in Trumpener, 181]). At least, these incipient debates were enough to make the seraglio catch the attention during this period; not until the eighteenth century would the seraglio become the definitive *topos* of the Muslim woman and indeed of the entire world of Islam.

Now to return to the Knight of Malta, whom we left panting over his imaginative glimpse of a seraglio in his lady's smile: that the seraglio is mentioned approvingly, even enviously, by the villain of the play clearly places it on the negative side of the text's officially declared values. There is a direct line of association from the Turkish seraglio, to Mountferrat, to Zanthia, who enters later in the same scene. Mountferrat's blandishments turn from Oriana, unattainable virtuous lady, to Zanthia, his "black swan," his "Pearle, that scornes a staine!" (i.e., because of her blackness no stain will show on her). Unlike Oriana in her relationship with the man who will become her husband, however, Zanthia perceives exactly how she is being used in a male economy, and retorts, "[L]ike a property, when I have serv'd / Your turnes, you'll cast me off, or hang me up / For a signe, somewhere." [17] Aware of this, she enters the game anyway, for she has her own desires. Knowing her ill worth in the European beauty market, Zanthia asserts an alternative standard of natural sexual beauty that is actually not without appeal to the play's audience:

> My tongue, Sir, cannot lispe to meet you so,
> Nor my black Cheeke put on a feigned blush
> To make me seeme more modest then I am.
> This ground-worke will not beare adulterate red,
> Nor artificial white, to cozen love.
> . . . . . . . . . . . . . . . . . . . . . . . . . . .
> . . . and yet, Mountferrat, know
> I am as full of pleasure in the touch
> As ere a white fac'd puppet of them all,
> Juicy, and firme . . . (I.i.172–182)

Moreover, Zanthia speaks for women's pleasure when she compares for Oriana the merits of husbands of various professions, concluding that a soldier's wife (as Oriana has been pledged to become) is best because he will not short-change her sexually. "Like a great Queen" she collects the booty he wins:

> He layes it at her feet, and seeks no further
> For his reward, then what she may give freely,
> And with delight too, from her own Exchequer
> Which he finds ever open. (III.ii.50–54)

"Be more modest," the aristocratic Oriana reproaches, unwilling to face the fact of female sexual desire that lower-class Zanthia raises: "Thou talkst of nothing." "Of nothing Madam? You have found it something; / Or with the raising up this pretty mount here,[18] / My lord hath dealth with spirits." Zanthia's double entendres in this scene with Oriana subtly align her with the privilege of male subjectivity (like Hamlet's when he abuses Ophelia with sexual puns), although this subjectivity is withheld from her by the overt declarations of representatives of the established order. Similarly, Zanche in John Webster's *The White Devil* (1612), black Moorish servant to the Venetian adulteress title character, makes numerous ribald puns and is castigated as Vittoria's "baud" (III.ii.273). Patriarchal authority in *The Knight of Malta* understands Zanthia's sexuality as transgressive behavior, castigating her as "bawd," "devill," "sinfull usher."

In fact, Zanthia's actions in the play constitute a systematic attack on the repressive ideal of femininity enforced by the Order of Malta. Members of the Order must take a vow of chastity upon being knighted, so woman's sexuality is the primary danger to their solidarity. The only tolerable woman is the completely "pure," passive vessel. Oriana, the Grand Master's sister, is such a conformist female. Nevertheless, she is vulnerable to suspicion at the first charge fabricated against her by Mountferrat: the charge is that she has conspired with the Turkish Basha of Tripoli to desert her country and faith. A hostile exterior world constituted by Muslims laps at the edges of the island, always threatening contamination through its weakest or basest members.

The language of the forged letter highlights the concupiscence of its true author—Zanthia. Yet it is this concupiscent element which is most damning for Oriana, since there is no defense against it for a woman. When Oriana opens her mouth to protest her innocence, her brother shuts her up with—"[T]hou faire sweet banke of flowers, / Under whose beauty Scorpions lie, and kill . . . I would not hear thee speak . . . thou shalt die" (I.iii.166–172). Nothing she can do or say will lift the charge; it must be decided by a duel between men.

By her act of creative writing, which produced the forged letter to the Basha, Zanthia exposes the oppressive contradictions of the Order's feminine ideal. She exposes how fragile is the European woman's position, how quickly Oriana, too, like the Moorish black woman, can be called a devil's "dam"—as she is in act II, scene iii. (This link between the moral "blackness" of the European woman and the physical-plus-moral blackness of the Moorish woman is obvious from the very title of *The White Devil*[19] and is reiterated by the numerous separate references to both Zanche and Vittoria as devils.[20]) Oriana may not get the hint about the precariousness of women's position, for she trusts in the system or God to vindicate her, but the unfairness of her predicament is made plain.

Oriana herself, as the embodiment of an oppressive ideal of femininity, comes under attack by Zanthia. In trying to draw Oriana into bed with Mountferrat, Zanthia wants to bring Oriana into a realm where she will acknowledge that the female desire she dismisses as "nothing" is "something."[21] To accomplish her design, Zanthia concocts a potion which she manipulates Gomera into giving to Oriana. This associates her with poison lore's *venefica*, or potion-maker. "In the Middle Ages and the Renaissance, the purpose of the potion is to govern male behavior, so it is a powerful symbol of female dominance and, conversely, loss of male control. The *venefica* is a stock character who represents the dark and devious underside of legitimate feminine roles: nurturer and healer" (Hallissy, 60). When Mountferrat is stymied by a setback to his villainy, he lashes out at Zanthia:

> . . . thou damn'd one, worse;
> Thou black swoln pitchie cloud, of all my afflictions,
> Thou night hag, gotten when the bright Moone suffer'd,
> Thou hell it self confin'd in flesh: what trick now?
> . . . . . . . . . . . . . . . . . . . . . . . . . . . . . . . . . . . . . .
> This sword shall cut thee into thousand peeces
> . . . . . . . . . . . . . . . . . . . . . . . . . . . . . . . . . . . .
> A sacrifice to thy black sire, the Devill. (IV.ii)

Nonplussed, she retorts, "Neither his sword, nor anger do I shake at."

Not only is Zanthia a threat to those representing order in the play, she is even too much for the villain to control. She truly constitutes a third term, a resistant alternative. "I have done too much," she blasts, "Far, far too much for such a thanklesse fellow"—it is her excess, her too-much-ness, that the play is able only incompletely to subdue. She throws Mountferrat's misogynistic accusations back in his face, exposing the fact that the negative feminine ideal is as much authored by men as the positive one:

> If I be devill, you created me,
> I never knew those arts, nor bloody practises
> ([Pox] o' your cunning heart, that mine of mischiefe)
> Before your flatteries won 'em into me. (IV.ii)

By combining the murderous *venefica* role with that of a sexually transgressive woman, the black Moor Zanthia embodies the most powerful evil force in the play, more powerful even than the villain Mountferrat, who is something of a coward.

If Zanthia attacks the feminine ideal with a sleeping potion, she attacks the author of that ideal with a more murderous and unambiguous weapon: she shoots him with a pistol. (So Zanche in *The White Devil* shoots Flamineo.) In the tumultuous climax at Oriana's dimly lit tomb, Zanthia does what she sarcastically describes as "a poor womans part, / And in an instant, what these men so long / Stood fooling for," wounding the soldier Gomera's right arm so that he drops his sword. She then aims at the general Norandine, but he disarms her (just as he has disarmed the Turks who have attacked Malta). Defeated, she still has the spirit to rebuke the men beaten with her: "From me learn courage" (V.iv.59). Zanche/Zanthia is certainly a termagant, although as a servant she does not have all the power or characteristics of the "overbearing Muslim noblewoman."

In fact, although on one hand Zanthia's vanquishment is accomplished in terms which condemn and marginalize her, on the other hand, the text seems to acknowledge her character as having an energy which cannot easily be fettered. In punishing Mountferrat by making him marry Zanthia and be banished with her ("Away French stallion, now you have a Barbary mare of your own, go leap her, and engender young devillings" [V.ii]), the knights really force him to fulfill his own false promise to her ("I vow by heaven / Malta I'le leave, in it my honours here, / And in some other Country, Zanthia make / My wife, and my best fortune" [I.i]), which makes the penalty an ironic victory for the Moorish woman. There is no prospect of conversion in this intermarriage, yet it is part of the restoration of order which also reunites Gomera with Oriana and their new child, and which promotes Miranda to knighthood. All along Zanthia has asserted her "black is beautiful" equality: "Am I not here / as lovely in my blacke . . ." (II.iii). Even Webster's Zanche[22] ends with dignity: "I am proud / Death cannot alter my complexion" (V.vi). Zanthia and Zanche are florid theatrical creatures, their blackness overworked for effect, but out of what Lemuel Johnson characterizes as the "exuberant curiosity and ignorance" of the "medieval-renaissance" view of the Negro, not the "pseudo-scientific and pathological malice" of nineteenth-century racism (33–34).

At the sentencing, however, *The Knight of Malta*'s Norandine makes Zanthia's villainous activity seem auxiliary when in fact Mountferrat has relied on her in his incompetence. At the same time, the general heaps insults on her drawn from the discourse of the *Malleus Maleficarum*[23] combined with that of the English wonder-cabinet of "savage" artifacts from Africa and the New World: "Wee'l call him Cacodemon, with his black gib there, his Sucuba, his devils seed, his spawn of Phlegeton . . . do ye snarle you black jill? she looks like the Picture of America" (V.ii). That snarl, mediated through Norandine's narration, is the last sound Zanthia makes, and her first descent into the dehumanization of the black African woman in Western cultural discourse. With her descends all that had been "too much" about the Muslim woman. As the echo of Zanthia's astute outcry, "If I be devill, you created me" fades, she sinks into incomprehensible, feral language, into the silence of Sycorax.

Donusa in Massinger's *The Renegado* (staged 1624) is something of a throwback, proving that the older model of the Muslim woman still has some life. She is a white devil on the Turkish side, covering her breach of Muslim morality with the haughty nerve of a Vittoria. Donusa cuts a figure familiar to us by now as a willful Muslim princess who pursues a Christian man, converts to his faith, and absconds with the jewels. She even contains shades of the *venefica*, for the Venetian gentleman Vitelli drinks moral "poison," he tells her, from "the alluring cup of your enticements," although he was a willing enough participant in the sexual affair (III.v). Her "wantonness" with Vitelli (forewarned by his Jesuit advisor against the fierce "lust" of "Turkish dames" who are like "English mastiffs" from too much restraint) is contrasted to the impassioned Christian chastity of his aptly named sister Pauline, object of unsuccessful seduction by Asambeg, viceroy of Tunis.

Two details only add an unexpected twist to this treatment of the theme. One is the introduction of the issue of liberty. Curiously, however, although there is a seraglio in the play, it is the kidnapped Pauline who is "mew'd up" in it by Asambeg, as a function of Islamic male sexual aggression against Christian order.[24] The Muslim Donusa has complete freedom of movement (within the expected limits of her royalty, that is) and is not subordinate to the authority of Asambeg or any other man. Thus we have on one hand a reiteration of one of the oldest "Muslim woman" types in Donusa, the overbearing Muslim noblewoman, and on the other the entirely new element of seraglio. That there is no attempt at congruence between their conflicting meanings exposes a jagged, fragmentary transition in the Muslim woman's image. The second addition is the use of the treatment of the Muslim woman explicitly to criticize the position of women in society—English society, that is.

"I have heard / That Christian ladies live with much more freedom / Than such as are born here," Donusa begins, addressing her eunuch Carazie. This would imply that Muslim women have less liberty, but ironically that initial set-up is inverted by the end of the following passage. She continues:

Our jealous Turks
Never permit their fair wives to be seen,
But at the public bagnios, or the mosques,
And, even then, veil'd and guarded. Thou, Carazie,
Wert born in England; what's the custom there,
Among your women? Come, be free and merry:
I am no severe mistress: nor hast thou met with
A heavy bondage.
Carazie: Heavy? I was made lighter
By two stone weight, at least, to be fit to serve you.
But to your question, madam; women in England,
For the most part, live like queens. Your country ladies,
Have liberty to hawk, to hunt, to feast,
To give free entertainment to all comers,
To talk, to kiss; there's no such thing known there
As an Italian girdle. Your city dame,
Without leave, wears the breeches, has her husband
At as much command as her 'prentice; and if need be,

Can make him cuckold by her father's copy.

Donusa: But your court lady?

Carazie: She, I assure you, madam

Knows nothing but her will; must be allow'd

Her footmen, her caroch, her ushers, pages,

Her doctor, chaplains; and, as I have heard,

They're grown of late so learn'd, that they maintain

A strange position, which their lords, with all

Their wit, cannot confute.

Donusa: What's that, I prithee?

Carazie: Marry, that it is not only fit, but lawful,

Your madam there, her much rest and high feeding

Duly consider'd, should, to ease her husband,

Be allow'd a private friend: they have drawn a bill

To this good purpose, and, the next assembly,

Doubt not to pass it.

Donusa: We enjoy no more,

That are o' the Ottoman race, though our religion

Allows all pleasure. I am dull: some music.

Take my chapines off. So, a lusty strain. (I.ii)

Donusa as the sultan's niece commands all the men around her, from the viceroy of Tunis to the war hero Mustapha, who has come to court her. Her command can deprive men of their tongues or testicles, depending on her mood. The Muslim woman, far from being deprived of "liberty," supposedly has too much, and this liberty is specifically sexual. She is set up as the picture of despotic decadence, served every luxury, indulged every whim, supposedly allowed every pleasure by a religion of concupiscence— and all this, Carazie says by way of hyperbole, is surpassed by the atrocious liberty of the English woman.

Carazie is being facetious, obviously, but the profound mistrust of women motivating his spoof of English manners seems to find a congenial audience. After the sycophantic flattery paid to one powerful woman in the court of Elizabeth, who was no feminist, James I was reputed to have developed a distaste for assertive ladies, and a sizable contingent of English society agreed with him. This is not to say that Jacobean drama is not polyphonic, with its multiple levels of language from street-talk to court-talk, its use of blank verse and vernacular prose—but the strident misogyny in many Jacobean plays cannot fail to impress.[25]

Donusa proceeds to justify every point in the diatribe about the excessive liberty of women by indulging in an illicit affair with the first man she sees on her outing to the market. Although she veils when she emerges from her palace, the only prison truly inhibiting her is the "cruellest of prisons, / Blind ignorance and misbelief" which she sheds with cries of "False prophet! / Imposter Mahomet!" (V.v).

This passage is an early example of a genre that was to become common in the next century, the use of "the East" to satirize and critique the home society of the writer. Yet in lampooning women's "liberty," this text also recognizes a new motif in the representation of the Muslim woman, the motif of enclosure. This motif activates a whole new scenario, one which includes, for the first time, the jealous Muslim man (here doubled as Asambeg and Mustapha) guarding the woman, veiling and enclosing her. This is the scenario of the seraglio. It is only loosely deployed in these plays so far, suggested, introduced. Little attempt to smooth out its contradiction with earlier patterns of representing the Muslim woman is made. Its similarity to structures which organize gender in European societies is testified by the prevalence of the theme of jealous husbands who lock up their wives in texts from Marguerite de Navarre's *Heptameron* (1558) to Molière's *L'école des maris*, *L'école des femmes*, and *Le Sicilien*,[26] over a century later. The merger of this theme with Islamic material signals that the harem as *topos* has been mobilized in the Western narrative of the Muslim woman. But it is still a relatively indeterminate site. How the harem will be furnished, what meanings will be fabricated for it, remains to be seen.

ROXANE: THE TERMAGANT'S LAST STAND

In Racine's plays, suffocating enclosure is the overriding metaphor for life and the structure for tragedy. The oppressive sense of enclosure in *Bajazet* is reinforced by Racine's neoclassical adherence to the unities of action, time, and space, and by the formal strictness of his alexandrine lines, producing a vastly different spectacle from that of Jacobean drama. The captivity of the hero at the mercy of an absolute power who tries to enforce both authority and erotic domination is what produces the tragic action, which, as Roland Barthes shows, is the same in nearly all Racine's plays (8–9). Specifically, the tragic conflict in Racine emerges from a relationship in which "A has complete power over B. A loves B, who does not love A" (Barthes, 24). In *Bajazet* (1672), Roxane is the powerful favorite of the absent Ottoman sultan.[27] She loves the sultan's brother Bajazet, who is imprisoned in the seraglio (there is no clear distinction here between "*sérail*" as palace and "*sérail*" as women's quarters). Bajazet loves Atalide, a cousin with whom he has been raised. In Roxane's love there is a defiance of the sultan's power, while Bajazet's love defies Roxane's power. Roxane toys with Bajazet, holding his death over him when she discovers his love for Atalide, but in the end, the sultan's will descends with the force of destiny, of the "*ciel*" everyone constantly invokes, leaving Roxane, Bajazet, and Atalide dead. Having indicted absolute power in the female form of Roxane, Racine preserves it in the male form of the king, and exalts its impersonal retribution as "destiny." Although Barthes sees sex as a function of the figure's position in the power dynamic (thus Roxane is a "viriloid" woman and Bajazet a "feminoid" man, 13) rather than as important in itself, it is still female power that receives the greatest chastisement, not only in *Bajazet* but for example in *Phedre* and in *Athalie* as well. The male figure of supreme power is doubled into two characters so that its lower order may be indicted while its higher order may survive the tragedy intact.

Although the unity of space is strictly followed in Racinian drama, Barthes distinguishes three sites within the one setting. The first, the Chamber, "vestige of the mythic cave, it is the invisible and dreadful place where Power lurks" (3). In *Bajazet*, it is the mutes and black Orcan who are sent forth from this site of power (the absent Sultan Amurath) to enforce its dread will (4). The second site, the Antechamber, as the stage proper where the tragic figure effuses language, mediates between the Chamber and the third site, the exterior world, through a Door. This Door is more often a veil, "an eyelid, a symbol of the masked gaze," which enables the invisible power to "spy on" those subject to it in the Antechamber (5). "The Racinian stage is thus a spectacle twice over: to the eyes of the Invisible and to the eyes of the spectator (the site that best expresses this tragic contradiction is the Seraglio of *Bajazet*)" (Barthes, 5). In this manner, voyeurism is established as the basic structure of viewing Racinian drama; *Bajazet*'s activation of the seraglio matter heightens the excitement of the voyeurism by making its object Islamic. Voyeurism is a rather new element in the material of the Muslim woman; at least it has never been so explicitly and fully realized in previous treatments. Here it is suddenly everything: mise-en-scène, structure, content, action.

The seraglio is a place of shadows, where figures wait in subjection for the will of the supreme power, "*ciel*," God, destiny, the father, the king, to burst upon them like a ray of the sun. This relation is doubled in *Bajazet*: Roxane has absolute power over Bajazet and the entire seraglio, but the absent Amurath has absolute power over Roxane, and she is part of his seraglio. In her pursuit of Bajazet there is a faint reminder of the sexually aggressive medieval queen, but very faint. As a figure of Muslim woman, Racine's Roxane is much reduced, even from Zanthia, in the extreme degradation of her mind. She responds to the male order by employing the master's tools of sadism. Her very cruelty arises from her acceptance and internalization of the master–slave condition, which artificial servility in women, as Mary Wollstonecraft will observe, "produces a propensity to tyrannize, and gives birth to cunning" (84). Her use of the master's tools only serves to affirm his power in the end. It is the sultan's brilliant *soleil* which eventually bursts upon Roxane's sealed-off shadow-play and makes it vanish in the blink of an eye. It is his will whose godlike machinery crushes and resounds in the end, leaving the imprint of Roxane's sado-masochistic character indelibly on the narrative of the Muslim woman.

While the veil is not literally named and the seraglio is not a graphic image in *Bajazet*, veil and seraglio constitute the very structure of the drama and its physical mise-en-scène. Seraglio is the place which cannot be seen, the forbidden place, the inner place, bearing allusion to the Freudian uncanny, "*ces lieux / Dont l'accès était même interdit a nos yeux*" (I.i.).[28] At the same time, because of its enclosure and subjection, it is the object of the gaze of the terrifying powers-that-be, and of the prurient spectator who desires the secret of its interior. It is the place where seeing without being seen becomes the ultimate exercise of power (one which Roxane knows how to use), and being seen without seeing the ultimate form of helplessness. Between these two absolutes is the veil, whose meaning depends on which side can see through it. The most helpless of *Bajazet*'s characters is Atalide because she is most blind to the machinations of those in power, always learning of them too late. Yet the most powerful figure in Bajazet is the most heavily veiled—the absent sultan. Unseen but seeing, he reaches out through his agent Orcan and strikes suddenly.

The existence of this same seraglio/veil structure in other of Racine's plays from *Britannicus* to *Athalie* shows that it is not exclusively produced by the manipulation of Islamic materials and allusions. The drama of absolute power and subjection enclosed in an erotically charged, violent, sealed space is first produced by archetypical Racinian conditions and then assiduously seeks out forms of expression, the most uniquely suited of which happens to construct an "Islamic" *topos*.

Obviously, however, these associations are not and cannot be accidental. The increasing political and economic power of Europe, in this case France, is also part of the conditions that cause the sudden ubiquity of the seraglio narrative in Western, here French, discourse. Such power requires that a "cultural space" (Behdad, 124) be created for it by discursive practices which explore themes of domination and subjugation of the Other. It is no coincidence, for example, that Tavernier and Chardin, whose travelogues were among the first in French to produce an image of the harem, were funded by Colbert, author of France's political expansionism and economic mercantilism. Tavernier dedicates his memoir to Louis XIV, remarking that *"il me semble que tous les Roys de l'Asie, et de l'Afrique ne sont faits que pour estre un jour vos Tributaires, et que vous estes destine pour commander a tout l'Univers"* (it seems to me that all the kings of Asia and Africa were not made but to be one day your vassals, and that you are destined to command all the universe) (Behdad, 123). The phrases *"il me semble"* and *"un jour"* (it seems to me, one day) remind one that these things have not been accomplished, are still in the realm of what might be, but the sweeping imperialist vision is clear nonetheless. As Ali Behdad puts it, "What does Tavernier wish Louis XIV or France to become if not a Grand Seigneur who has political and economical sovereignty over his Asian and African slaves?" (124) The feminization of the Orient implied in relation to a virile Western master makes the harem as a discursive structure uniquely suited to the imaginative interpretation of the realities of expansion.

Although what is called "the Age of Reason" had already begun, Racine's texts emerge from a sociopolitical context that passionately rejected the perfectibility of man (let alone woman), the reasonability of God, and the accountability of king. What are the milieux, in the sense of "the locus of certain habits of thought, certain implicit taboos, certain 'natural' values, certain material interests of a group of men actually associated by identical or complementary functions" (Barthes, 156), in which Racine writes? Racine's own life orbited around two places besides the theater, the court of Louis XIV and Port-Royal. Toward each he had the relation of an indebted son, now in defiant disfavor, now humbly conciliatory. He was educated at Port-Royal, center of Jansenism, an austere Catholic sect which stressed predestination and total dependence on divine grace. Although his former teachers had grave doubts about the probity of the theater in general, Racine himself believed that his later plays instructed piously. He wrote, for example, in the preface to *Phèdre* that "vice is here painted throughout in colors that make us see and hate its deformity. This is the proper end that every man who works for the public should propose to himself. . . ." (quoted in Durant, 139). He owed his livelihood to the patronage of the Sun King, who did not exactly tolerate dissent, having, for example, revoked the Edict of Nantes, which tolerated Huguenots.

The court of Louis XIV, especially the later decades of his reign, was highly centralized, rigid in its hierarchy, severe in its patriarchal authority. The king manipulated the upper ranks of the townspeople in order to control and contain the power of the nobles, whose rights in the *parlements* were hotly contested and curtailed. These upper burghers prominent in Louis' court, from whose ranks playwrights such as Racine and Molière were drawn, were precisely the sector of society least tolerant of the political influence of aristocratic women. It was their moral code which rebuked the political ambitions of lady courtiers, mocked the philosophical aspirations of the *Précieuses* and *Savantes*,[29] and generally condemned the religious hypocrisy, sexual promiscuity, and sumptuary display of noblewomen. It is easy to see in Roxane the negative female ideal around which king and court, from a combination of class and patriarchal motivations, could unite in execration. The misogynistic nature of the condemnation of Roxane is disguised and softened by her foreign Islamic identity, allowing even French noblewomen to be as horrified as their male counterparts by her grasping ambition and crude tyranny, as relieved as they by her ultimate debasement and death.

In *Bajazet*, the termagant is toppled. Not just because she is killed in the *denouement*, but because she is now bound up by the seraglio structure. Lashed to her place by its veils, Roxane has lost the primal power of the medieval Muslim woman. She can only pace and stalk within narrow forbidding corridors, her former mobility gone. Only a helpless female anger, twisted into sadism, remains of the termagant's powers.

The Islamic association fortuitously redoubles the effect of elements already present in Racine's material without reference to Islam. "Seraglio" is merely another word, an exotic new word, for something formed from an indigenous process, from a new sense of France's relationship to racial others and French society's reconsideration of the female. That is why, although Racine stresses in his preface to *Bajazet* how attentive he was to Turkish history and customs, Corneille and others "criticized Racine for not having created in his play a single character 'who has the feelings that he ought to have, that people at Constantinople have. Though wearing Turkish dress, they all express the feelings common in France'" (cited in Rodinson, 39). The allusion to Islamic or Turkish forms is a pure exercise of cultural power. The fact that Racine can cull and select a setting from the contemporary Ottoman court with as much prerogative as he can choose an ancient Greek or biblical setting shows a certain mastery over the contemporary Ottoman culture. Without question, a contemporary French setting could not have been chosen with such impunity to explore the issues that Racine's texts examine, since the weightiest fact of late seventeenth-century French sociopolitical life was absolute despotism.

In *Bajazet*, the Islamic surface fuses with the deeper structures. The text's fusion of the two is such that readers of French after Racine will inevitably associate the dark, erotic cruelties of arbitrary power with Turkish seraglios. The contemporary Turkish setting has already become inert ground, a resource to be mined, a site on which conflicts born of European conditions can be played out. This is quite unlike either the moments of equivocality and fluctuation produced by the trembling equilibrium of world power during the Renaissance or the medieval invasion of Europe by Islamic romance material.

## *Chapter Four*

# THE MUSLIM WOMAN FROM ENLIGHTENMENT TO ROMANTICISM

# *"Je la fis entrer dans les appartements secrets"*

*Knowledge and a Gun*

If European culture in the seventeenth century discovered the seraglio or harem and located the Muslim woman in it, the Enlightenment declared her unhappy there. Seventeenth-century imaginations were drawn to the seraglio (still the more common of the two terms) in part because of its explanatory force for questions emerging within European society, but they did not think of questioning the validity of the old structures. *The Renegado*, for example, contains a capsule satire of English women's manners but is certainly no radical exposé of the oppressive conditions that produced those manners. *Bajazet* accepts the basic cosmological framework of arbitrary despotism even while projecting its fear onto a foreign setting. When philosophical thought began to question the basis of previous knowledge, however, this acquiescence changed. Beginning with the method of deductive reasoning, the Enlightenment declared an epistemological clean slate and opened the way for a radical critique of entrenched systems—political, economic, religious, social. Deductive reasoning and natural law theory had begun in the seventeenth century with Bacon, Descartes, and Locke, but reached full expression in the eighteenth century. Later, liberal theorists

such as Paine, Jefferson, and Condorcet expanded the "rights of man" doctrines further into arguments for individual freedom and universal equality.
Economic theory reflected these changes too as the middle class pushed
laissez-faire, promoting "the invisible hand" [1] of unregulated individual-
istic capitalism as the most "Natural" market force, as opposed to state-
directed mercantilism. Evaluations of foreign peoples and civilizations
could now (to some extent) free themselves from older spoken and unspo-
ken strictures. Given the eighteenth-century thinkers' radical questioning
of preexisting systems, especially political and social systems, it is not surprising that the view of the seraglio and the image of the Muslim woman
also changed.

From 1704 to 1717, Antoine Galland published his multivolume French
translation from Arabic of the Arabo-Perso-Indian folktale cycle, *The Thousand and One Nights*. He carefully expunged explicit sexual details, especially
those emphasizing an active female sexuality, and otherwise crafted the stories to contemporary European tastes (Melman, 65). Before *Mille et une Nuits*
was even finished, its first English version hit the streets (1706–1708).
Hackneyed as the Grub Street translation was, it served the English reading public right through the generation of the Romantics. Translations—
from Galland, not from Arabic—into other European languages surfaced
almost immediately. After the *Nights* tradition was inaugurated, texts with
Oriental themes flooded the European markets, extending from popular
tales of magic and romance to philosophical treatises based on the premise
of travel as a mode of cultural relativism.

The influence of Galland's *Nights* on the Western image of Islam is ex-
tensive, but somewhat outside the scope of this research. Of interest here
is the fact that the cultural production of the Muslim woman exploded and
created a new popular image for her.

Several new relevant motifs emerge in Western discourse during the
eighteenth century. First, the Muslim woman's "feminization" continues.
That is, the basic premise for her portrayal becomes her helplessness and
increasingly subdued speech; her textual presence seems to shrink. The aggressive, active, forward quality assigned to the Muslim woman in earlier
literature is driven into latency. Now passivity becomes her prominent and
fundamental quality.

Next, she becomes oppressed. In the seventeenth century, as soon as it
entered the Western discourse on Islam, the seraglio/harem began to be an
oppressive place. In the eighteenth century, the Muslim woman becomes its

inmate definitively—and the seraglio inmate's lack of liberty turns into an issue in a century veering toward revolution. "From the Enlightenment onwards, the harem came to be . . . a metaphor for injustice in civil society and the state and arbitrary government" (Melman, 60). In some texts, the felt need for transgressing an oppressive system offers a way for the Muslim woman's waning aggressive side to surface. As a stand-in for the bankrupt old order of pre-Enlightenment Europe (safely contained within a Western critique of a tyrannical Islamic Other), the seraglio seemed ripe for overthrow.

Finally, the sexuality of the Muslim woman is increasingly organized as a scopophilic experience, both voyeuristic and fetishistic. Sexuality has been an important part of her portrayal from very early on, but until now she has primarily been actively seducing, rather than receptively seductive. Now she emphatically becomes the erotic object of male visual pleasure. Such a transformation follows inherently from the cementing of the seraglio in the dominant (i.e., male elite) Western discourse as a structure which operates on the basis of teasingly concealing and revealing the woman, both delaying and heightening the male gaze through narrative technique. Subtly, the veil begins to slip into the place of a defining metaphor.[2]

As all these elements slide into position, the Muslim woman in her reduced and oppressed capacity begins, paradoxically, to occupy a more focal place in the overall Western narrative of Islam. The dominant, institutionalized, Western male perception of the Islamic world increasingly characterizes it as impotent, unproductive, ineffectual. This view is reflected in a general feminization of the Islamic Orient in cultural discourse. The Muslim woman, as the most feminine part of that effeminate world, therefore becomes its exemplary manifestation.

A range of conditions predisposed European societies to selective retention and reiteration, through the massive production of Orientalia, of a specific kind of "knowledge" about the Muslim woman. In large part this selectivity came from a condition that Edward Said does not hesitate to call Western "cultural strength," ponderous as that term may be (40). In the seventeenth century, even sixty-five years after the Battle of Lepanto, the experienced traveler Henry Blount could write, "He who would behold these times in their greatest glory could not finde a better Scene then Turkey. . . . ," adding that the Turks "are the only moderne people, great in action . . . whose Empire hath so suddenly invaded the World, and fixt it selfe such firm foundations as no other ever did" (Chew, 101). Blount's assessment reflected the conventional secular judgment, not an aberrant view, in his time. But by the advent of the next century, no one would easily confuse the Turks with the "only moderne people" in the dawning age of European power. Knowledge, and a gun, changed that.

Muslim "cultural strength" had indeed seen better days. While the Turks proved they still had some kick left by attacking Russia in 1709 and Austria in 1716,[3] their empire was mostly riding on dwindling momentum from past glories. Their military technology was dismally outdated, their heavy artillery outstripped by lighter European guns—and everybody knew it. The great Safavid dynasty of Persia fell to the Afghans in 1736. In India, the Moghuls declined under Aurangzeb (d. 1712). The Barbary states in North Africa maintained a precarious independence from Turkey but did not amount to much on the scale of world power; neither did the inner kingdoms of Africa. European ascendancy—political, military, economic—became as obvious to Europeans as the converse decline in Muslim power, so that Samuel Johnson's Abyssinian Prince Rasselas can ask "By what means . . . are the Europeans thus powerful? or why, since they can so easily visit Asia and Africa for trade or conquest, cannot the Asiaticks and Africans invade their coasts, plant colonies in their ports, and give laws to their natural princes? This same wind that carries them back would bring us thither." That wind may have blown in both directions two hundred years before, but it clearly did not in the eighteenth century. "Knowledge," his guide replies, is what makes Europeans more powerful, and "knowledge will always predominate over ignorance, as man governs the other animals."

It has become apparent, eminently so to the Europeans themselves, that Europeans are indeed "another order of beings," as the guide puts it, meant to "govern" the lower orders (30). Gone was the day when Europeans approached the Islamic world with a keen sense of the inadequacy of their knowledge about it. The first chair in Arabic had been created in Paris at the new College de France in 1539; Oxford followed a hundred years later; in the interim Arabic and Turkish studies had been inaugurated in Leiden, Lorraine, and Rome (at the College of Propaganda). By the turn of the century Europe had assembled the tools of representation and classification, had achieved the material conditions that enable the prerogative of scrutiny and information gathering, and was ready to conquer Islam discursively. What could be considered the first encyclopedia of Islam, *Bibliothèque Ori-*

*entale*, was issued in 1697,[4] followed in 1708 by Simon Ockley's *History of the Saracens*. "In such efforts," Said writes, "Europe discovered its capacities for encompassing and Orientalizing the Orient. . . ." by a "triumphant technique for taking the immense fecundity of the Orient and making it systematically, even alphabetically, knowable . . ." (65). By the middle of the eighteenth century, we can finally say that Orientalism as a discipline for knowing and making the Orient has been deployed.[5] It is deployed because it can now be deployed, as it could not before, by a hand that is able.

The eighteenth century was the scene of broad changes not just in the various European nations' relations with the Islamic world, but in the social organization of gender within European societies. This period witnessed a great increase in the number of conduct books and a curious change in their content to a focus on "a new kind of woman" more than on the ideal aristocratic man (Armstrong 1987b, 99). Nancy Armstrong shows that the ideal of the conduct book, and of the chronologically overlapping novel of manners which developed throughout the eighteenth century and peaked in the period from 1760 to 1820, was a female composed of two sets of virtues. The first set comprised passive virtues such as modesty, humility, honesty, and obedience to male authority. The second—this is the novelty—comprised the active domestic virtues of the competent housewife. This new feminine ideal was promoted at first alongside, then in opposition to, the older cultural ideal of the accomplished aristocratic woman, whose sumptuary self-display performed an economic function and preserved her family's position in the complex web of courtly alliances which were the nexus of a declining form of power. The new ideal "is not a woman who attracts the gaze as she did in an earlier culture, but one who fulfills her role by disappearing into the woodwork to watch over the household" (Armstrong 1987b, 119). Her virtues are precisely those that would enable the middle-class male to devote his undivided attention to the business of capitalist production, the same economic production that was creating greater levels of contact between the West and the Islamic world and gearing Europe for colonization of that world.

Yet Armstrong hits a perplexing hurdle in her argument. The creation of this new feminine ideal is unmistakably suited to the needs of the bourgeoisie, yet the middle class as a distinct, self-conscious socioeconomic group grounded in full-fledged industrialized capitalist production did not exist until the nineteenth century. The new female both preceded and accompanied the emergence of the middle class. "If changes in socioeconomic categories came after similar changes in the categories governing female education, we must ask . . . what the new domestic ideal said to a heterogenous economic group that ensured this ideal would keep on making sense well into the nineteenth century" (102).

A similar question perplexes my argument about the sudden explosion of harem discourse in the eighteenth century. The instinct of a critic of Orientalism is to see European imperialist power over the Islamic world as materially enabling the production of an inferior, debased Muslim woman in Orientalist discourse. Yet this production, which does indeed valorize and rationalize European domination, appears well before the material apparatus of imperialism and colonialism is in place. It appears before a single European ruler has invaded or conquered or administered Muslim lands. It certainly appears before Napoleon's penetration of Egypt, which Said regards as seminal in the establishment of European modes of producing the Orient. What function could this harem discourse have fulfilled earlier, that it could continue to fulfill after imperialism and colonialism had been fully installed?

The narrative of the Muslim woman had to be more than just a function of European relations with the Islamic world. It was also a function of specific kinds of desire in the discourse of sexuality within European societies, in the "deployment of sexuality" and the creation of new forms of pleasure and desire that Michel Foucault insists occurred during this same period (in *The History of Sexuality*).[6]

The Muslim woman, like the now-castigated aristocratic woman, provided discourse with a negative ideal. She had, however, the added advantage of being safely foreign and therefore even fairer game for condemnation. For what are the disapproved traits of the aristocratic woman? She was skilled in cosmetic self-display, engaged in frivolous amusements, flaunted her sexuality, instigated corrupt desires in men, and functioned as the object of the male gaze. She aroused the wrong kind of desire. These were the very traits assigned to the Muslim woman in the harem discourse. Moreover, moralists now rebuked the "cloistered virtues" that used to be the ideal for young aristocratic maidens as selfish and wasteful of energies that were better spent in maintaining a home and children or acquiring an education in thrifty domesticity (Armstrong 1987b, 106). Hence the vehemence of disapproval for the Islamic harem, otherwise difficult to account for given the cultural relativism of the age, which tended to look more open-mindedly on the different sexual standards of other "climates." Writers of the discourse of domesticity abhorred the political and economic

motives of aristocratic marriage and the adulterous lifestyles it spawned; they advanced companionate marriage free of "lewdness" as a sober alternative which was more equitable for the woman, more respectful of her "affective individualism" (Flynn, 73). Thus women were being offered certain freedoms and advantages, while at the same time a new form of desire was being produced that enclosed them more securely in the domestic sphere. Armstrong ventures, as an answer to the question posed above, that the proliferation of discourse producing the new female was a response to the social fragmentations of the eighteenth century:

> The authors of conduct books were acutely sensitive to the subtlest differences in status, and each represented his or her readers' interests in terms of a differential system that opposed country and town, rich and poor, labor and leisure. . . . the representation of any male role automatically defined a partisan position. . . . The female, in contrast, provided a topic that could bind together precisely those groups who were necessarily divided by other kinds of writing. Virtually no other topic appeared to be so free of bias toward an occupation, political faction, or religious affiliation. In bringing into being a concept of the household where socially hostile groups felt they could all agree, the domestic ideal helped create the fiction of horizontal affiliations that only a century later could be said to have materialized as an economic reality. (106–107)

Lucky for Armstrong that she covers herself with "Virtually!" For the discourse of the debased Muslim woman even more effectively fulfills the functions Armstrong lists.

The Muslim woman and the imagined harem in which she was now definitively enclosed serve as a negative counterimage for the ideal Western female in the home, an image immensely capable of providing satisfaction for readers of any religious, political, or occupational affiliation. She could at once arouse the wrong, passé desire and serve as an object lesson in the right kind of desire, the kind Armstrong insists was generated in eighteenth-century domestic fiction. Her discourse helped formulate a comfortable notion of European superiority over non-Europeans. Upon this notion, not only disparate groups within a single European society, but groups across a Europe erstwhile divided by internecine warfare,[7] could happily agree. Thus the discourse of the debased Muslim woman helped generate a supportive cultural environment for the colonization of Islamic lands which would not materialize in earnest until the nineteenth century.

We must acknowledge, however, a dissenting voice.

## Lady Mary: Live from the Bagnio

It is obvious that by the time Lady Mary Wortley-Montagu, nee Pierrepont, traveled to the Ottoman Empire in 1717 as the wife of the English ambassador/Levant Company representative,[8] the Western narrative of the oppressed Muslim woman was operative: Lady Mary exerted particular effort to rebut it. Her letters were circulated among a select group of wits in London and on the Continent until 1763. Then they were published, and caused an even wider stir. Lady Mary's "Turkish letters" induct an aristocratic Western woman into the new, so far male, subgenre of harem discourse, and initiate a female tradition of harem descriptions that continued to develop outside the dominant, institutionalized male tradition. They also constitute a "defense" of sorts, not only of the Islamic Other, but also, by implication, of the female in Augustan English culture. Lady Mary's writing seeks out affinities which undermine the distinctness of categories that men of her society used to devalue both groups.

With relish Lady Mary debunks one stereotype after another about the Muslim woman. She hurries to amend the "vulgar notion" that Muslims do not believe women have immortal souls (101). She mobilizes the Enlightenment's language of rationalism in defense of the Turks, as in her remarks to the Abbé Conti comparing Christian and Islamic sexual ethics. One unrealistically extols "perpetual virginity," while the other considers the sexually active married state most natural. "Which divinity is most rational I leave you to determine," she writes, leaving little doubt about her own opinion (102). This approval for an Islam which, in its ostensible lack of superstition and mystery as well as its balance of spiritual and sensual values, "approximated the Deism of most Enlightenment philosophers," became a common discursive practice in the eighteenth century (Rodinson, 47). Now that Islam's political and military threat to Europe had abated, and before subduing and administrating it became the prevailing concern, Enlightened Europeans could be magnanimous about the religion without their fundamental loyalties being called into question. At the same time, Lady Mary's "Islam" offers some critique of the Enlightenment cult of Reason, in the name, perhaps, of a waning aristocratic élan: "I am allmost of opinion they have a right notion of Life; while they consume it in Music, Gardens, Wine, and delicate eating, while we are tormenting our brains with some Scheme of Politics or studying some Science to which we can never attain . . . I had rather be a rich Effendi with all his ignorance, than Sir Isaac Newton with all his knowledge" (Lewis, 31).

Of course, there is a class element to this, for as a member of an aristocratic elite she was very comfortable with a lifestyle which maintained great distinctions of wealth and power between people. Yet her defiant tone can also be read as a defense of the devalued feminine in Augustan society, in which "women, considered sensible but not reasonable, were all but denied status as human, that is, rational beings" (A. R. Richardson, 14). She presses the very language of Reason into the service of a challenge to her culture's prevailing idea of both the Islamic and the female Other.

Perhaps the distinguishing feature of Lady Mary's language is her ability to locate congruences between the European and Islamic elements she experiences, points of overlap or convergence in which she and the Other become permeable substances, partaking of each other not as hard polished fantasms but as mutually vulnerable, porous bodies. Despite her short stay in the Ottoman Empire, for example, she learned Turkish well enough to appreciate poetry and to converse without translators. When she visits a certain Lady Fatima a second time, after having learned Turkish, she says "now I understand her language, I find her wit as engaging as her beauty. She is very curious after the manners of other countries and has not that partiality for her own so common to little minds"—she was not unlike Lady Mary, in other words (111). Lady Mary's Greek maid then comments in Italian that Lady Fatima must be Christian by her beauty and manner; when Fatima insists on a translation, she receives this intended compliment with a gracious smile and says that her mother was a Polish Christian. Having introduced Fatima as an example of a Turkish lady, Lady Mary dexterously shows the slippage of distinct racial categories, unraveling them through multiple interpretations of multiple languages. The final turn is an English interpretation of the entire visit to her sister, Lady Mar, to whom she quips at the end, "'Tis well if I don't degenerate into a downright story-teller"!

The body is the paramount site of the kind of permeabilities Lady Mary's writings explore. Her stay in the Ottoman Empire coincided with her second pregnancy and childbirth; one letter, written as she entered her ninth month, seems to end with intimations of labor; she must stop writing, she says, to send for her midwife! (106). Turkish women seem robustly rational even in childbirth: "What is most wonderful is the exemption they seem to enjoy from the curse entailed on the sex. They see all company the day of their delivery and at the fortnight's end return visits, set out in their jewels and new clothes" (105). At first this appears a typical traveler's observation from the outside: "I wish I may find the influence of the climate in this particular, but I fear I shall continue an English woman in that affair . . ." (105). But it is transformed into corporeal reality for Lady Mary when she is able to put it in practice. Childbirth "is not half so mortifying here as in England," she tells her sister five weeks after delivering, mainly because she has allowed the Turkish practice to transform her sense of her body and liberated herself from the English custom of lying-in (106). By far the most radical and unique indication of Lady Mary's openness to the convergences of "Eastern" and "Western" is her inoculation of her young son against smallpox. She reports "a set of old women who make it their business to perform this operation" (her first mention of nonaristocratic Turkish women) and describes how they open veins with large needles to "engraft" against the disease, which had already disfigured Lady Mary in England. Rather than mistrust these "old women" of a lower class and a foreign culture, or fear contamination from their "large needles," or disparage their unheard-of medical arts, she actually has the operation done on her "dear little son" and later on her infant daughter (although she brings a male European doctor to do it), decades before the scientific "discovery" of the smallpox vaccine in Europe (99).

Another of Lady Mary's "permeabilities" is her experimentation with Turkish women's dress, which leads her to an insight overlooked by male travel writers: Turkish women have "more liberty than we have," she declares (knowing it is a provocative declaration), because the "perpetual masquerade" of their veiled street appearance allows them to pursue the very same kinds of liaisons as Englishwomen pursue but with more security from men's prying (96–97). Seeing the veil thus from a woman's eye view, from the inside out, prevents it from becoming the defining metaphor through which she perceives the Muslim woman. There is little voyeurism in her description, since the frustration of the gaze that met Western males regarding Muslim women, with its heightening of eventual or imagined visual pleasure, was not part of her experience. The whole harem fantasy of male sexual promiscuity she flatly demystifies, reporting briskly,

'Tis true their law permits them four wives, but there is no instance of a man of quality that makes use of this liberty, or of a woman of rank that would suffer it. When a husband happens to be inconstant (as those things will happen) he keeps his mistress in a house apart and visits her as privately as he can, just as 'tis with you. Amongst all the great men here I only know the *tefterdar* [i.e., treasurer] that keeps a number of she slaves for his own use (that is, on his own side of the house, for a slave once given to serve a lady is entirely at her disposal), and he is spoke of as a libertine, or what we should call a rake, and his wife won't see him . . . (97)

Rather than activate a sense of the exotic, rather than set things Turkish up as acutely different, she asserts their normality and affinity with the home values. With phrases like "just as 'tis with you" and "or what we should call a rake" Lady Mary attempts no less than the translation of cultural particularity, of social idiom, from one locality to another. "Thus you see, dear sister," she concludes from Adrianople in April 1717, "the manners of mankind do not differ so widely as our voyage writers would make us believe" (97).

She sees the harem, not as an exotic *topos*, but as a type of aristocratic household that works in ways perfectly understandable from her own Augustan perspective. Even the seraglio of the sultan, which, she admits, "is so entirely unknown amongst us," she demystifies, remarking that the company of the sultan surrounded by all his ladies is "neither better nor worse than the circles in most courts, where the glance of the monarch is watched and every smile waited for with impatience . . ." (109). Lady Mary empathizes with the Sultana Hafise,[9] from whom she gleans this description, not only as one member of an aristocratic order understands another (knowing the adversity that can befall courtiers), but as one noblewoman understands another (fully aware of women's vulnerability within that ruling class). "Neither have they much to apprehend from the resentment of their husbands," she notes to her sister, "those ladies that are rich having all their money in their own hands, which they take with 'em upon a divorce with an addition which he is obliged to give 'em." She probably has in mind her own disturbing financial dependence on her husband[10] (97).

All the same, Lady Mary's letters from Turkey are very much crafted literary works, "exhibitionistic and self-conscious," and for all her lambasting of earlier male writers on the Orient, her writing partakes of a rich intertextuality (Halsband, 13). In her famous description of the bagnio at Sophia (April 1, 1717), for example, she weaves back and forth between her own fresh, immediate observations and deeply allusive evocations of Western male traditions. "I was in my travelling habit, which is a riding dress, and certainly appeared very extraordinary to them, yet there was not one of 'em that showed the least surprise or impertinent curiosity but received me with all the obliging civility possible," she begins, drawing attention to herself as the visual object, as the strangely attired Other (Melman, 91).[11] She narrates how, near the end of her interlude in the bathhouse, the women tried to persuade her to undress and bathe, and stopped only when she opened her skirts and showed them her stays: "they believed I was so locked up in that machine that it was not in my power to open it, which contrivance they attributed to my husband." So here it is the Turkish women who see the English woman as deprived of a liberty they consider basic! "I believe in the whole there were two hundred women and yet none of those disdainful smiles or satiric whispers that never fail in our assemblies when anybody appears that is not dressed exactly in fashion," she continues, again imaginatively switching places with the Turkish women, placing herself in the position of a stranger at a European court.

Her initial physical description of the women, "all being in the state of nature, that is, in plain English, stark naked," is brisk, forthright, unexotic. Then she is awakened to the potential for erudite allusion:

> They walked and moved with the same majestic grace which Milton
> describes of our General Mother. There were many amongst them
> as exactly proportioned as ever any goddess was drawn by the pencil
> of Guido or Titian, and most of their skins shiningly white, only
> adorned by their beautiful hair . . . perfectly representing the figures
> of the Graces. . . . I had wickedness enough to wish secretly that
> Mr. Jervas [12] could have been there invisible. I fancy it would have
> very much improved his art to see so many fine women naked in dif-
> ferent postures, some in conversation, some working, others drink-
> ing coffee or sherbet, and many negligently lying on their cushions
> while their slaves (generally pretty girls of seventeen or eighteen) were
> employed in braiding their hair in several pretty manners. In short,
> 'tis the women's coffeehouse . . . (91)

The evocation of prelapsarian Eve is significant, for it alludes to the old disruptive quality (the evil Muslim woman being compared to Eve in medieval texts such as Chaucer's) but in so gentle a manner as to rewrite Eve into a dignified queen rather than the mother of sin, simultaneously giving and denying access to Eve's disruptive quality. This allusion gains depth when read with her later comment, quoted above, that Turkish women seem to be exempt from the curse on women—that is, the pain of childbirth to which Eve was sentenced for her sin. The references to Titian evoke a Tasso-esque appreciation for "Islamic" sensuality (albeit stripped of the active components of Armida). What's more, the lack of a defining and ordering male perspective on this abundance of womanly forms seems to allow a benign limbo-space for female homosocial pleasure. However, Lady Mary then adopts a male point of view, that of Jervas, and momentarily freezes the women into idealized aesthetic objects that would "improve his art." This "wicked" desire is as close as she gets to incorporating the male position of the voyeuristic observer into her own narrative—for to be voyeuristic, the look has to be forbidden, and there is nothing forbidden in her looking or her presence, as the women's nonchalance at her being there shows. Moreover, in the interest of creating her *tableau vivant*, Lady Mary is not above refining the "truth" of the women, for according to Billie Melman it is highly unlikely that the bathers were entirely nude—Ottoman women usually bathed with linen wrappers around their waists and lower torsos (91). Finally, Lady Mary returns to her deployment of congruences; in calling the bathhouse "the women's coffeehouse" she seeks cultural affinities that minimize the Otherness of the Muslim women. Interestingly, the affinity evoked by "women's coffeehouse" is one that translates between men and women, rather than between "Eastern" and "Western."

If the customs of one's home nation are no longer the sole revealed standard for everyone, the moral values of other nations are to be judged not by how closely they adhere to one's own, but by how they fulfill the "natural" needs and rights of "man," which can be determined by the deductive reasoning of an unprejudiced mind. This is the kind of mind Lady Mary describes Lady Fatima as having, and this is the kind of mind Lady Mary hoped to show in her own writings on Turkey. Lady Mary's "defense," so to speak, of the Turkish woman draws upon an intellectual background of cultural relativism and natural law theory, but manipulates those traditions in order to try to admit devalued categories (English women, Turkish men, and Turkish women) into the charmed androcentric (actually andro-Eurocentric) circle of rational beings.

Lady Mary is also out of sync with the majority of writers and readers of eighteenth-century "Oriental tales" because she fails to meet their expectations of exoticism[13] and voyeurism. She does not set up the harem or the Muslim woman as a negative model (nor as a positive ideal, either), despite her advocacy for women's education—which has rather a Renaissance than an eighteenth-century ring about it. Nonetheless, she is a participant in the Age of Reason. She aims her debunking arsenal at the narrow, parochial, scholastic mind that rejects not only deductive reasoning, but empirical evidence, because they do not fit its preconceptions. This older mentality would probably revel in the severe moral conservatism, hierarchalism, and exoticism of Racine's *Bajazet*.[14] Lady Mary's reasoning, however, presents Islamic sexual ethics as "rational"; her empirical evidence shows the seraglio as ordinary and pleasant. Rejecting scholastic hierarchalism, which declared certain categories of behavior immoral based on Revelation, natural law theorists of the seventeenth century made "Nature" the arbiter of moral value. As a woman contesting a male tradition which devalues her, Lady Mary deliberately uses natural law theory and reason to challenge that devaluation. She simultaneously asserts that Turkish life and Turkish women are quite reasonable and rational, and that even when they are not, they have more joy in them anyhow; that stance contains implied affirmations of English women's value.

The sumptuary display of the aristocratic Turkish women Lady Mary encounters, and their leisurely, insular lifestyles, understandably rouse no deep ire in her. Nor does she try to mask the privileged political position which allows her to see Turkey from a specific vantage, as when she notes the expensive garments at Sultana Hafise's place which "seemed [so] negligently thrown on the sofa" that "I don't doubt these rich habits were purposely placed in sight" of the English ambassador's wife. She has no interest in writing a new feminine ideal that would cut across class and factional affiliations to produce a domestic woman suited for middle-class modes of economic production. Nor do emerging notions of affective individualism excite her to abandon traditional vertical hierarchies of status and therefore to see the gradations of status in Ottoman society and household as inherently evil; in this she is rather a relic of an *ancien régime* than a cutting-edge radical.

Later readers of Lady Mary's letters would completely overturn her underlying assumptions and read her writings through the grid of subsequent harem discourse, dismissing what is most original in them as regrettable eccentricities and pressing the rest into the service of voyeuristic Romantic banalities like Ingres' painting *Le Bain Turc.*

## Roxana, or the Unfortunate Slave

Natural law theory could also be developed in opposition to Lady Mary's views on the harem: it could be used to condemn the seraglio as a perversion of Nature. This was the more established view in the eighteenth century. After retreating from the traditional Christian excoriation of Islamic sexual standards as too worldly and sensual, Enlightenment thought paused for a moment to laud Islamic sexuality as "rational"—then found another reason to disdain it. During the "pause" mode, Islamic sexual mores seemed to represent the avant garde of European thought about sexuality. But as Enlightenment thinkers plunged beyond natural law theory toward more revolutionary vistas, Islamic sexual life came to represent hated aspects of the old order they attacked.

Disapproval for nonmonogamous sexuality was not the driving logic behind this attack, for the promiscuous nonmonogamous sexuality in the South Pacific, the West Indies, and equatorial societies was often represented as a "Natural" sexual utopia. Authoritarianism was these critics' target. The idea of Islamic sexuality in this period was not the medieval one of diffuse promiscuity but one of sexual activity locked up, regulated, and institutionalized. The seraglio/harem became the quintessential, arch-representative scene or locale of the Islamic world, and it was a horrible place.

Montesquieu definitively develops this *topos* in *Lettres Persanes* (1721), an epistolary treatise about two "Persian" aristocrats, Usbek and Rica, who travel to Europe, critique its old institutions, and gain a liberal education whose lessons are brought painfully home to them by a violent revolt in Usbek's harem back in Persia.[15] *Lettres Persanes* "is one of those rare works which contain within themselves the whole history of an epoch. Its internal development prefigures the course of European history in the eighteenth century: it begins in exoticism and ends with revolution" (Berman, 5). It was enormously popular, spawned dozens of imitations, and created a fresh after-wave of Orientalia from the street to the court.[16]

In *Lettres Persanes*, Montesquieu extends natural law to espouse a theory that makes of individual rights the basis of a sound polity. Relationships should be governed by the consent of the individuals involved, he advances. Any system which alienates individuals from their natural selves is unsound. Sexuality is a primary form of expression for this natural authenticity; sexual life in *Lettres Persanes* is therefore important both in itself and as a pattern for political life. "The model of the seraglio he creates typifies the unity of private and public life," Marshall Berman points out. "Thus the freedom or repression, equality or inequality in a state is a function, not of its merely political organization, but of the structure of its personal and social life as a whole" (7). Usbek's seraglio is an unsound sexual/social/political system because it alienates its members from their true selves. The harem is repressive for the women, whose veils, curtained litters, and seclusion are symbols of an unnatural alienation; it creates an entire set of mutilated, frustrated men, the eunuch-guards (Letter 34); finally, it even alienates its master, enslaving him to his jealousies and depriving him of the capacity for joy (no. 38).

Samuel Johnson would echo these criticisms of a repressive closed system in *Rasselas* (1759). The "happy valley" where the Emperor of Abyssinia confines all his children is a perfectly engineered self-contained society in which no expense has been spared to make "seclusion pleasant" and create a "blissful captivity"; here is Johnson's critique of the Enlightenment doctrine of human perfectibility (3). Satiety in this Eden deprives Prince Rasselas of the capacity for desire and reduces him to the bestial level of the mountain goats he observes, so he escapes, along with his mentor, his sister, and her maid. In one segment of the Candide-like quest of these innocents abroad, the maid is captured and taken to the seraglio of an Arab nomad. The Arab man—who is something of a philosopher himself—suffers from a nausea produced by the debased, enslaved condition of the women in his life:

> Whatever pleasures he might find among them, they were not those
> of friendship or society. When they were playing about him he looked
> on them with inattentive superiority: when they vied for his regard he
> sometimes turned away disgusted. As they had no knowledge, their
> talk could take nothing from the tediousness of life: as they had no
> choice, their fondness, or appearance of fondness, excited in him nei-
> ther pride nor gratitude; he was not exalted in his own esteem by the
> smiles of a woman who saw no other man . . . (104–105)

Although the maid is not mistreated, and although the women are happy and compliant, this system is unsound because it lowers the human potential of both women and men. The women's lives consist of "childish play" and needlework. Living on a sensuous level only, the women in the harem are similar to the goats in the happy valley: "They ran from room to room as a bird hops from wire to wire in his cage. They danced for the sake of motion, as lambs frisk in a meadow" (103). Their intellects are completely retarded by their confinement; they cannot read, have "no ideas," and "hardly names for anything but their cloaths and their food" (104). Johnson's focus is on the diminished intellectual faculties of harem women rather than the erotic abjectness of their status. Nevertheless, his seraglio is the epitome of a master—slave structure, a negative utopia that embodies all the horrors of the old-guard system against which Enlightenment writers unleash their pens.

It was Montesquieu who had originally and decisively established the "harem" theme. "A repressive system . . . fails to fulfill its own immanent standard: it is incapable of satisfying any of its members, even the most privileged; precisely when it appears most stable, it is actually decomposing from within" (Berman, 16). In *Lettres Persanes*, Rica, a bachelor, comes to see all this clearly. Usbek resists these lessons of liberalism because his rationalizing apparatus is too strong. He continues to speak of his harem with pious hyperbole as a holy place, *"le séjour de l'innocence"* (the bower of innocence), and so forth (no. 26). The absent master still enforces his will through his black underlings (like Amurat of *Bajazet*), but the dissonance between natural law and the law of the harem begins to eat away at Usbek's seraglio. Usbek's response is to unmask his apparatus of repression, which until then had been covered with benevolent rhetoric (as in *"je voudrais vous faire oublier que je suis votre maître pour me souvenir seulement que je suis votre époux"* (I wish you to forget that I am your master and to remember me only as your husband) (no. 65). Usbek retreats from the liberalism he and Rica have explored in Europe and becomes a profoundly pessimistic reactionary.

Finally, the harem spins irretrievably out of control. Usbek loses authority over the word: a mysterious letter circulates in the harem while the eunuchs are unable to determine its author or addressee; Usbek's letters of instruction remain neglected and unopened for weeks; there is a flurry of writing from eunuchs, slaves, and women unheard from before. Usbek loses sexual control of the women, too: Zelis drops her veil in the mosque; strange men are found climbing over the wall or hidden within walls; finally, Roxane's adultery is revealed. The last letter in the collection is hers, written after she has killed the guards who killed her lover, and after she has poisoned herself. "I have reformed your laws by those of nature," she declares, reclaiming her true, free self. *Lettres Persanes* is "the first manifesto" of radical individualism (Berman, 33).[17]

If the *Lettres Persanes* is a manifesto of radical individualism, is Roxane the first radical individual? Does this work reinvent the Muslim woman in the Western narrative of Islam as the liberated self or the affective self in revolt? That may be the surface meaning of the text, its overt philosophical conclusion, but that is certainly not how the text operates on the meta-narrative of the Muslim woman. Roxane may become a liberated self at the end, but that is not because of any "slippage" of Othered categories that can be cleverly deconstructed (as Trumpener suggests, 181)—it is because she is *supposed* to revolt at the end, to fulfill Montesquieu's plans for the work, to manifest his philosophical argument.[18] The shake-up of master–slave categories is the conspicuous point of the treatise, not its sly subversive secret, not the point at which it unravels, and not the source of the greatest insights the text can provide about the Muslim woman.

A reading of Roxane need not restrict itself to Montesquieu's intentions any more than a reading of Bramimonde or Armida is restricted to "Turold's" or Tasso's intentions. The medieval meta-narrative of the Muslim woman affects her conversion in the *dénouement* from an active, disruptive female to a passive, submissive one, yet it is the first formulation, the aggressive Muslim woman, which seeps out of the text, subverting its surface meaning. In the case of *Lettres Persanes*, the Muslim woman begins as submissive and subjugated, and is transformed at the end into an active, disruptive female; nevertheless it is still the first woman, the oppressed harem slave, who remains as the text's vivid and lasting contribution to the meta-narrative of the Muslim woman. It is the harem slave who seeps out of the text into the reams of popular Orientalia spawned by *Lettres Persanes*. In no small part because of Montesquieu's erotic obsession with her, it is she who becomes part of the subtext of all subsequent treatments of the Muslim woman.

Three factors support this reading. First, both the substance of the wives' letters and their positioning and proportion within the larger text definitively construct the Muslim woman as submissive harem slave. Second, although Usbek and Rica are considered stand-ins for European men, mouthpieces for Montesquieu's criticism of French society, their Persian-ness is much more than a transparent device or convention. The descriptions of Persia are also seriously intended as descriptions of Persia. So the Muslim women are not just literary devices but serious ethnographic portraits.[19] Third, *Lettres Persanes'* development and enlargement of the "harem slave" type of the Muslim woman is evident from its influence on subsequent Western "harem" discourse; its harem slave is cited and recited as subtext, accruing authority each time, becoming an inextricable part of the intertextual web of Orientalism.

To begin with the first factor, only 11 out of 161 letters are written by Usbek's wives, in a text where writing is power. Of these, the first seven carry submission to masochistic extremes—even while Montesquieu subtly foreshadows the coming disturbances, as any masterly writer would.

One cluster occurs at the beginning of the work (Letters 3, 4, and 7) and includes one of the classic titillating passages in the text (no. 3), recounting the women's competition for Usbek's favor:

> *Il fallut nous dépouiller de ces ornement qui t'étaient devenus incommodes; il fallut paraître a ta vue dans la simplicité de la nature. . . . tu portas tes curieux regards dans les lieux les plus secrets; tu nous fis passer en un instant dans mille situation différentes: toujours de nouveaux commandements et une obéissance toujours nouvelle.*

> (We had to remove all that ornamentation which had wearied you, and to appear before your gaze in the simplicity of nature. . . . Your curious gaze penetrated to the most secret places; you made us take a thousand different positions; ever new commands brought ever new compliance.)

Zachi is masochistically aroused by her own description of Usbek's mastery and the erotic servility of his women. The *tableau vivant* she paints is one of the text's two or three vivid moments of pure voyeurism, designed to place the reader in the viewing position of Usbek designated by the intimate second-person pronoun "*tu.*" Even though the writer is a woman, instead of describing her own actions and those of her companions by placing the women in the subject position, she places herself and the other women in subordinate grammatical positions, bending over backward to admit the reader into voyeuristic rapport with herself as object. Also in this group, Fatima, who writes only once in the whole work, expresses her complete emotional dependence on Usbek (no. 4).

The second cluster, in the middle of the work (nos. 47, 53, 62, and 70), includes Zelis' diligent plan for "consecrating" her seven-year-old daughter to the "inner apartments" of the seraglio so she can be molded into submission at an early age (no. 62). Zachi describes with sentiments of utter conformity another type of suffocation experienced by the harem inmates, relating an occasion when they nearly drowned in order to avoid the dishonor of being seen while crossing a river in their litters; her response was to faint (no. 47).

Moreover, besides the five who write letters, the seraglio contains countless women who are presented to us only through the narratives of others. If the five wives speak in the voice of submission, the remainder are represented as abjectly silent. Such is the concubine inspected for purchase by the Chief Eunuch, in another passage inviting the reader's participation in voyeuristic pleasure. The reader is brought to peek through the keyhole, so to speak (no. 79):

> *Je la fis entrer dans les appartements secrets, je la déshabillai, je l'examinai avec les regards d'un juge, et plus je l'examinai, plus je lui trouvai de graces. Une pudeur virginale semblait vouloir les dérober à ma vue; je vis tout ce qui lui en coutait pour obéir: elle rougissait de se voir nue . . .*

> (I conducted her into the secret apartments, undressed her, and examined her with the eyes of a judge. The more I looked the more graces I found in her. A virginal shame seemed anxious to hide them from my view, and I saw how much it cost her to obey. She blushed at seeing herself naked . . .)

Again, the woman is the direct object. This time, the reader is invited to share the grammatical position of "*je*" with the eunuch and to share in his sexual frustration as well, for just as the eunuch can do nothing with the slave girl except as his master authorizes, the reader can only participate vicariously in the scene as authorized by the master-writer, Montesquieu.

Roxane, the wife who rebels, writes nothing before the last pages of the text, but she is written about twice by Usbek (nos. 20 and 26). At the very end (when the women have been forbidden to write) she suddenly bursts into language with two defiant letters. Her revolt does not depart from the terms of the master–slave discourse; it simply inverts it. What Usbek feared most from her was sexual infidelity, so she meets his expectations with sexual infidelity. The women have been masochistic; in revolt she turns sadistic. And why, if she has killed the guards, does she poison herself as well? She is a harem slave to the end, and cannot imagine herself alive outside the terms of the harem. Moreover, there are many women in the harem, but only one revolts (perhaps one and a half; Zelis in her final letter declares outrage at Usbek's tyranny). The rest remain forever harem slaves.

As for the Persian-ness of Usbek and Rica, it is at once a convention and more than just a convention. In one sense, when Usbek discredits the scholasticism of the "Mollack" at Com, who is obviously conceived very much more as a pope or bishop than as an actual eighteenth-century Shiite mullah,[20] Montesquieu is aiming barbs at the obscurantism of Christian churchmen. Once this satirical purpose is accomplished, however, the Islamic material is not discarded as mere device, but retains credibility as a realistic description of Islam. The Mollack is also supposed to be a mullah. This is evident in Montesquieu's exhaustive attention to "authentic" data on Persia, such as his careful listing of the Islamic lunar months, attention which seeks to establish his ethnographic authority on things Islamic. Besides critiquing French and European society from the "outside," then, Usbek and Rica do offer a substantive European critique of Persian and "Asiatic" society from the "inside." Of course, both analyses are really Montesquieu's, so that the terms of inside and outside are really reversed.

However, there is no question of parity or parallel between the European and the Persian terms in this comparison, which actually contains not two, but three terms. On the one side, there is the existing European order, the old degenerate order which is under attack. There is also the implied field of new European ideas: natural law theory, and even beyond it, empiricism, utilitarianism, and Montesquieu's brand of radical individualism. On the other side, there is only one static Persian order, which is associated with the discredited old order of Europe. The Islamic order is timeless and inert; it encounters no new ideas. Rica marvels, for example, that he has seen the tax system change four times in his three-year visit, while "[t]axes are levied in Turkey and Persia today just as they were when the empires were founded" (no. 138), and "a rather sensible European" discusses with Usbek why governments change in Europe but not in Asia (no. 103).

The point is, the ubiquitous descriptions of the Muslim woman as harem slave (which emerge not only from the letters of the women themselves but also, and primarily, from Usbek's master discourse), are intended to stand as a representation of Muslim women, and not simply as a literary pretense for discussing European women. In fact, the Muslim women are Muslim women more completely than Usbek and Rica are Muslim men. For Usbek and Rica are simultaneously Persian men and Montesquieu's mouthpieces, while Zachi, Zephis, Zelis, Fatima, Roxane, and the nameless rest are too specifically designated as Other to be identified with as subjects. They are too much the objects of the voyeuristic male gaze of both the projected reader and the various letter writers (Usbek, the Chief Eunuch). They are too debased and naked. They are too exotic and foreign, even in their form of rebellion (poison, with its association to witchcraft). They cannot possibly be subjects like Usbek and Rica.

Besides, what is emphasized about them is their plurality. It is the plurality of the named wives, added to that of the unnamed concubines flitting around the huddled harem throng, that underlines their insignificance in the marginal space of the text. For the harem drama is a story subordinate to the main, "masculine" theme of the treatise, the part which garnered it any respect it had—Usbek's and Rica's critique of the West.

The third factor, the subsequent life of *Lettres Persanes*' Muslim woman, shows that she lives on in the legacy of this text as harem slave and not as radical individual. When Rousseau says, "I would want a young Englishwoman to cultivate pleasing talents that will entertain her future husband with as much care as a young Albanian cultivates them for the harem of Ispahan" (*Émile*, V, 374), he is referring to none other than *Lettres Persanes*. For why Ispahan? Why not Istanbul? The vogue for "Ispahan" was created by *Lettres Persanes*. Everyone in Rousseau's contemporary audience knew that. "*Comment peut-on être Persan?*" (How can anyone be a Persian?), a *bon mot* on cultural parochialism extracted from the *Lettres* (no. 30), had circulated among the wits of Paris and London and found its way into Rousseau's writing. Rousseau was certainly acquainted with the Montesquieu *oeuvre*, and is speaking in the above passage specifically of the talents for which Usbek praises Roxane in Letter 26:

> *Quand vous relevez l'éclat de votre teint par les plus belles couleurs; quand vous vous parfumez tout le corps des essences les plus précieuses; quand vous vous parez de vos plus beaux habits; quand vous cherchez a vous distinguer de vos compagnes par les graces de la danse et par la douceur de votre chant; que vous combattez gracieusement avec elles de charmes, de douceur et d'enjouement: je ne puis pas m'imaginer que vous ayz d'autre objet que celui de me plaire . . .*

(When you enhance the brilliance of your complexion with lovely coloring, when you perfume all your body with the most precious essences, when you dress in your most beautiful garments, when you seek to distinguish yourself from your companions by the charm of your dancing or the delight of your song, when you graciously compete with them in beauty, sweetness, and vivacity—then I cannot imagine that you have any other object than that of pleasing me.)

*Lettres Persanes'* vivid representation of the Muslim woman as harem slave partakes of the "self-containing, self-reinforcing character of a closed system" that is Orientalism (Said, 70). It was intended to be read, was read, and amazingly, is still read as straight ethnography as much as philosophy or anything else. The clincher is that even modern scholars will enter into the text's assumptions about the Muslim woman as if they were self-evident.

"For, though eighteenth-century French women obviously enjoyed freedom undreamt of by their Persian counterparts . . ." Katherine M. Rogers offhandedly begins a sentence in a *Philological Quarterly* article entitled "Subversion of Patriarchy in *Les Lettres Persanes*" (68). How does she know this? If she is dealing with any work besides *Lettres Persanes*, she does not feel it necessary to cite it as evidence. "Though women in Europe were not actually deprived of their liberty, they were nevertheless . . ." (68) she continues, as if Persian women were irrefutably deprived of their liberty—again, no evidence necessary. "Cultivated Frenchmen," she goes on, "who not only associated with women whom they had to respect, but were intellectually committed to ideas such as the equal value of all human souls, the sacredness of marriage, and universal human rights to liberty and self-fulfillment, had to work harder at rationalization than their Persian counterparts" (69). Plainly, eighteenth-century Persian men did not associate with women whom they had to respect, they opposed the equal value of human souls, and all the rest. A twentieth-century English translator of Montesquieu, George Healy, inserts confident footnotes such as "Persian women are much more carefully confined than Turkish or Indian women," and "The Persians wear four" face veils, in the present tense, without feeling obliged to distinguish either between fictional and real eighteenth-century Persians, or between either of those and present-day Persians (15 and 41).

*Lettres Persanes* was so potent in configuring its harem slave that her after-image has nearly erased the previous history of the Muslim woman within Western discourse (let alone the history of real Muslim women). All other images became nearly immaterial to the text's contemporary and subsequent audience. *Lettres Persanes* knocks history out cold.

Daniel Defoe's *The Fortunate Mistress, or Roxana* (1724, only three years after *Lettres Persanes*) builds on the tradition of the two French Roxanes and

draws upon the matter of the Muslim woman in eighteenth-century discourse. Defoe's heroine is never actually named, but acquires the name
Roxana involuntarily: a Maltese man-of-war assaults a Turkish ship bound
for Egypt, and the women on board are stripped of their rich garments and
enslaved. The heroine's aristocratic lover buys her a Turkish slave from
among these nameless women, and she gets the luxurious outfit in the bar-
gain. Donning it and improvising a seductive mock-Oriental dance, she becomes the life of the party, stirring one male onlooker to cheer, "Roxana!
Roxana! by —," "with an oath, upon which foolish accident I had the
name of Roxana presently fixed upon me all over the Court end of town
as effectually as if I had been christened Roxana" (170). "Roxana" knows
very well that her dance (invented by "a famous master at Paris," 170) is
"exploitatively Orientalist rather than genuinely Oriental because it gives
back to the largely male audience its own preconceptions, confirming its
voyeuristic, indeed salacious, attitude toward an Orient associated with
harems, male dominance, women deliciously compliant or sexually forced";
she laughs at a man who swears he saw it performed in Constantinople
(Trumpener, 189). She maximizes the advantages that accrue to her from
the dress, the dance, and the name Roxana, even though the rapidity and
radicality with which the name takes over her life makes her uneasy.

The Fortunate Mistress finagles her way around the pitfalls of the
female condition, slipping in and out of many identities, relationships,
houses, countries, continents. She rejects a marriage proposal because "the
very nature of the marriage contract was, in short, nothing but giving up
liberty, estate, authority, and everything to the man, and the woman was indeed a mere woman ever after, that is to say, a slave" (142). In other words,
the "situation of the seraglio lives on here as a metaphor; London is clearly
not far from Paris or from Persia" (Trumpener, 187).

The name "Roxana" with its allusive intertextual history, as well as the
history of the Turkish garment, stripped from the marginal enslaved Muslim woman in the text, return to trap the heroine in the fate of the Roxanes. The nameless Muslim woman's opulent dress in this text signifies not
only that particular woman's subjection within her own society to a male
economy that reduces her to property and sensuosity, but her vulnerability
to a predatory European economy that is now able to subject her kind
globally (recall Zoraida's rich dress, spared by the French pirates). The
name and the dress of the Muslim woman end the Fortunate Mistress' exhilarating picaresque adventures and confine her in the wretched female

condition she had avoided for so long. When her long-lost daughter and
alliterative namesake Susana identifies "Roxana" as her mother by the name
and the dress (or the name of the dress, since that is really what "Roxana"
is), murderous consequences follow. These force "Roxana" into a miserable life and end her story with an unspecified "dreadful course of calami-
ties" (322).

The entrance of the Muslim woman's dress into European society at
once fixes her meaning as harem slave and pinpoints the place where that
meaning is most serviceable to Western patriarchy. For the English ideology of gender during this period was "a system at war with its own imperatives. At the same time that women were being granted certain freedoms,
they were nonetheless being contained by categories of domestic use that
assumed spheres of influence circumscribed by domestic necessity" (Flynn,
74). Certain freedoms: women were being recognized as "affective individuals" in their own right (perhaps due to the long-term influence of the early
Puritans), and companionate marriage free of physical coercion and abuse
was being advanced, certainly by Defoe himself, among others. Contain-
ment: in return for the ostensible lifting of overt physical coercion, women
were to "voluntarily," affectionately, resubmit to patriarchal authority after
all the reasonable grounds for the recycled Christian limitations on their
liberty were amiably explained to them (Flynn, 74). This system both requires that women be seen as equals—else its religious underpinnings fall
apart—and demands that they be subservient and separated in a feminine
domestic sphere—or its proto-bourgeois, early capitalist material imperatives crumble.

Now the Muslim woman as harem slave is a perfect didactic tool for
such an ideology of proper female conduct. By producing the seraglio as a
less benevolent patriarchal system with a cruder repressive apparatus for
domesticating women to a degrading extreme (such as that recalled by the
unnamable, humiliating physical punishment, implicitly flagellation, administered to Zachi and Zelis by the eunuchs at Usbek's order), harem discourse rationalizes for European women and men the kinder, gentler sup-
pressions of patriarchy at home. It releases a whole series of soothing
rationalizations from the point of view of patriarchal authority: at least our
women are "free"; at least our women are autonomous individuals with
souls, and not animals; at least we have a single sexual standard; at least we
Christians do not treat women as mere sexual playthings. The underside is:
of course it is not possible that women be "free" the same way men are

"free" to follow the will of their autonomous individualities, or wives would not obey their husbands; of course women must be kept economically dependent and legally subordinate to male authority within a separate domestic sphere, and the fiction of their willing submission be maintained; of course certain sensual "lewdnesses" that must be excluded from respectful companionate marriage and decent society in general will need to be sought elsewhere, creating the alluring whore/boring virtuous woman duality.

It is through Roxana that "Defoe explores most relentlessly the contradictions of a sexual economy that demands subordination and self-determination while he emphasizes the impossibility of attaining enough domestic security to make possible the ideological fiction of correct conduct" (Flynn, 88–89). The Muslim woman's dress in "Roxana's" story exposes these fraying contradictions. Through its intertextual reference to the other Roxanas, the ghosts of the two Roxanas summoned by the curse of the man at the party, the dress invokes the harem discourse that is supposed to rationalize by contrast the English woman's happier subordination. It is a sartorial evocation of all that is excluded from the ideal of the proper female and the companionate marriage: sensuality, sexual promiscuity, sumptuary luxury, wild abandon—and naked slavery.

The Fortunate Mistress mistakenly thinks she can, through masking herself in the fascinating dress of the Other, thumb her nose at propriety and enjoy the complete sexual liberty, the whore side of the duality, forbidden to proper women. She does not realize that the dress is a body bag discursively sewn by men, and forgets that it was handed to her at the cost of the bodily enslavement of the marginal Muslim woman in the text. The seamy underside of the dress, its affinity with the repressive ideology, is revealed when the dress rises to punish her for her transgressions against proper female conduct. If that makes it sound like the dress has a life of its own, this is justified by Defoe's text, in which the physical material of the dress must be hidden from Susana and becomes an almost animated article impossible to hold down.

The Muslim woman by the mid-eighteenth century becomes the prime model of the enervated, disabled, oppressed creature, the definitive victim of a tyranny that just won't laissez-faire, the devalued treasure of a market that refuses to open to the invisible hand. She is the emblem of the frustrating Islamic world that had threatened Europe from the late seventh to the early seventeenth century and that was becoming attainable for the first time. The Peace of Paris among the European powers in 1763 "presumed that much of the world was theirs to do with as they wished" (Woodruff, 66). The English had already procured a monopoly on the African slave trade with the Treaty of Utrecht (1713). (The black Moor became an entirely contemptible or pitiful figure, less a "Moor" or Muslim than a pagan Negro.) The profits from this trade in part built the English fleet up to surpass all others by mid-century, so that even if Asian lands were not yet conquered, most Asian waters were. France and Britain fought over India during the War of the Austrian Succession (1740–1748), with a belated British victory in 1760. But neither India nor Africa, though they might overlap with "Islam," had the unique relationship that the Islamic heartland had with Europe:

> It lay uneasily close to Christianity, geographically and culturally. It drew on the Judeo-Hellenic traditions, it borrowed creatively from Christianity, it could boast of unrivaled military and political successes. Nor was this all. The Islamic lands sit adjacent to and even on top of the Biblical lands; moreover the heart of the Islamic domain has always been the region closest to Europe. . . . Access to Indian (Oriental) riches had always to be made by first crossing the Islamic provinces and by withstanding the dangerous effect of Islam as a system of quasi-Arian belief. (Said, 74–76)

Now this world was finally vulnerable to European mastery—academic, military, naval, economic. Now its vaunted virility was sapped, and it could be reconceived as emasculated, castrated—as a woman. And not as an aberrant overbearing woman, but as a "feminine," powerless, conformist.

The frustrating thing was that she—it, the core Islamic world—was still in some sense closed to Europe, had not succumbed in all its fleshy materiality as easily as, say, the pre-Columbians of America, or even the Africans or Indians. Europe was not *there* yet, did not own the body of the land. And increasingly, it needed to. That is, European nations, Britain and France especially, developed strong ideological and economic motives for conquering the Islamic heartland. Accelerated industrialization in the latter years of the century, especially in England, created a spiraling need for markets and raw materials that fed the engines of colonization. The nearby Islamic world was extremely well suited to fulfill this need, for one thing. The amalgamation of discourses that made up Orientalism fulfilled ideological imperatives, for another.

From being a distinct character in the texts of earlier centuries, the Muslim woman in this period is usually one of a plurality of Muslim women who hover nearly namelessly, facelessly, in the harem-margin of the text. She is a diaphanous non-being who reveals what Islamic despotism does to effeminate Oriental man. She is a lesson in what Enlightened Western man congratulates himself he has been able to avoid—although he is not above deriving voyeuristic pleasure from her, both as narrator and reader. Narratively contained within the scopophilic form of voyeurism, she is masochistic in her subjugation and sadistic in her rebellion (if she has any). Lady Mary's old-guard aristocratic female dissenting voice notwithstanding, the Muslim woman is, in a word, a harem slave. She awaits rescue. The Romantics will rescue her. But first, she must endure Rousseau's pontifications and Mary Wollstonecraft's quarrel over her.

## PRECURSORS OF ROMANTICISM:
### ROUSSEAU'S HAREM AND ITS CHALLENGER

He was perhaps the quintessential Enlightenment philosopher, and Freedom was his byword. "The problem is to find a form of association which will defend and protect with the whole common force the person and goods of each associate, and in which each, while uniting himself with all, may still obey himself alone, and remain as free as before" (*Social Contract*, I, vi, 174). Rousseau's solution was the General Will, a seemingly genderless formula that makes the rulers and the ruled one. This is the foundation on which Rousseau built civil society, the proposal which inspired the French Revolution. It is a radically egalitarian foundation which eliminates the very language of domination and submission from the political order: "Since no man has a natural authority over his fellow, and force creates no right, we must conclude that conventions form the basis of all legitimate authority among men" (I, iv, 169).

But let us not generously mistake Rousseau's literal "man" for a generic one. The philosopher set his fundamental axiom of individual autonomy aside for two kinds of people: women and Orientals.

For Rousseau, sex is not socially constructed but biological; it precedes and determines social relations . . . and it implies conquest. "*L'attaque et la défense, l'audace des hommes, la pudeur des femmes, ne sont point des conventions, comme le pensent tes philosophes, mais des institutions naturelles dont il est facile de rendre raison et dont se déduisent aisément toutes les autres distinctions morales*" (The attack and the defense, the audacity of men, the modesty of women—these are by no means conventions, as your philosophers think, but natural institutions which are easily accounted for and from which all the other moral distinctions are readily inferred) writes Julie, and Rousseau indisputably agrees (I, Lettre XLVI, 165). As for Orientals, Rousseau believed that liberty was not "the fruit of all climates" (*Social Contract*, III, vii, 226), concurring with Montesquieu's geographic and racial determinism.[21] Rousseau articulates in Book V of *Émile* his belief in an original purity of races, each race having its peculiar temperamental, as well as physical, stamp (453). He admits the theory is confounded by the continual mingling of races (which, fortunately, allows the Persians to "lose their former ugliness every day"); nevertheless, Orientals are not racially suited for republics.

Just as biology renders women unfit for egalitarian systems, so race and geography render Orientals unfit. If Orientals are Naturally despotic and women are Naturally meant to be ruled despotically, what could make more sense than adopting the (ostensibly) Oriental seclusion of women as a model for European women?

Rousseau's harem is a location for the displacement of the master–slave relations he so effectively erases from public life. He constructs this harem by explicitly prescribing it (e.g., in Book V of *Émile*, 382–384; *Letter to D'Alembert*, VIII, 88, IX, 100); by evoking it with the language and imagery of enclosure and irreducible binaristic difference in which women are enveloped in every single writing; and by invoking its name and vocabulary when speaking of his experiences with women in the *Confessions*. Rousseau's thoughts on the home, women, and the Orient converge around the model of the passive secluded Muslim woman. Though she is never actually named or mentioned in his writings, she presides at the shadowy intersection of his "Orient" and his "woman." Rousseau's dream of domesticity depends on the harem slave.

This domestic dream is a new idea. When Rousseau writes glowingly of "a very little, but clean and comfortable apartment" (*Émile*, V, 413), something is changing. "Very little" rules out an aristocratic home, and "comfortable" rules out the peasant. Privacy had not been a value for a class whose livelihood was predicated on public service, whose rank was based on the publicity of their ancestors' virtue and the publicity of their births and marriages. Neither had it previously been important for the lowest classes, who ground out a subsistence in sites of production where a distinction between public and private was still rudimentary. Rousseau, within the larger context of eighteenth-century social and economic change, writes the home into existence for Europe's emergent middle class as a private sanctum. This home is carefully separated from the public sphere—from politics on the aristocratic side, and from economic production on the peasant side. And every item prescribed in Rousseau's agenda, from breast-feeding to a kitchen garden to a decrease in the number of domestic servants (*Émile*, IV, 346) is designed to keep people (especially women) in that sanctum. Rousseau approves of Robinson Crusoe's enforced isolation, during which he learns the value of walls and of the middle-class domesticity that he spurned in leaving his father's house (*Émile*, III, 185). He prefers domestic recreation—strolling through an enclosed garden or reading a novel—to outings to the decadent theater. Hospitality, as Rousseau sees it, has degenerated—except among Asians, who have a strong sense of domesticity (*Rêveries*, Neuvième Promenade, 134).

Finally, Rousseau carves out the home through sheer force of imagery. In the *Confessions*, he intermingles the description of his physical housing and his psychic state, giving the home more importance than it ever had in literature as a mere location. His first room with Mme de Warrens had a view of a brook and garden which "strengthened my inclination to tender emotions!" (III, 107); when he returns to find her in a debased condition, his room "was the darkest and gloomiest in the house" (V, 182). Lovingly he describes the "wild and retired asylum" of Les Charmettes (V, 231), where "My dear little room was my only recreation" (VI, 280). He waxes lyrical about his Montmorency apartment as "earthly paradise": "It was delightfully neat, with furniture in blue and white. In this profound and delightful solitude, in the midst of woods and waters, to the accompaniment of the songs of birds of every kind, surrounded by the perfumes of orange blossoms, I composed, in a continued state of ecstasy, the fifth book of 'Émile.'. . ." (X, 539–540). He adores groves and precipices, dark forests and mountains (IV, 178), cozy rooms and multilevel gardens (X, 538). His prose writes home.

The genre of the novel, at whose birth Rousseau assisted, espoused the new notions of private virtue and domestic women, as set against the aristocratic tradition of public virtue based on rank. Speaking about the rise of domestic literature in Britain, Nancy Armstrong maintains that it substituted the language of emotion and behavior for that of the sociopolitical order: "At the site of the household, family life, and all that was hallowed as female, this gendered field of information contested a dominant political order which depended, among other things, on representing women as economic and political objects" (15). (It is easy to see how this substitution occurs in Samuel Richardson's *Pamela*, for example, for the serving maid is able to marry Squire B because her private virtue proves to have more moral authority than the public, political-economic characteristic of high birth.)

The purpose of Rousseau's new home is to nurture better specimens of men, as opposed to the effeminate courtiers of the Regency early in the century, and the libertine *philosophes* of its middle decades. Everything is arranged around the purpose of inculcating "virtue," including women: "If you wish then that they [men] should be noble and virtuous, let women be taught what greatness of soul and virtue are" (*Discourses*, First Discourse, II, 17). Given Rousseau's emphasis on childhood as a formative stage, this education of women is a requisite for producing the kind of men that he wants. Woman is the new transmitter of virtue, then—but the ultimate aim is virtue itself. She is to be used for arousing man's love for virtue in the private realm, just as patriotic symbols are to be used for arousing the people's love of the fatherland in the public realm.

Confounding love for virtue with love for the medium—woman—is dangerous. Love then erupts as an erotic impulse, no longer confined by reason. This, as Lord Bomston reveals, is Saint Preux's monumental frailty: "*Savez-vous ce qui vous a fait aimer toujours la vertu? Elle a pris à vos yeux la figure de cette femme adorable qui la représent si bien, et il seroit difficile qu'une si chère image vous en laissat perdre le gout. Mais ne l'aimerez-vous jamais pour elle seule . . .*" (Do you know what has always made you love virtue? In your eyes it has taken on the form of that lovely woman who typifies it so well, and so dear an image could hardly let you lose the inclination for it. But will you never love virtue for its own sake . . . ? [V, Lettre I, 5]). And if it is dangerous for a man to forget that woman is only a vehicle to virtue, it is even more perilous for a woman to forget. When woman has the temerity to seek virtue for her own ends, she becomes a viper poisoning man's virility and her sexuality becomes a disruptive force, like the Parisian woman who "gathers in her apartment a harem of men more womanish than she . . ." (*Letter to D'Alembert*, IX, 101).

In contending that gender organization in French society (far from having deplorable affinities to the Persian confinement of women, as Montesquieu suggests) gave women too much freedom and emasculated men, Rousseau struck a chord. The French Revolution vented its anger against the too-free woman with the guillotining of Marie Antoinette, but the chastisement of power-brokering females was not limited to the Revolutionary government. Both Napoleonic and counter-Revolutionary writers called on women of the aristocracy to withdraw from courtly power mongering into the sphere of household duties.

Rousseau posits a problem: how can man's erotic impulse be released enough to let him love virtue with more than his reason, through the medium of woman? And how can woman's erotic impulse be released enough to let her inspire this love without spinning both sexes into the vortex of libertine sexuality? He posits a solution: all may be achieved by releasing the erotic only within heavily guarded walls—by haremizing women.

"Let us follow the indications of nature, let us consult the good of society; we shall find that the two sexes ought to come together sometimes and to live separated ordinarily" (*Letter to D'Alembert*, IX, 100). By minimizing the physical space and the actual duration of the meeting of the sexes, Rousseau proposes to nip the danger of eros. So he invents anew the women's quarters, citing the example of the ancient Golden Age "Persians, the Greeks, the Romans, the Egyptians" (*Letter to D'Alembert*, VIII, 89). Thus, the evidence of Julie's regeneration as a wife and mother is that she not only has a secluded garden (IV, Letter XI, 304), but lives, as a rule, in her women's quarters (IV, Letter XV, 331), to which Saint Preux and even her husband are admitted extremely rarely (V, Letter VI, 356). Her big mistake as a girl had been to allow a man to cross the boundaries of this enclosure, in the grove and the boudoir.

If the home and its women's quarters express enclosure, another of Rousseau's images is a crucial factor in his differentiation between the sexes: the image of the veil. It is a favorite metaphor in his political writings for deceit, dissimulation, Machiavellian sophistication. There he prefers openness, naked truths, the dropping of masks. For issues of sexuality, however, the veil is good. Saint Preux early in the romance with Julie says, "*[J]'avois couvert mes regards d'un voile et mis une entrave à mon coeur*" (I had veiled my eyes and fettered my heart [I, Lettre XIV, 59]); he should have kept it that way, but then he kisses her, and the membrane is removed. "*Mon oeil osa contempler ce qu'il ne falloit point voir*" (My eye dared to look upon what it was not supposed to see [II, Lettre I, 3]). "*O ma Julie! ... le voile est déchire ... je te vois ... je vois tes divins attraits!*" (Oh my Julie! ... the veil is torn away ... I see you ... I see your divine features![22] [II, Lettre XXII, 153]). If he and Julie are to resume any semblance of normal life, Claire tells him, "*Il s'agit de cacher sous un voile éternel cet odieux mystère*" (It is now a matter of concealing this odious mystery under an everlasting veil [III, Lettre I, 4]). It is not merely the class difference between Julie and Saint Preux which makes their love dangerous, it is love itself. Even if they were marriageable peers, like Émile and Sophie, the erotic impulse would have to be carefully veiled by limiting the sexual contact between husband and wife. The only way eros can be aroused and controlled at the same time, Rousseau concludes, is by unleashing it within strongly guarded—manned—walls: within the ha— har—home.

Within this highly controlled patriarchal enclosure, good wives ought to become erotic objects for their husbands' gratification, because "[b]y en-slaving decent women only to gloomy duties, we have banished from mar-riage everything which could make it attractive to men." He rejects the prudery of (Puritan or Calvinist) "Christianity" in favor of the pragmatic sensuality of the Orient: recall his statement, "I would want a young En-glishwoman to cultivate pleasing talents that will entertain her future hus-band with as much care as a young Albanian cultivates them for the harem of Ispahan" (*Émile*, V, 374). It is obviously Usbek's harem at Ispahan, not any real Persian seraglio, to which Rousseau alludes, calling on the inter-textual authority of Orientalism to make up Oriental "reality" (see Said, 72). Yet, while he unquestioningly adopts the image of the Muslim woman as harem slave from Montesquieu, Rousseau misses the whole point of *Let-tres Persanes*—that a man cannot espouse ideals of liberty in public life while practicing despotism in his personal life.

In Rousseau's personal life, relationships to women are imagined within harem contours:

> Mademoiselle Galley, Mademoiselle de Graffenried, Mademoiselle
> de Breil, Madame Basile, Madame de Larnage, my young pupils,
> even the piquant Zulietta, whom my heart can never forget. I saw
> myself surrounded by a seraglio of houris and by my old acquain-
> tances, the liveliest desire for whom was no new sensation for
> me. My blood became heated and inflamed, my head swam . . .
> (*Confessions*, IX, 441)

"I am sorry to be obliged to describe so many girls in love with me . . ." (IV, 148). Sure he is. With Thérèse, his servant-class mistress, he can bring himself to do the Squire B thing only after twenty-five years. Late in his ca-reer, Rousseau adopts the Armenian costume, which is associated by everyone with the Orient and Islam, as shown by Lord Marshal's comment upon seeing it, "Salaam alek" (XII, 624). Did he choose an Oriental costume, over anything else he might have contrived, purely for medical reasons?[23] Terry Castle notes that "exotic costumes marked out a kind of symbolic inter-penetration with difference—an almost erotic commingling with the alien. Mimicry became a form of psychological recognition, a way of embracing, quite literally, the unfamiliar" (61–62). This costuming, combined with his East-evoking language (veil, seraglio, harem) and with his explicit prescription of a sort of cloistering for women, suggests that what Rousseau embraced of the Orient was an Oriental harem-master alter ego—the ostensible opposite of all things political advocated by him.

For effeminacy, irrationality, superstition, slavery, and darkness make up Rousseau's Orient. This Orient, in relation to Europe, is more despotic and politically primitive (*Émile*, IV, 224) despite its longevity (*Social Contract*, II, vii, 197); more virile, jealous, and brutishly sensual (*Émile*, IV, 215, and V, 429–430); about equal in religious sincerity (*Émile*, IV, 309); less civilized in letters (First Discourse, I, 4); strangely appealing in some aspects of lifestyle such as hospitality, dress, household arrangements, and sexuality. Its men are tyrants (*Émile*, II, 130), its polity nothing but "totally arbitrary government"[24] (*Émile*, IV, 224). Its women are "poor slaves"—this is the one direct reference to Muslim women (*Émile*, IV, 305)—silent, abject, seductive, and hidden in harems. Montesquieu's Muslim woman is a harem slave too, but she still retains a flicker of rebellion; Rousseau pushes the harem woman's dark active element much deeper, almost irretrievably, underground.

Rousseau goes beyond the cool cultural relativism of the Enlightenment to highlight the mystique and exoticism of the Orient, fermented in a proto-Romantic sensibility. He describes Zulietta, the dark beauty with "large, black, Oriental eyes": "The young virgins of the cloister are not so fresh, the beauties of the harem are not so lively, the houris of paradise are not so piquant. . . . The great ones of the world ought to be her slaves; sceptres ought to be laid at her feet" (VII, 328–329). He who endows woman with a numinous nimbus of feminine mystique and who makes the Orient the nexus of extreme racial difference would naturally produce the most highly exoticized and eroticized (pseudo-) "Oriental" woman yet.

If Rousseau frequently speaks of things Oriental within the framework of a language of domination and submission, he almost never speaks of relations between the sexes without this language. Rousseau's earliest sexual feeling is aroused by a spanking from a young schoolmistress, Mlle Lambercier (*Confessions*, I, 13). He is fond of maintaining that women dominate men, "govern" them ("Dedication" to the Second Discourse, 36), have "empire" over them (Second Discourse, I, 70). Coquetry is woman's weapon, and "it is by dispensing it artfully that she makes the strongest chains for her slaves" (*Émile*, V, 384). This power turns out to be an artfully disguised, retractable condition, dependent on the benevolence of husbands, "solely exercised within the limits of conjugal union" ("Dedication," 36); otherwise it is an insubordination from "the sex which ought to obey" (Second Discourse, I, 70). Saint Preux is fond of calling Julie "*cruelle*," of theatrically obeying her "commands" (I, Lettre XIV). Walking in the garden, Saint Preux—who is now "*noir comme un More*" (black like a Moor [IV, Lettre VII, 51])—and Julie can only think in terms of "*ésclaves*," "*tyran*," and "*prisonniers*" (slaves, tyrant, prisoners [IV, Lettre XI, 135–136]). At the same time, Julie says of her lover, "*[I]l est maître de mon coeur et de ma personne*" (He is the master of my heart and of my person [I, Lettre LVIII, 221]). Rousseau can only conceive of the sexual relationship in absolute terms of domination and submission, however mitigated by the fragrant foliage of affection. The "nature" of the male–female relationship imposes this master–slave language, so alien to Rousseau's civil society.

In a way, Rousseau is less hypocritical than the eighteenth-century writers who posit the harem as a negative counterimage of all the qualities of the new feminine ideal. By pointing out that the Western separation of women into a privatized sphere is actually similar to the Eastern harem (or at least to Western notions of it), he only admits what other writers mask with rationalizations and ethnocentric arrogance. Of course, he would still see European women in the system of his devising as better off than "real" Muslim women in "real" harems because their masters would be more benevolent.

But the existence of a despotic harem in the personal realm disables the egalitarianism of the public part of Rousseau's system. He can never even seem to make it work with the women he himself creates: his ideally educated Sophie dies young; so does the repentant paragon Julie. The inherent failure of Rousseau's harem is apparent when he narrates a marginal incident in which male–female, master–slave, and Western–Oriental binaries operate. "If there is one circumstance in my life which well describes my character," says Rousseau, "it is that which I am about to relate" about his tryst with the Oriental-eyed harem beauty Zulietta (*Confessions*, VII, 329):

> I entered the room of a courtesan as if it had been the sanctuary of love and beauty; in her person I thought I beheld its divinity. . . . Suddenly . . . I felt a deathly chill run through my veins; my legs trembled under me; and, feeling ready to faint, I sat down and cried like a child. . . . I said to myself: This object, which is at my disposal, is the masterpiece of nature and love; in mind and body, every part of it is perfect; she is as good and generous as she is amiable and beautiful. The great ones of the world ought to be her slaves; sceptres out to be laid at her feet. And yet she is a miserable street-walker, on sale to everybody; a merchant captain has the disposal of her; she comes and throws herself at my head, mine, although she knows that I am poor, while my real merits, being unknown to her, can have no value in her eyes. In this there is something incomprehensible. Either my heart deceives me, dazzles my senses, and makes me the dupe of a worthless slut, or some secret defect, with which I am unacquainted, must destroy the effect of her charms, and render her repulsive to those who would otherwise fight for the possession of her. I began to look for this defect with a singular intensity of mind . . . (329–330)

He becomes obsessed by the suspicion that something renders her condescension to be with him less than free. Like Usbek, he "realizes that a woman can satisfy a man only when she gives herself to him freely" (Berman, 24). The complete power he claims over this object at his disposal creates in him feelings of emptiness like Usbek's, a "whimsical melancholy," jealousy, and ultimately, dependence. He finds a defective nipple— so she isn't free—and has the "stupidity" to mention it to her. She coldly turns him away: "Give up the ladies, and study mathematics." But he reconciles himself to her lack of freedom and finds a kind of pleasure in her servility which inspires servility in himself. He begs, reproaches, regrets, awaits, is uneasy, flies to her on the appointed day . . . only to find she has flown the coop.

". . . I could have consoled myself for the loss of her; but I confess that I have never been able to console myself for the thought that she only carried away a contemptuous recollection of me," he concludes (VII, 331). He had entered the bower of all that his own rhetoric hallows—and nothing happened, except that the fantasy collapsed, entrapping him. It turns out to be a rather hollow harem. "Ah, dear Usbek, if only you knew how to be happy!" laments Zachi (12). "*Mon cher ami,*" sighs Julie from the depths of Rousseau's heart, "*il n'y a point de vrai bonheur sur la terre*" (There is no true happiness on earth [IV, Lettre XV, 194]).

Despite Rousseau's exhaustive rationalizing apparatus for the haremization of women, despite the "*mille guirlandes de vigne de Judée, de vigne vierge, de houblon, de liseron, de couleuvrée, de clematite, et d'autres plantes de cette espèce, parmi lesquelles le chevrefeuille et le jasmin daignoient se confondre*" (a thousand garlands of woody vines, wild grape, hops, convolvulus, bryony, clematis, and other plants of this kind, among which honeysuckle and jasmine condescended to twine [*Julie*, IV, Lettre XI, 127–128]) with which he beautifies Julie's life of complete domestic sequestration, he puts no real checks on the power of the husband and gives the woman no individual autonomy whatsoever. A woman cannot even appeal over her husband's head to religion for power. Religion is what her husband says it is: "Since women are not in a position to be judges themselves, they ought to receive the decision of fathers and husbands like that of the Church" (*Émile*, V, 377). What if a man is not a good or beneficent governor, does she have any means of correction or source of appeal besides her own manipulative arts? Not at all, so "she ought to learn early to endure even injustice and to bear a husband's wrongs without complaining" (*Émile*, V, 371). For Rousseau, all woman has is beauty (which is variable and temporary at best) and guile; Rousseau seems to think it is enough. "This peculiar cleverness given to the fair sex is a very equitable compensation for their lesser share of strength, a compensation without which women would be not man's companion but his slave" (*Émile*, V, 371). "Good-sirs!" as Pamela would say, "I don't know what to say to this!—It looks a little hard, methinks!—This would bear a smart Debate, I fansy, in a Parliament of Women" (Richardson, 371).

Mary Wollstonecraft begins the "smart Debate." She takes Rousseau to task for proffering glib rationalization, not equitable compensation, and for making Western woman into just that unnameable thing: a harem slave. "The *rights* of humanity have been . . . confined to the male line from Adam downwards," she writes (*A Vindication of the Rights of Woman*, 1792), demanding that women at last be admitted to those rights enlarged by political theorists since Locke. Wollstonecraft castigates Rousseau and a host of lesser figures of the Enlightenment and the Revolution for contradicting the very values they passionately argue when they create a second standard and a separate sphere for women. Rousseau, she says, does an admirable job in educating his ideal man, Émile, but fails his own criterion with his ideal woman, Sophia: "Is this the man who, in his ardour for virtue, would banish all the soft arts of peace, and almost carry us back to Spartan discipline? . . . How are these mighty sentiments lowered when he describes the pretty foot and enticing airs of his little favourite!" (107). Rousseau's creation of Sophia is "grossly unnatural"; he cripples her intellect, maims her higher spirit, and incapacitates her for the nobler virtues, all to make her "a more alluring object of desire, a sweeter companion to man, whenever he chose to relax himself" (108).

Wollstonecraft explicitly invokes "slavery." Lest her use of the term be taken for hyberbole, she very specifically says, "When therefore I call women slaves, I mean in a political and civil sense, for indirectly they obtain too much power, and are debased by their exertions to obtain illicit sway" (292). The smug superiority of those who hold up the lot of European women as better than that of harem women is sheer hypocrisy, she reveals.

The most scathing analogy Wollstonecraft can engage to expose the injustice of Western men's treatment of Western women is the seraglio. Like Rousseau, she has no direct sustained discussion of the seraglio itself, but its image recurs with such regularity in the margins of her writing as to give it significance in her thought. What Wollstonecraft calls the seraglio is the epitome of both class and gender oppression: it exemplifies the profligate, empty-headed, lavish lifestyle of the aristocratic lady who is both exploited as a woman and exploitative of the underclasses. It is a place of unnatural and degrading female artifice:

> Women ought to endeavour to purify their hearts; but can they do so when their uncultivated understandings make them entirely dependent on their senses for employment and amusement, when no noble pursuits set them above the little vanities of the day, or enable them to curb the wild emotions that agitate a reed. . . . Nature has given woman a weaker frame than man; but, to ensure her husband's affections, must a wife . . . condescend to use art, and feign a sickly delicacy. . . . In a seraglio, I grant, that all these arts are necessary; the epicure must have his palate tickled, or he will sink into apathy; but have women so little ambition as to be satisfied with such a condition? Can they supinely dream life away in the lap of pleasure, or the languor of weariness, rather than assert their claim to pursue reasonable pleasures,

and render themselves conspicuous by practising the virtues which dignify mankind? Surely she has not an immortal soul who can loiter life away merely employed to adorn her person, that she may amuse the languid hours, and soften the cares of a fellow-creature who is willing to be enlivened by her smiles and tricks. . . . (112–113)

The seraglio is a place where women are devoid of the values Wollstonecraft cherishes: virtue, modesty, self-reliance; clean, healthy, vigorous bodies; independent minds and immortal souls. Lady Mary's emendation on that last point has been forgotten through the intervention of Montesquieu, Johnson, and Rousseau. Seraglio women's spiritual dimension is vestigial or nonexistent; they live at a childish or even a bestial level:

> . . . strength of body and mind are sacrificed to libertine notions of beauty, to the desire of establishing themselves. . . . And this desire making mere animals of them, when they marry they act as such children may be expected to act—they dress, they paint, and nickname God's creatures. Surely these weak beings are only fit for a seraglio! Can they be expected to govern a family with judgement, or take care of the poor babes whom they bring into the world? (83)

The possibility that the seraglio is merely another kind of household where women also govern families, raise "babes," and attend to the details of domestic production does not come up because it is incompatible with what the harem has come to mean. The harem is, self-evidently now, a place where none of those good middle-class things can be properly achieved. Wollstonecraft adds new elements to the composite picture of the Muslim woman: physical weakness ("sickly delicacy") as well as incompetence in domestic management and child rearing. The picture is a composite because the Muslim woman is not named. She is merely one in the plurality of shadowy "beings" that fill the seraglio, as in *Rasselas*.

Those two social critics, Lady Mary and Mary Wollstonecraft, each read and write the seraglio in ways that give the Islamic Other and the Muslim woman very different valuations. Wollstonecraft endows the seraglio with irreducible specificity and almost monstrous difference—though not from things as they are, but from things as they should be. Lady Mary emphasizes empathetic congruence. Lady Mary accepts a "reasonable" separation of spheres as part of her aristocratic identity and uses her privileged information about the seraglio to contest Eurocentrism, with its voyeuristic exploitation of the foreign female. Wollstonecraft rejects the separation of spheres and uses her inherited Eurocentric construct of the seraglio to contest the androcentrism of the ideology of her class. Wollstonecraft was a supporter of the middle-class revolution in France that stood for the ideals of individual rights, egalitarianism, and national authenticity, disenchanted though she was with the actual progress of the revolution. From her position, Lady Mary seems to speak from a decadent, inauthentic, and patrician cosmopolitanism—just the kind of aristocratic woman whom the Revolution would chasten and vanquish.

Two things are happening in the passage from Wollstonecraft. On one hand, the contempt for the foreign Other which her projected reader is expected to feel at the mention of the seraglio is being forced back upon the West, as Wollstonecraft goads the reader to see the abominable affinities between two gender systems which should (self-evidently) be as far apart as light and darkness. On the other hand, the seraglio may indeed be an analogy for the condition of a class of Western women . . . but after the analogy is over, as with Montesquieu, it is still also a seraglio. Through Wollstonecraft's work, the Muslim woman is cemented even more firmly into the Western imagination as a harem slave.

Wollstonecraft's use of the dominant male construct of "seraglio" reinforces the thickening web of Orientalist tradition with its rigid binaristic differentiation between the West and the Islamic Orient. For example, her comparison of seraglio inhabitants to animals echoes Johnson, whom she certainly read, and who also calls them "childish," as does Wollstonecraft in the above passage. Her idea of how harem women pass their days seems to leap from other texts: "they dress, they paint" she says, recalling Usbek's description of Roxane (Letter 26); "the epicure must have his palate tickled," she writes, calling to mind the wives' beauty contest for Usbek (Letter 3); harem beauties "feign a sickly delicacy," she notes, echoing Johnson—"One sometimes pretended to be hurt that the rest might be alarmed" (*Rasselas*, 103); she remarks that "they supinely dream life away in the lap of pleasure"—Johnson again—"Part of their time passed in watching the progress of light bodies that floated on the river, and part in marking the various forms into which clouds broke in the sky" (*Rasselas*, 104). She cites with exasperation Rousseau's instruction that "a girl should be educated for her husband with the same care as for an Eastern harem" (191)— prolonging the life of a passage that has traveled from a fictional satirical text (Montesquieu's) into a didactic one (Rousseau's), into hers—and its life is not over yet.

Thus while Wollstonecraft challenges the use or value given the seraglio by authors such as Rousseau, she accepts the content or meaning of seraglio as authorized by a Western male tradition that denies autonomy to a cultural Other as surely as it denies autonomy to the Western woman. This unexamined acceptance inaugurates an intra-Western debate over the harem in which one side defends the right of the Oriental potentate, its surreptitious Other self, to his gloriously barbaric, romantically "heroic" mode of mastery over women, while the other side deploys the apparatus of superior Western moralism to liberate the harem slaves. For example, the Romantic painter Delacroix is attracted by the very traditionalism and restriction of women that he finds in the supposed harem visit which inspired his *Women of Algiers* (1835), remarking in his journal, "It's beautiful! It's the way things were in Homer's day! The wife in the woman's quarters, looking after the children, spinning, or embroidering gorgeous fabrics. That is woman as I understand her!" (Djebar, 55)—and not far from how Rousseau creates her in Sophie. Charlotte Brontë articulates the other position in *Jane Eyre* (1847), when Jane says to Rochester, "I'll be preparing myself to go out as a missionary to preach liberty to them that are enslaved—your harem inmates amongst the rest. . . . I'll stir up mutiny; and you, three-tailed bashaw as you are, sir, shall in a trice find yourself fettered amongst our hands . . ." (322). In this scenario, the Western woman, "unable to defeat patriarchy at home . . . takes advantage of the position of power imperialism offers to strike a blow against a less empowered man, the colonized subject," over the head of the mute Muslim woman.[25]

But this is a little ahead of the text at hand. The Muslim woman in Wollstonecraft's scenario is not yet even rescue-able. She is immersed in her own servility, not only an "insignificant object of desire" in a male economy (Wollstonecraft, 83), but also an inert, silent body tossed from side to side in a self-sustaining quarrel among Westerners convulsed by the French Revolution. Her silencing occurs within discursive practices that create "cultural space" (Behdad, 124) for European dominance over the Orient. For while intellectuals influenced by the French Revolution argued over the inconsistency of excluding women from "liberty, equality, fraternity," the inconsistency of these principles of autonomy with the continuing colonization of civilizational Others escaped them.

If the image of the Muslim woman in the Renaissance period defies linear charting, oscillating indeterminately rather than making a discernible progression, there is no avoiding the fact that in the following century her course plummets. The stalking, scheming figure of Racine's Roxane, who was herself a devolution of an earlier Muslim termagant, has disappeared down a dark corridor. In her place, seductive, servile, half-sleeping sickly forms languish in sensual stupor.

"Montesquieu's odalisk," Billie Melman pronounces, "resembles her predecessor, the seductive houri of the anti-Saracen polemic" (71). She most certainly does not. The medieval anti-Saracen polemic contains no such thing as a seductive houri; its Muslim women are not passively seductive but active, intimidating seducers. They are "wanton," they gaze and grasp, shout and smite; they sit on Sir Bevis' bed and kiss hard. They do not do needlework. But on the eve of Napoleon's invasion of Egypt, the Muslim woman in Western discourse is lying supine, completely emptied of volition, ready to submit to erotic conquest.

## ROMANTICISM

### Zuleika, Mute and Motionless

The late Romantics liberate the harem slave from the harem—and deliver the coup de grace to the Muslim woman. Their texts are strewn with her body. The basic paradigm is established in Byron's "Turkish" tales and reaches its frenzied climax in Hugo's lyrical "oriental" poems. There is a Romantic hero, a noble, tormented, disenchanted man capable of great deeds. There is a Muslim woman, an angelic paragon of numinous feminine nothinghood, a shimmering fetish object for both the competing males within the narrative and the projected male reader. She is held captive or enslaved or otherwise oppressed by a Muslim villain, a cruel, tyrannical, but worthy enemy for the hero. This conflict of obvious Oedipal overtones, with a son-like figure contesting the authority of the father-like despot by stealing his woman, has significance for Romantic writings generally, but when Islamic material is involved, the texts activate unique characteristics that are my concern here. The typical landscape of the Romantic harem drama is the feminized Orient, fetishized and inviting possession; or emasculated Greece, enslaved and awaiting liberation;[26] but the harem serves as emblematic *topos* for both geographical locations. There is a great battle in which the man of lofty spirit and troubled soul hurls himself against the forces of darkness. Though doomed, he achieves Promethean heights and breaks open the interdiction of the harem. Meanwhile, the Muslim female is completely killed to subjectivity, "ere her lip, or even her eye, / Essayed to speak, or look reply" (*Bride*, 2.XXII). She is frozen into the pure form of an object:

> Zuleika, mute and motionless,[27]
> Stood like that statue of distress,
> When, her last hope forever gone,
> The mother harden'd into stone;
> All in the maid that eye could see
> Was but a younger Niobe. (*Bride*, 2.XXII)

And/or she is drowned, stabbed, strangled, or otherwise eliminated.

The first stage of the "rescue from the harem" is idealization of the Muslim woman's femininity, for the paltry painted creatures of Johnson's or Wollstonecraft's seraglios are hardly worth rescuing. Idealization involves aestheticizing and fetishizing her body. Voyeurism was the predominant way in which the Muslim woman became an object of visual pleasure in eighteenth-century texts, but fetishism is the predominant mode in Romantic literature.[28] If the object is to be idealized, she can no longer be just an abject sex-slave, up whose skirt the male hero wants to peek for a forbidden erotic thrill (recall the eunuch's "examination" of the Circassian concubine in *Lettres Persanes*, for example). She is now a glamorous, shining prize to be sought after and acquired through virile competition with other members of the male world; she is, in Freudian terms, a substitute for the phallus.

The second stage is the actual "rescue," the panoptic conquest by the Romantic hero. The founding paradigm for this exploit is Napoleon's entrance into Egypt, although—actually, *because*—that adventure failed as a military tactic against England. In failing it revealed the glory no less than the folly of the Romantic hero's visionary (con)quest to open up new expanses of cognitive territory. For Napoleon's project to dominate Egypt was as intensely a project of the mind as of the military, a project "to render it completely open, to make it totally accessible to European scrutiny"; it was to result in a "great collective appropriation of one country by another" (Said, 83–84), similar to the male appropriation of the feminine in the Romantic text.

At the third stage, the material presence of the Muslim woman is some-how "deadened"—that is, absented or discarded. For if she is a fetish-substitute for the phallus (by definition unattainable, as Lacan establishes), she can only be sought after, and never fully possessed. She evaporates as soon as she is acquired; this is enacted in the narrative as her death or elimination.

While cantos 5–8 of Byron's *Don Juan* (1821–1823) took a playful ap-proach to the grand Romantic harem drama, his *The Giaour*[29] (1813), *The Bride of Abydos* (1813), and *The Corsair* (1814) iterate the theme in full serious-ness. In their distinctive way, Victor Hugo's poems in *Les Orientales* then re-iterate it. In the first three works, the hero is Greek or "Greek in soul" (*Bride*, IV), which always, for Byron, means the self that is struggling to re-gain its natural freedom. (Significantly, two of these heroes are also men of the sea, in an era when Britain's undisputed mastery of the seas is what clinched its ascendancy among European powers and enabled the com-mencement of its global colonial enterprises.) The hero's virtue and love of liberty, his "pursuit for masculine self-possession" (Ross, 29), manifests it-self in a panoptic metaphor:

> . . . my tongue cannot impart
> My almost drunkenness of heart,
> When first this liberated eye
> Survey'd Earth, Ocean, Sun, and Sky,
> As if my spirit pierced them through,
> And all their inmost wonders knew!
> One word alone can paint to thee
> That more than feeling—I was Free!
> E'en for thy presence ceased to pine;
> The World,—nay Heaven itself, was mine!
> (*Bride*, 2.XVIII)

The "spirit" of the hero is a possessive, knowing, "piercing" gaze which operates on land and woman. In Byronic language there is a conflation of Eastern woman and Eastern landscape. For example, Dudu, one of the harem beauties in *Don Juan*

> . . . was a soft Landscape of mild Earth,
> Where all was harmony and calm and quiet,
> Luxuriant, budding . . . (VI.53)

"For where is he that hath beheld / The peak of Liakura unveiled?" asks the narrator of *The Giaour* (p. 241), a text in which the only other contest over veiling is that involving the Eastern woman. *The Bride of Abydos* opens with a challenge to the reader's powers of knowing and piercing the land, a Napoleonic theme that reverberates throughout Byron's work ("The clouds above me to the white Alps tend," he says in *Childe Harold's Pilgrimage*, "And I must pierce them, and survey whate'er / May be permitted" [109.117–119].) The land of the East is a paramount field for this kind of quest for heroic self-possession. "Know ye the land," the narrator repeatedly asks, "Know ye the land . . .

> Where the light wings of Zephyr, oppress'd with perfume
> Wax faint o'er the gardens of Gul in her bloom (*Bride*, I)

—upon which Byron affixes a footnote, the first of copious many, telling us that "Gul" is the rose, thereby ostentatiously declaring that *he* certainly knows the Orient. This more than hints at a rivalry with the reader, constructed as male, whose eye peruses the Byronic page in its own quest for knowledge. The rose is an obvious emblem of femininity, and "Gul" begins the name of more than one Byronic harem woman; a metonymic relationship is established between the Orient and woman; both are positioned as objects in the field of sight of the hero. Grammatically, the land is a direct object and the feminine element is the object of a dependent clause in the series of sentences beginning "Know ye."

The Romantic hero's strength of vision is tested against male challengers (Ross, 32). For there is another contestant for possession of the land and the woman, the Muslim male, and his rivalry is also expressed using the metaphor of the gaze. The first speech Giaffir (the villain of *The Bride of Abydos*) utters is to declare his exclusive scopic property in his daughter:

> Woe to the head whose eye beheld
> My child Zuleika's face unveil'd! (III)

The rivalry between him and the Romantic hero is clearly scopic:

> On Selim's eye he fiercely gazed;
> That eye returned him glance for glance
> And proudly to his sire's was raised,
> Till Giaffir's quail'd and shrunk askance. (V)[30]

Likewise, the Corsair "glared on the Moslems' eyes some Afrit sprite" (IV) in his moment of defiance against Seyd Pacha. "I know him by the evil eye," cries the villain of *The Giaour*, searching for his adversary across the battlefield. This "Black Hassan" is so fierce a foe that even lolling on the ground after death and defeat he glowers, "his unclosed eye / Yet lowering on his enemy," so that it is he who actually exhibits the evil eye (p. 242). The structure of the gaze that objectifies the Muslim woman is the same whether it comes from the hero or the villain. Though diametrically opposed in value, they mirror the same will to conquest and domination in relation to the land and the woman. "Yet did he but what I had done, / Had she been false to more than one," the Giaour unambiguously declares, prioritizing his homosocial identification with his rival "black Hassan," who drowned his wife for her adultery with the Giaour (p. 246).

Most of Hugo's *Orientales* in fact work by projecting Western identity onto the Muslim male alter ego. How else to explain poem after poem of eroticized violence all figured as Islamic assaults on Christians in an age when the tenor of the times was set by Napoleon's invasion of Egypt? How else to explain the lurid revelry in carnage in *"La Ville Prise"* (1825) than between the reverberating contexts of Napoleon's slaughter of the surrendered inhabitants of Jaffa in his 1799 Syrian maneuver and the escalating French campaign to take Algeria (conquered in the 1830s and officially annexed in 1842)?

In *Crie de guerre du Mufti* (1828), the speaker eggs on the Muslim hordes with *"Écrasez, ô croyants du prophete divin, / Ces chancelants soldats qui s'enivrent de vin, / Ces hommes qui n'ont qu'une femme!"* (Crush, o believers in the divine prophet, these faltering Christian soldiers, who are enervated with wine, these men who have only one woman!). In the terms of Orientalism, it is the Islamic world which is effeminate, enervated by addiction to sensual pleasures. In *Chanson de pirates* (1828), Muslim corsairs boast

> *Nous emmenions en ésclavage*
> *Cent chretiens, pêcheurs de corail;*
> *Nous recrutions pour le sérail*
> *Dans tous les moutiers du rivage.*

> (We will take into slavery
> One hundred Christians, pink complexioned sinners
> We will recruit for the seraglio
> With every roll [of the waves] on the shore.)

They seize a young nun, assuring her that "*[c]e n'est que changer de couvent,/Le harem vaut le monastère*" (Nothing is going to change but the convent; the harem will become your cloister) in a mirror-image reversal of the rescue from the harem.

Exactly who the hero is in these poems of pseudo-Islamic conquest becomes clear in *Bounaberdi* (1828), when the Arab male speaker calls Napoleon "*sultan des francs d'Europe*" (sultan of the Franks of Europe) whose gaze "*[e]mbrasse d'un coup d'oeil les deux moities du monde*" (encircles in the flash of an eye the two halves of the world). The Romantic hero in Hugo's poems is so successful in appropriating the cognitive territory of his enemy that he can appropriate his identity as well. As Napoleon proclaimed to the people of Alexandria on July 2, 1798, "*[N]ous sommes les vrais musulmans*" (We are the true Muslims) (Said, 82).

This victorious *vrai musulman* sent for Egyptian women to sample, on the one hand, and dangled European mistresses on the other—but the latter had brothers, husbands, fathers, whom he had to take seriously, while his dalliances with the former had no consequences—for him. One sixteen-year-old Egyptian female whom he used was killed by local authorities for collaboration with the invader, after he discarded her. Byron has a strikingly similar experience in Greece. His sexual affair with "a Turkish girl" is discovered, upon which she is "sewn up in a sack, to be thrown into the sea," but Byron is able "to prevent the completion of the sentence." He sends her to friends in Thebes where "she died, a few days after her arrival, of a fever—perhaps," he flippantly adds, "of love" (quoted from Thomas Medwin's *Conversations with Lord Byron*, in Meyer, 675). He thus manages to suggest that she pined away for want of her hero, just as his Zuleika-types do in his Turkish tales.

These paradigmatic stories demonstrate the reciprocality of French and Egyptian patriarchal domination, but equality between the two systems is out of the question. Western "liberation" of the inert Muslim woman in nineteenth-century Orientalist discourse always overwhelms the native patriarchal structure it simultaneously reinforces because it has the upper hand militarily, economically, politically, culturally. The Romantic hero's vision is simply superior in the quality, not the kind, of its penetration.

As an object of this possessive desire expressed through the gaze, the Muslim woman acquires a status of sorts that she did not have in eighteenth-century texts. She emerges from the horde of faceless insignificant women that populate Enlightenment harems to become the one Muslim female in the text again.[31] She is lifted from her abjection in *Lettres Persanes* and from her brutish existence in *Rasselas* (which were reinforced by the marginalia of numerous other eighteenth-century writers). Yet the Romantic Muslim woman does not seem to resemble her seventeenth-century or Renaissance predecessors, and she certainly seems farthest removed from her most memorable medieval predecessors: as execrable as they are in their overbearing wantonness, she is exemplary in her femininity.

What continues from eighteenth-century discourse is the use of the harem as a negative ideal to make the glorified domesticity of the ideal Western woman look benign by contrast. The Romantic's rescued harem woman is in fact the best candidate for Western-style domesticity, since she rejects only the more extreme and humiliating elements of her indigenous type of seclusion and does not take advantage of the generous admission of Western women to affective individualism by expecting the kind of actual equality Wollstonecraft demanded. This allows the Romantic male to enjoy the best of both worlds.

No Romantic hero would want as a companion one of those sniveling harem slaves painted by the eighteenth-century discourse, for then she would not be able to give herself to him freely and appreciate his greatness of soul. She would not be able, as Selim wants of Zuleika, "To soothe each sorrow, share in each delight, / Blend every thought, do all—but disunite" (*Bride*, 2.XX). Yet "The Haram's languid years of listless ease / Are well resigned for cares—for joys like these." They are indeed—but there is no need to go all the way, Byron implies, and make the woman have intellectual ambitions of her own—like the English "bluestockings" he detested. He comes right out and says it in a footnote on Zuleika's harem amusements: "many of the Turkish girls"—he would know, of course—"are highly accomplished, though not actually qualified for a Christian coterie. Perhaps some of our own *"blues"* might not be the worse for *bleaching*" (256). You can take the woman out of the harem, in other words, but there is no need to take the harem out of the woman; in fact, why not inject some harem into European women for good measure? The rescued harem damsels retain some of that Islamic mystique, then, that makes them more desirable from a Western male heterosexual point of view—that paradoxically submissive yet well-cultivated sexuality. These are the sons of Rousseau.

The Romantics empty the woman of volition to make her a pure vessel of inspiration for man's life and art. To serve so, she must be drained of subjectivity. "[I]n the metaphysical emptiness their *'purity'* signifies [women] are, of course, *self-less,* with all the moral and psychological implications that word suggests" (Gilbert & Gubar, 21). Gulnare approaching the Corsair in his cell is not even a "she" anymore but an "it," not because of subhuman brutishness but for her angelic translucence:

> . . . 'tis an earthly form with heavenly face!
> . . . . . . . . . . . . . . . . . . . . . . . . . . . . . . . . .
> That form with eye so dark, and cheek so fair,
> And auburn waves of gemm'd and braided hair;
> With shape of fairy lightness . . .
> (*Corsair,* 2.XII)

Zuleika too gives off "Beauty's heavenly ray"—

> Such was Zuleika—such around her shone
> The nameless charms unmark'd by her alone —
> The light of love, the purity of grace . . .
> (*Bride,* 1.VI)

—while of Leila the narrator says, "through her eye the immortal shone" (*Giaour,* p. 240).

Of earlier manifestations of the Muslim woman, only Cervantes' Zoraida had similarly appeared to the Captive like "some goddess from heaven" in her beauty and "perfection" (*Don Quixote,* 416). She too was idealized and romanticized and made an object of visual pleasure and pity. But the marks of her erasure were fresh; traces of her speaking self were visible in her words, traces of her troublesome Morisco identity resurfaced in her handwriting. The Zuleikas do not write or speak except to hasten their deaths. "In silence bow'd the virgin's head, / And if her eye was filled with tears, / That stifled feeling"—not only she "dared not shed," but the poet rather sadistically aestheticizes: "So bright the tear in Beauty's eye / Love half regrets to kiss it dry" (*Bride,* 1.VIII).

Zuleika's body is idealized, killed into "a statue of distress," made an aesthetic commodity. Leila's drowned body is carried through the fragmented narrative of *The Giaour,* passed from narrator to narrator . . . beginning with Byron, who in his Advertisement, invents a whole supposed tradition, a pseudo-history, of a "Musselman manner" of throwing women into the sea for infidelity. In "advertising" Leila's story, Byron creates her as an aesthetic and literary commodity and draws attention to the heroism of his own real-life Giaour episode.[32] What's more, Leila is one of Byron's Muslim women who actually has an interesting story to tell—she disguised herself as a Georgian page and escaped black Hassan's harem to meet her Christian lover. This makes her exclusion from language even more striking.

From the point of view of dramatic action, there is no reason why the tale could not have been called *Leila*, and mediated through her subjectivity, instead of being called *The Giaour* and mediated through male narrators. But of course there is every reason. For the Romantic hero operates from a subject position that is "socio-historically determined as masculine," and the Romantic poet writes "to establish rites of passage toward poetic identity and toward masculine empowerment" (Ross, 29). Leila is not allowed her version of the story because to tell the story is part of the quest for self-possession which is figured so necessarily as masculine by male writers in the Romantic era.

Byron's literary output is a major factor in creating what I see as the paradigmatic Romantic view of the Muslim woman. Perhaps because of this, he is also among the first to satirize the harem drama, in *Don Juan*. Having "been there, done harem" (so to speak), he can afford to run ahead of his time and parody it. Harem spoofs in the twentieth century, such as the films *Lost in a Harem* (1944), starring Abbott and Costello, and *Don Juan de Marco* (1995), starring Johnny Depp, bear Byron's imprint. The satirizing of the harem adventure does not negate the core Romantic view of the Muslim woman; indeed, it is predicated upon this view.

Byron seems to be the father of many of the images in Victor Hugo's construct of the Orient. Hugo aestheticizes the dead bodies of Muslim women thrown in the Bosporus in *Claire de Lune*. "*La lune était sereine et jouait sur les flots*," he begins. "Bright shone the merry moonbeams dancing o'er the wave."[33] A "sultana" is leaning from a window strumming a guitar, semiconscious of another sound—"*[u]n bruit sourd frappe les sourds echos*" (that sound that echoes dull and low). Idly, lyrically, alliteratively, the poem wanders through the possible sources of the muffled sounds, then reveals the answer after a series of negations whose sole purpose is to provide aesthetically pleasing parallels to the sounds:

> *Qui trouble ainsi les flot près du sérail des femmes?* —
> *Ni le noir cormoran, sur la vague berce*

*Ni les pierres du mur, ni le buit cadence*
*D'un lourd vaisseau, rampant sur l'onde avec des rames.*

*Ce sont des sacs pesants, d'ou partent des sanglots*
*On verrait, en sondant la mer qui les promène,*
*Se mouvoir dans leurs flancs comme une forme humaine.*
*La lune était sereine et jouait sur les flots.*

(Who thus disturbs the tide near the seraglio?
'Tis no dark cormorants that on the ripple float,
'Tis no dull plunge of stone—no oars of Turkish boat,
With measured beat along the water creeping slow

'Tis heavy sacks, borne each by voiceless dusky slaves;
And could you dare to sound the depths of yon dark tide,
Something like human form would stir within its side.
Bright shone the merry moonbeams dancing o'er the wave.
[49])

The whole poem is a set of frames within frames. The sultana is framed within her window, and her idle mood of half-conscious curiosity frames the inquiry about the noises. Finally, the first line is repeated as the last, so that the heavy human-shaped sacks from which sobs can be heard (by no one in particular, since the grammar reinforces anonymity) as they float out from the seraglio to the sea are framed within perfect lyrical closure. It is as an inert body that the Muslim woman bears the visionary load of the Romantic hero.

A nimbus of idealization now fixes the woman "to her place as bearer of meaning, not maker of meaning" (Mulvey, 7). The meaning that the Muslim woman bears in these Romantic texts is apparent from the unmistakably fetishistic nature of the gaze directed at her. This fetishistically organized visual pleasure associates the Muslim woman with an assortment of classically phallic body parts. There is a preponderance of white feet, long necks, milky arms, and cascading hair. So Wollstonecraft had good reason to catch Rousseau's fascination with his little Sophie's pretty foot—in this, as in so many things, he sets the mold for the male Romantics. Leila's flowing hair "swept the marble where her feet / Gleam'd whiter than the mountain sleet." "As rears her crest the ruffled Swan," no less, "Thus rose fair Leila's whiter neck" (*Giaour*, p. 241). We have already encountered Gulnare's "auburn waves of gemm'd and braided hair," but must not forget her "white arm" or "naked foot, / That shines like snow, and falls on earth as mute" (*Corsair*, 2.XII). And who could match the *"pied d'albâtre"* (alabaster foot) of Hugo's *Sara la Baigneuse*? This bathing beauty inspires foot fantasies in a class by herself as she lies *"toute nue"* in her hammock, white skin delicately moist, dangling a dainty foot in the fresh trembling water, dreaming appropriately of *"sandales / De drap brode de rubis"* (sandals of ruby-worked cloth) and fantasizing about being spied on by two eyes gleaming from between the trees—apparently the position of the poet (p. 128).[34]

Moreover, given the parallel that critics such as Marlon Ross have drawn between the Romantic poet / hero and the capitalist / industrialist (32–33), it is not surprising that the fetishized body of the Muslim woman becomes a *commodity*. She is the trophy competed for by two men in a struggle for "cognitive hegemony" (Ross, 31) that also reflects a struggle for material hegemony—the clash of empires that rearranged the globe in the nineteenth century. If in this struggle the Romantic hero reprises the role of the knight from medieval romance, as Ross suggests, the Muslim woman does not reprise her medieval role as overbearing female enemy. Rather she is removed from the locus of dramatic action: the sultana in *Claire de Lune* can only wonder vaguely about the meaning of the dull sounds she hears; Zuleika from her harem wonders how Selim fares; Gulnare and her handmaids are locked in the harem as the fight flares between Seyd Pacha and the Corsair. She is a translucent symbol suspended above the significant action and inspiring it, rather like Aude than Bramimonde.

What better figure to use as an empty vessel than the recycled harem slave? For the women of one's own society (in this age of incipient Western feminist claims to liberal individualism) might not be so easy to discard after their purpose had been served. As Byron well knew, the material presence of the Annabellas and Adas, the Augustas and Astartes, was difficult to encompass.

The harem and its symbolic extension, the veil, constitute the supreme silencing mechanism; there is nothing quite analogous to it in the other foreign cultures represented in Romantic texts. Using the harem as an excuse, the Romantic narrator can perform a "symbolic laryngectomy" (Busia, 90) on the Muslim woman more completely than he can ever silence a Western woman. Then he can step back and blame this silencing on the harem master, the Muslim male who technically enforces Muslim female silence in the plot.

The Muslim woman materializes in the texts of Byron framed and suffocated by the harem: in *The Giaour, The Bride of Abydos,* and *The Corsair,* the name of the Muslim woman is not mentioned until the name of the "Haram" has been pronounced. In Hugo's *Le Voile,* the woman is boxed in by her four brothers, who surround her and her words like a narrowing frame; the veil is a symbolic extension of the forbidden and forbidding harem wall.

Hugo heightens the moment of the sister's violent death by having the poem begin when the brothers have just accosted her. She sounds nervous from the start: "*Qu'avez-vous, qu'avez-vous, mes frères? . . .*" (What has happened, my brothers?).[35] "*N'avez vous pas leve votre voile aujourd'hui?*" (Hast thou, since the dawn / To the eye of a stranger thy veil withdrawn?), the first brother confronts her. She has come from the bath—"*Je revenais du bain, mes freres, / Seigneurs, du bain je revenais*"[36] (I was returning from the bath, my brothers, my lords, from the bath I was returning)—with its suggestion of wet, promiscuous, female nudity lyrically inverted and repeated. Hugo then circles from terse brother to brother, inserting the sister, with her rising panic, in between: "*Grace! tuerez-vous une femme / Faible et nue en votre pouvoir?*" (Mercy! Would you kill a woman weak and helpless in your power?) Finally all four thrust with their daggers and she falls bleeding, pleading, dying at their feet: "*Car sur mes regards qui s'etaignent / S'etend un voile de trepas.*" An English translator renders it thus:

> Mercy! Allah! have pity! oh, spare!
> . . . See! I cling to your knees repenting!
> Kind brothers, forgive me! for mercy forbear!
> Be appeased at the cry of a sister's despair,
> . . . For our mother's sake relenting.
> O God! must I die! They are deaf to my cries!
> . . . Their sister's life-blood shedding;
> They have stabbed me each one—I faint—o'er my eyes
> . . . a veil of Death is spreading! (88)

At least death is a veil she will not be able to lift, the last brother remarks with satisfaction, his barbaric code of honor satisfied. The poet/speaker uses the Islamic Otherness of the brothers and the premise of their primitive enforcement of the veil to mask the desire he has adroitly erected for the rape of the sister.

This is the meaning of the rescue from the harem, a feature unique to the representation of the Muslim woman in Romantic texts. It entails the replacement of the harem master by the Romantic hero as possessor of the woman. Even if this possession does not fully succeed in physical terms, it is accomplished in terms of cultural or cognitive triumph. For example, Gulnare is returned to Seyd Pacha after the Corsair rescues her from the burning harem, yet the superiority of his masculine presence over Seyd's has been indelibly established. The Corsair rescued her in the first place because of superior chivalric values: "Man is our foe, and such 'tis ours to slay; / But still we spared—must spare the weaker prey"... values that idealize women's "defenceless beauty" (*Corsair*, 2.V). Gulnare, carried to safety in the Corsair's arms, finds "*that* robber thus with gore bedew'd / Seem'd gentler then than Seyd in fondest mood" (2.VII). Here, then, is the qualitative difference: the hero's values make women dependent and idealize their dependence; the villain's values only make them dependent, without idealization. The hero's superiority is thus truly a victory of ideas, of the word, of the capability for rationalization: it is a cognitive colonization of the mind. Here we witness a triumph of Orientalism, of a Napoleonic deployment of the tools of classification and knowledge for the purpose of conquest.

And of course, after she is rescued, the Muslim woman is generally discarded. Zuleika dies of grief at the moment the hero's life is over, there being no further purpose to her uncognizant existence:

> That grief—though deep—though fatal—was thy first!
> Thrice happy! ne'er to feel nor fear the force
> Of absence, shame, pride, hate, revenge, remorse!
> (*Bride*, 2.XXVII)

In *The Giaour*, Leila is drowned. *Don Juan's* Leila is foisted off on an English lady who will educate her. *The Corsair's* rescued Gulnare vanishes without explanation from the narrative. Hugo's "*Orientales*" are littered with female corpses ("*que j'en ai vu mourir de jeunes filles!*"—How many young girls have I seen die there! [*Fantomes*]). Since the man has incorporated all that the Romantic hero needs of feminine feeling, an inconvenient feminine body, a material presence, has become superfluous. The male scopic encompassing of new social and mental territory has been established, so the female symbolic function is finished; the woman becomes dross. To keep her physical presence after that point would be to allow her corporeality to come to the fore, which for Romanticism's notion of the feminine is rather disgusting.

The Romantic hero, alas, never explicitly has sex with his Muslim woman, at least not graphically, not within the narrative frame. (Don Juan with Dudu is a discreetly disguised exception that proves the rule.) That experience must await the adventurer of the high imperialist era (the last half of the nineteenth century to about 1914).

*Monstrosity, Mutation, and Woman's Blood*

The subjectivity of the Other puts up one last struggle before its total Romantic eclipse, inspiring a disquieting, uncanny thrill in those few writers whose work encountered it. As one might expect, the texts of female Romantic writers[37] overlap with some aspects of the standard male harem drama while diverging from it in others. At least in Mary Shelley's *Franken-stein* (1818), the marginal Muslim woman survives the rescue from the harem. But in order to do so, she must run away from *herself*—a flight which reduces the project of rescue to ruins.

In chapter 13 of *Frankenstein*, during the course of the monster's narration of his life, there appears the interpolated tale of Safie, a Turkish-Arabian woman who turns out to be intimately connected to the monster's education and development. The monster has discovered the De Lacey family, a blind old man and his son and daughter, living in pastoral exile, and hides in a hovel attached to their cottage from which he can observe their lives. One day a lady in a "dark suit" and "thick black veil" arrives; by way of greeting she can only pronounce the name of the son, Felix. This is Safie, whose perfidious Turkish father is the cause of the De Laceys' miserable exile from society. She has abandoned her father and rejected his world, and comes to be tutored into the domestic affective individualism of a Western "angel in the house." By paying attention through a chink in the wall to the lessons Felix gives Safie, the monster learns language. Convinced by these lessons of the validity of its civilizing mission, he tries to insert himself into the society of the family using its very terms, only to be cruelly and utterly rejected.

Although Shelley's creation of Safie deploys many of the conventions of the standard Romantic Muslim woman material, it can also be read as a sideways critique. To begin with, Shelley's choice of Safie's name is surely not random. Although it is in fact a Turkish name,[38] its evocation of "Sophie" is too striking to be ignored. Sophie is Rousseau's model for the ideally educated woman: Mary Wollstonecraft derides Rousseau's agenda for female education by pointing out that he makes of Sophie little more than a harem slave. Why should Wollstonecraft's daughter Mary Shelley not rewrite Sophie through the mediation of her mother's liberal individualist agenda for the reeducation of women? Shelley puts forth her own program of education for Safie, one which gives her access to speech and language and, ostensibly, to an individual subjectivity—which, however, proves costly and impossible to sustain under its heavy load of contradictions.

Safie's inklings of the possibility of female freedom also come from her mother, a Christian Arab enslaved by the Turks.[39] The "texts" this woman bequeaths to her daughter before her death (like the posthumous legacy of Wollstonecraft to her daughter) "taught her to aspire to higher powers of intellect, and an independence of spirit, forbidden to the female followers of Mahomet" (108). Shelley is here the inheritor of her mother's assumptions. To presume the existence of an Islamic interdiction on female aspiration to "intellect" and "spirit" is the only possible conclusion a reader of Wollstonecraft can come to about the status Muslim women.

That assumption, and the one made in the subsequent description of Safie ("who sickened at the prospect of again returning to Asia, and being immured within the walls of a haram, allowed only to occupy herself with infantile amusements, ill suited to the temper of her soul, now accustomed to grand ideas and a noble emulation for virtue," 108), are the direct offspring of the eighteenth-century Orientalist authority which created the Muslim woman as harem slave. To paraphrase Spivak on the "worlding" of the "Third World," these are the intertextual repetitions that "haremize" the harem in Western discourse.

To cement *Frankenstein's* "haremization" of the "female followers of Mahomet" (who in the proper sense are actually absent from this text, because Safie was raised as a Christian by her mother), Orientalism takes an active hand in its plot. Felix instructs Safie from the writings of Constantin de Volney, author of *Voyage en Égypte et en Syrie* (1787) and *Considérations sur la guerre actuel de Turcs* (1788). These are works upon which Napoleon relied in preparing for his invasion of Egypt. Volney, who was "canonically hostile to Islam," "eyed the Near Orient as a likely place for the realization of French colonial ambition. . . . What Napoleon profited from in Volney was the enumeration, in ascending order of difficulty, of the obstacles to be faced in the Orient by any French expeditionary force" (Said, 81). This is the author through whose text, *Ruins of Empires*, Felix teaches Safie the history of the world, and by implication, her place in it.

Ironically, Felix says he chose Volney "because the declamatory style was framed in imitation of the eastern authors" (105). In other words, Felix seems to think that because its author masks himself in the florid narrative style of his male Islamic Other (just as in his poems Hugo masks himself in the lurid bloodthirsty voice of his Islamic speakers), Safie ought to be better able to form her new self from the knowledge imparted by the text—knowledge permeated by its superior overview of "slothful Asiatics" (105). So Safie is to mutate into "a domesticated Other that consolidates the imperialist self" (Spivak, 253). Only the monster realizes the alienation this produces, when he says, "As I read, however, I . . . found myself similar, yet at the same time strangely unlike the beings concerning whom I read" (112).

As Gayatri Spivak points out, Shelley "*cannot* make the monster identical with the proper recipient of these lessons" (258). Neither can she bring herself to make the Muslim woman their recipient; the proper "Muslim woman" remains somewhere beyond, in Asia, involuntarily immured in a harem and forcibly occupied with infantile amusements. So who is on the scene immured behind walls, secluded, oppressed? Who can only look out onto society from between chinks in a wall not unlike the celebrated latticework windows through which harem women peek? None other than the monster. We can therefore attribute a kind of metonymic relationship between the monster and the Muslim woman proper, between whom Safie, as a kind of mutant-hybrid Christian-Muslim, is the link.

Although the monster learns to speak by listening to the lessons given Safie, Safie gains access to language at a cost. First, the password which gains her admittance to the realm of language is the name of Felix. It is perhaps only through the Name of the Son that she could have left the world of Islam for the world of Christianity—for the world, moreover, of post-Revolutionary heroic soul-searching among the rebel sons of the era. As soon as she enters the cottage, she kneels at the feet of the De Lacey father, who raises her: submission to a newer, kinder, less physically overbearing patriarch in place of her old degenerate father is another price of her admission. To the new patriarchy she brings her "jewels," just as did the Muslim women characters of earlier centuries (111); lest the meaning of this cost be unclear, we are told that when Felix assisted her imprisoned father he saw "that the captive possessed a treasure [Safie] which would fully reward his toil and hazard" (108).[40] And indeed, when Safie arrives at the De Lacey house, her "angelic beauty" becomes the treasure of their home; she becomes for Felix "my sweet Arabian," his domesticated exotic property.

Note how far we have come from the conventions of the medieval "enamored Moslem princess": is Safie the termagant's last sigh? It is Safie's father who is imprisoned in a Christian land, rather than Felix in her father's land. The woman has been stripped of the initiative in sexual pursuit and takes no part in the conflict between the men (i.e., her father's legal battle in Paris). No monumental struggle is required to tame and assimilate the bristling presence of the Muslim woman; she has been pared down and made jejune for easy digestion. For finally, the ultimate cost of Safie's access to the world which permits her a liberated individuality is the exclusion of the monster itself, and by metonymic connection and implication, the monster-woman who is the Muslim woman left behind—left behind in "Asia," deliberately left behind in the medieval subtexts of Romanticism. To be saved from the monstrous fate of the harem slave as created by Montesquieu, Johnson, Denis Diderot,[41] William Beckford[42]—and further to be saved from the dubious "rescues" of Byron and Hugo which so inevitably end by discarding her corpse—Mary Shelley's Safie must flee the monster forever.

And in fact, when Safie comes face to face with the monster, she turns on her heel and rushes from the cottage: it is the last time she appears in *Frankenstein*. The whole De Lacey family quits the area. Felix appears once more within sight of the monster and narrates Safie's "horror"—but after all, we know nothing directly of her own reading of the monster (119). The monster returns to the cottage one last time, to burn it to a crisp, just as he burns himself on the Arctic tundra outside the frame of the text.[43]

The dilemma posed by Safie's face-off with the monster, which challenges the edifice of affective individualism built up by the myth of "a modern Prometheus," is "the tangential unresolved moment in *Frankenstein*" (Spivak, 258). The unresolvability of this moment is the point where Mary Shelley diverges from the male Romantics. For the success of the civilizing mission, the course in Volney, the heroic quests of the Felixes and other Giaours—all are ultimately disrupted, their contradictions exposed, their claims to universality debunked, by the excluded monster (metonymically recalling the Muslim woman) and its impossible claim to subjectivity at the very center of Shelley's text.

A trace of that subjectivity comes back to haunt even Byron. It surfaces almost despite him in *The Corsair*'s Gulnare. This "dark-eyed lady" first ap-

pears as a "defenceless beauty," a "trembling fair" in the rescuing arms of
Conrad the Corsair (2.V). Though the Gulnare Conrad saves from the
burning harem is "Haram queen," she is "still the slave of Seyd," "a favor'd
slave at best." The first hint that she is anything more than Byron's other
"trembling fairs" comes when she ventures to visit Conrad in Seyd's dungeon. Yes, she has the white arm and snowy foot and all that—but as she
bends over his vulnerable sleeping form the narrator exclaims, "Ah! rather
ask what will not woman dare?" (2.XII). Gulnare follows up this sudden
narrative thought with a startling suggestion: "I have power" . . . but it turns
out only "to soothe the Pacha in his weaker hour." Or so it seems. "I am a
slave," she abjectly states, and reiterates, "I am his slave," informing Conrad of her slavish strategy to save him (2.XIV). And yet "my soul is nerv'd
to all," she furtively declares, "Or fall'n too low to fear a further fall,"
putting into dramatic form Wollstonecraft's psychological insight that
women's servility "produces a propensity to tyrannize, and gives birth to
cunning" (84).

The visit to the doomed Christian captive is a prerogative of the old enamored Moslem princess: the trip usually resulted in her persuasion to his
religion. Gulnare too converts to the hero's religion. If we search for her
thoughts on the Romantic creed of freedom rather than for those on Christianity, we find the necessary transformation realized when she tells him her
secret belief: "I felt—I feel—love dwells with—with the free." Then she
leaves, dropping one tear on his chains. This provokes an extraordinary
invective on the part of the narrator:

> Oh! too convincing—dangerously dear—
> In woman's eye the unanswerable tear!
> That weapon of her weakness she can wield,
> To save, subdue—at once her spear and shield:
> Avoid it—Virtue ebbs and Wisdom errs,
> Too fondly gazing on the grief of hers!
> What lost a world, and bade a hero fly?
> The timid tear in Cleopatra's eye.
> Yet be the soft triumvir's fault forgiven;
> By this—how many lose not earth—but heaven!
> Consign their souls to man's eternal foe,
> And seal their own to spare some wanton's woe!
> (*Corsair*, 2.XV)

This tirade attempts to reduce even the lofty Cleopatra to a doe-eyed oda-lisque . . . and it is strangely disproportionate to Gulnare's lowly powers as a harem slave. The passage seems to spring from a deeper source. The choice of the word "wanton" in the last line hints at the older subtexts from which this outburst may be drawing, since "wanton" was the term of choice to describe the Muslim woman in many medieval romances. In fact, the al-lusion to Cleopatra has similar implications, for this powerful pagan pre-decessor was frequently and aptly invoked in medieval representations of the Muslim woman. Despite her unconvincingly painted "timidity," the great queen seems out of place standing next to the defenseless harem damsel. On a similar note, even the meek Zuleika somehow induces men-tion of Eve:

> Fair as the first that fell of womankind
> When on the dread yet lovely serpent smiling
> Whose image then was stamp'd upon her mind—
> But once beguiled—and evermore beguiling.
> (*Bride*, 1.VI)

This links her ever so subtly to her wanton foremothers, to their monstrous element, to the Lamia tradition in Romantic poetry.

Gulnare bears a more telltale residue of this shadowy past. "I do mis-trust thee, woman!" Seyd snaps (3.V). She cannot forgive him this. His sus-picion and threats are what push her over the line from merely begging for mercy for Conrad to plotting her master's demise. Her plot to kill Seyd in his sleep does not mesh with Conrad's code of chivalry, but she is fevered:

> That hated tyrant, Conrad—he must bleed!
> I see thee shudder, but my soul is changed—
> Wrong'd—spurn'd—reviled—and it shall be avenged—
> (*Corsair*, 3.VIII)

Possessed, almost demonically, by her awakening to new emotion ("Alas! *this* love—*that* hatred are the first—"), Gulnare echoes Montesquieu's Rox-ane, justifying her "crime" with revolutionary rhetoric ("Those tyrants, teasing, tempting to rebel— / Deserve the fate their fretting lips foretell"). Conrad now begins to be uneasy at Gulnare's appropriation of his language of heroism. Men fighting men in the open is one thing:

To smite the smiter with the scimitar;
Such is my weapon—not the secret knife—
Who spares a woman's seeks not slumber's life.
Thine I saved gladly, Lady, not for this—
Let me not deem that mercy shown amiss. (3.VIII)

The concurrence of Conrad, Seyd, and the narrator in mistrusting Gulnare implicitly endows her with a secret power and exposes the real seams of the Romantic harem drama: it is not really about a contest between two men, Eastern and Western; it is about the proper masculine way to gain self-possession and world possession, as opposed to the effeminate Oriental way—usually embodied in the Eastern man, but here shockingly usurped by Gulnare. For Gulnare's motives are not appropriate for a woman. Though awakened by love of Conrad, Gulnare knows her love is hopeless (he loves another, a Greek maiden, Medora). Still she wants to act, to save Conrad and kill Seyd—only she no longer wishes it for Conrad's sake, but for her own aroused sense of individuality, to "avenge" her own changed "soul."[44]

And act she does, but her action occurs outside the narration. It is through Conrad's eyes that the reader learns of it:

Again he look'd, the wildness of her eye
Starts from the day abrupt and fearfully.
She stopp'd—threw back her dark far-floating hair,
That nearly veil'd her face and bosom fair,
As if she late had bent her leaning head
Above some object of her doubt or dread.
They meet—upon her brow—unknown—forgot—
Her hurrying hand had left—'twas but a spot—
Its hue was all he saw, and scarce withstood—
Oh! slight but certain pledge of crime—'tis blood!
(3.IX)

She has dared to write her own sign on her own face with her own hand, staining its shining whiteness, destroying the blankness that made it a symbol and a fetish and an object of male scopophilia.

The mere suggestion of Gulnare's self-possessing action had shrunk and shriveled Conrad's manhood: "Gulnare—Gulnare—I never felt till now / My abject fortune, wither'd fame so low" (3.VIII). Now she appears,

and the spot of male blood shed by her hand takes on powerful significance. It seems to contain the horror of female sexuality, to be the uncanny sight of a castration wound, to shake the whole foundation of the
Romantic hero's endeavor:

> He had seen battle . . .
> . . . . . . . . . . . . . . . . .
> But ne'er from strife, captivity, remorse—
> From all his feelings in their inmost force—
> So thrill'd, so shudder'd every creeping vein,
> As now they froze before that purple stain.
> . . . . . . . . . . . . . . . . . . . . . . . . . . . . .
> Blood he had view'd—could view unmov'd—but then
> It flow'd in combat, or was shed by men! (3.X)

His whole quest is undermined, and he almost changes places with her:
"He veil'd his face, and sorrow'd as he passed," momentarily pushed into a
humiliated feminine position of veiling and sorrowing. His formerly "iron
hand" (3.VII) now "Had lost its firmness, and his voice its tone" (3.XVII).

Conrad's Greek girlfriend, too, seems to suffer from Gulnare's grasp at
subjectivity. Medora appears to be sacrificed in the place of the Muslim
woman, whose requisite dead body is otherwise missing from this tale.
Greece in Byron's writings is an intermediate place between the polarities
of Occident and Orient, masculine and feminine; its specific meaning varies
according to context. Here the Greek woman functions as a backup, quasi-
Muslim woman, for she lives in harem-like seclusion in a "tower" resem-
bling Zuleika's tower in *The Bride of Abydos* and dies in a swoon, like Zuleika
(like medieval Aude, too), from the sheer mental impact of the male
conflict from which she is physically distanced. Gulnare after her soul-
change contrasts herself to Medora ("I rush through peril which she would
not dare" [3.VIII]) and scorns the Greek's tame domesticity: "An outlaw's
spouse—and leave her lord to roam! / What hath such gentle dame to do
with home?" (3.VIII).

Just as the hero's masculinity is threatened when Gulnare enters the
realm of significant action, so key elements of her Romantic femininity as
rescued harem damsel drop away. As soon as she first mentions her resolve
to murder, she momentarily disappears as the object of Conrad's gaze, not
even bothering to await his word, and he is disoriented:

She turn'd, and vanish'd ere he could reply
. . . . . . . . . . . . . . . . . . . . . . . . . . . . . . . .
'Twas dark and winding, and he knew not where
That passage led; nor lamp nor guard was there
He sees a dusky glimmering—shall he seek
Or shun that ray so indistinct and weak? (2.IX)

Next, the spot of blood on her face "banish'd all the beauty from her cheek!" Now far from appearing an angel in Conrad's eyes, she is almost— a monster. And then that same blood-mark magically connects her with the overbearing Muslim noblewoman from whom the harem slave is normally so severed, as her behavior suddenly takes on characteristics of the all-but-forgotten termagant:

She clapp'd her hands—and through the gallery pour
Equipp'd for flight, her vassals—Greek and Moor
. . . . . . . . . . . . . . . . . . . . . . . . . . . . . . . . .
No words are utter'd—at her sign, a door
Reveals the secret passage to the shore
. . . . . . . . . . . . . . . . . . . . . . . . . . . .
And Conrad following, at her beck, obey'd
Nor cared he now if rescued or betray'd;
Resistance were as useless as if Seyd
Yet lived to view the doom his ire decreed.
(3.XII)

So she has vassals, all of a sudden, she who was but "a slave unmurmuring," "a toy for dotard's play" (3.VIII). So she commands the secret passageways, opened by her sign of blood, a sign she wrote by her own hand, bypassing the "words" of the world of men. Just as Bramimonde could give the towers, just as Gyburc could command the fort, just as Floripas could overthrow her father, for one blood-spotted moment Gulnare rules the place "as if Seyd."

The text reveals that Gulnare is reaching for the great Romantic male goal, the power of self-possession, by putting the same line in her mouth that each Romantic hero must sooner or later utter: "I am not what I seem" (3.XIV). Compare this cry, for example, to the hero Selim's "I am not, love! what I appear" (*Bride*, 1.XIV); to the opacity of the Giaour; to the Corsair's troubled depth of soul. Gulnare's spot of blood clouds her feminine translucence, momentarily gives her the dimensionality and complexity lacking in Romantic females. Gulnare somehow, impossibly, has both the wronged innocence of Christabel and the snake-eyed malice of Geraldine.[45] That spot is a trace, like the telltale *"macange"* and *"marfuce"* that surface in Zoraida's speech and handwriting: a residue that opens a rich vein from Gulnare's suppressed textual history.

Then the veil drops again, like a bandage, binding the allusive flow of this drop of blood. One minute Conrad is morosely evaluating his heroic quest and looking with horror at the woman-turned-monster at his side:

Ah! since that fatal night, though brief the time,
Had swept an age of terror, grief, and crime.
As its far shadow frown'd above the mast,
He veil'd his face, and sorrow'd as he past;
He though of all—Gonsalvo and his band,
His fleeting triumph and his failing hand;
He thought on her afar, his lonely bride:
He turn'd and saw—Gulnare, the homicide! (3.XIII)

The next minute she "drops her veil and stands in silence by"; she looks up, meekly seeking some sort of "answer" from Conrad, a woman defenseless, fair, trembling once again, once again appealing to his sense of chivalry for pity. He seals her lips with a kiss that "even Medora might forgive," a kiss that was "The first, the last that Frailty stole from Faith" (3.XVII). And she is inexplicably out of the picture after that kiss.

Medora we know has died. When Conrad reaches home and discovers her death, we know he disappears mysteriously into the sea. But what happens to Gulnare? She is neither present nor absent. Byron drops her cold, drops her into a textual black hole, without plot explanation—verisimilitude or no verisimilitude. The prospect of an active Muslim woman is too much for him to accommodate, just as it was too much for medieval texts to accommodate. The difference is that Byron, compared to medieval text-makers, has a much more powerful and sophisticated cultural apparatus with which to bind this woman's unruly image into its required position in his age's text.

Gulnare is a troubling spot of complexity and opacity amid the central Romantic representations of the Muslim woman. The ubiquitous harem slave and rescued harem damsel overpower her. Yet the dynamism of these

two character types comes from the ebbing of their blood, comes from
their helplessness as they blanch and faint all over Romantic narratives. *"Ne
fuyez pas mes mains qui saignent"* (Do not avoid my bleeding hands), begs the
sister in *Le Voile*. Balzac's *Girl with the Golden Eyes* expires in a bath of blood of
multiple dagger wounds, leaving the prints of her hands and feet all over
the divans of her harem-prison. Such are the dire cultural spaces Western
discourse has prepared for the Muslim woman by the mid-nineteenth century. The historical variety of prototypes has been reduced to a single
harem woman who combines the most rigidly controlling mythic elements
of "Orient" and Occident: submissive erotic willingness and domesticated
female numinosity. The shifting of the core paradigm is complete: the basic mold of the modern Western representation of the Muslim woman has
been cast. It remains only for the engines of the imperialist-capitalist system to mass-produce this Muslim woman with more and more efficiency,
ingenuity, and tenacity. Western representations of the Muslim woman
continue to multiply and develop in the nineteenth and twentieth centuries.
The twists and turns of this later development are worth understanding,
particularly as they veer into the contemporary world and come between us
as human beings. This book sets out to establish the prehistory of the modern image and therefore stops here.

## Chapter Five

# CONCLUSION

There should be disarray. What had appeared natural, timeless, and uniform—the image of the Muslim woman in Western culture—should by now have materialized as a shifting, contingent, heterogeneous jumble. Muslim women assemble and disperse in the textual landscape of Europe: the blond and the dark-haired, the milk-white and the black-skinned, the meek and the wild-eyed. Eve, Semiramis, and Cleopatra swim in a drop of blood upon their cheeks. Giantesses swing cudgels over half-built harem scaffoldings; termagants shriek expletives from castle parapets; matrons address the knighthood of Orange in banquet halls; wantons bed-hop and continent-hop. Princess brides and winsome witches crisscross the Mediterranean Sea by water and by air; blackamoor bawds forge letters from bashaws; oppressed slaves slink through seraglios to paint and primp and plot; virginal damsels saved by *giaours* pine and die. The veils and vestments of these fictional women are strewn across cognitive expanses from Poitiers to Ispahan, tugged and stolen and transferred from one body to another; their jacinths and scattered rubies and pearl necklaces loop from Roncesvals to Damascus; their epistles, runes, and letters trail through Western cultural space from Algiers to the Alps.

If my dismantling activity works, for those who read it the stranglehold of the uniform image of the Muslim woman in Western culture will be

loosened. The homogeneity of the modern Western narrative will dissolve
into historical specificities, or at least into a handful of narratives more di-
verse than the one now on hand. The dominant narrative of the Muslim
woman in Western discourse from about the eighteenth century to the
present basically states, often in quite sophisticated ways, that the Muslim
woman is innately oppressed; it produces Muslim women who affirm this
statement by being either submissive nonentities or rebellious renegades—
rebellious against their own Islamic world, that is, and conforming to
Western gender roles. Their oppression is often figured as sexual oppression, and the corresponding submission or rebellion figured as sexual submission or rebellion. It is produced mainly in ways that are pleasurable
from a heterosexual male perspective, and that rationalize and justify Western interests in the material domination of the Islamic world.

Criticism of the Western narrative of the Muslim woman—a very slim
sheaf in the first place—has not attended to the historical genealogy of this
narrative. Such criticism has addressed the past two to three hundred years
of Western representations as manifestations of Orientalism, a broad term
for discourse that codifies "knowledge" about the "Orient" from a position of Western cultural hegemony and material dominance over that
"world." [1] As such, this criticism cannot offer explanations of Western images of the Muslim woman prior to the period of early modern Europe. For
to keep applying the Saidian critique of Orientalism farther and farther
back in history pushes the premise of Western cultural hegemony over the
Orient beyond its verifiable boundaries. Even to keep terming early Western discourse about the Islamic world "Orientalist" encourages that illu-
sion. It is clear that before the eighteenth century, Western cultural dominance over the Islamic world does not really exist. In the European Middle
Ages, the terms of cultural power are reversed (although not exactly sym-
metrically), with the Islamic world commanding the upper hand. During
what may be considered the middle centuries of Islam (roughly the fourteenth to the seventeenth C.E.), the relationship teeter-totters and varies
with local conditions. Neither circumstance could produce a hegemonic
discourse.

So the Orientalism critique is not an adequate methodology for studying the representation of Muslim woman in Western texts of those centuries. At the same time, feminist studies of the relevant texts tend not
to take methodological cognizance of the Islamic cross-connection. They
also tend to study the image of women only as a gender category within the

*oeuvre* of a particular author, or within a particular genre or national literature. To address the genealogy of the Muslim woman in Western literature,
then, I have had to braid together three strands: the discourse of Western
relationships with Islam, the Western discourse on gender, and the significance of particular texts against the background of these discursive and material conditions.

These are enormous, diffuse, and unwieldy variables to bring together.
There is no possibility of comprehensiveness or definitiveness. Knocking
out the heavy, blank firewall separating the modern Western narrative of
the Muslim woman from its history will, however, make room for more
refined exploration of this cultural space. In particular, the connections between Western representations of the Muslim woman and Western gender
discourse in general should open up a whole field of inquiry.

Explorable tangents abound in many directions. In the direction of
genre, I have brushed up fleetingly against historical chronicles, ecclesiastical literature, travel writing, imperialist archives, commercial advertise-
ments, and popular culture; there are also traditions of painting, photogra-
phy, and film representing the Muslim woman. In another direction, there
are obviously myriad national literatures I have not mentioned that would
yield rich and varied perspectives: Russian literature is one example, with
its unique relationship to the Central Asian Muslim milieu; American literature is another glaring case. And many of the national literatures from
which I have sampled texts would respond to a finer sweep. In the direction of subject matter, there is the tangent of the Muslim woman of the Indian subcontinent and the Indian woman in general; the tangent of the
Muslim African woman and the African woman in general; the tangent
of the Malay and Indonesian Muslim woman; the tangent of the Jewish
woman, especially the Sephardic woman; the Christian Arab woman; the
European woman kidnapped into the harem and the obvious question of
the Muslim male sexual threat; and so forth. Toward some of these valuable subjects-in-themselves I have inserted arrow marks where they inter-
sect with my text, but there are too many to have done so for all.

My narrative is not complete. It stops about a hundred years before the
point I initially wanted to reach. It stops with the Romantics not only for
the fullness of logistical reasons external to my text, but because by that period the basic paradigm has congealed which is still operative (though not
entirely unchanged) today. The Muslim woman begins to be oppressed; her
veil drops over her; the harem hardens into stone; the white-man's-burden

ideology begins to cast its lengthening shadow upon her; things begin to look familiar. It is the dis-Orienting of this familiar paradigm that I wanted to accomplish by reaching back behind it and exposing its scaffoldings and splintered planks. The age of high imperialism (the last half of the nineteenth century to 1914) does bring important developments in the representation of the Muslim woman, as does the age of Western colonial administration of the Islamic heartland (unabashedly defined as the Arab world), which lasts until the beginnings of decolonization in the 1940s. However, a great deal of what is manifested during those decades is elaboration, refinement, and revision of the paradigm whose basic components are in place by the beginning of the nineteenth century.

Real changes in Western representation of the Muslim woman do not occur until decolonization struggles alter the material conditions of discourse, until the Muslim world, and the Muslim woman, begin to speak back in the language of the colonizer. After 1963 (Algerian independence) and 1967 (the birth of the PLO), a new hint of terror tempers the contemptuous tone of Western representations of the Muslim woman, whose breasts become grenades, whose body is wired into Cold War firepower. Further, since 1979 (the Iranian Revolution and American hostage crisis in Tehran) and ever since the West christened the post-Cold War late-1980s and 1990s the "Islamic Threat" era, the image of the Muslim woman has mutated rapidly. In a *New York Times* photograph a black-veiled Iranian aims a gun point-blank into the camera: she is obviously no Zuleika.

Still, these new images are being quickly absorbed into the paradigm of the oppressed Muslim female, although the capacity of that paradigm to process them has not been fully established. It is a very rigid and narrow paradigm. For all that Western culture retains today of its own ebullient parade of Muslim women is a supine odalisque, a shrinking-violet virgin, and a veiled victim-woman. Bramimonde and Belakane are nowhere to be found in the modern Western cultural vocabulary; Alatiel and Armida, Zenocrate and Zanthia, are gone; plucky Nicolette, fierce Floripas, and wise Arabel have been banished, just when they might have been most useful in making up new myths of the Muslim woman under the changing material conditions that beleaguer Western cultural authority.

# Notes

## Chapter 1

1. As in Bijoux's perfume advertisement in *Vogue*, April 1992, contrasting a "submissive" "Muslim" woman with a carefree "American" (as if those were mutually exclusive categories) woman—who uses their perfume, naturally.

2. In an episode which aired January 10, 1992 on Channel 11, WPIX, New York, a fat sheik-cat kidnaps Heathcliff's girlfriend-cat and takes her to his harem to be his twenty-first wife-cat.

3. For example, Armenian princesses in medieval romances may be Christian but still belong to the category of "the Muslim woman" because of their strong association with an Islamic milieu and Islamic civilization.

4. The couplet describes the Muslim princess of Antioch's captivity under the Christian knight Tancred, with whom she falls in love after he conquers her city and kills her father the king.

## Chapter 2

1. Such in fact was the response when I posed the question to a large undergraduate class at Rutgers University in 1993 while teaching the *Roland* epic.

2. Oxford version.

3. References at the end of quotations from *Roland* are to laisse numbers; the English is Harrison's translation.

4. Consider that, despite the famous halt to their northward expansion at Poitiers in 732, Muslims ruled Provence for eighty years—longer than the modern state of Israel has existed.

5. This Greek word of unknown etymology was synonymous with "Arab" in pre-Islamic times but became an all-purpose word for Arabic-speaking Muslims of indeterminate race as used by medieval writers. From the twelfth century onward it pretty much means "Muslim," although other words can mean "Muslim" too, such as "Turk" and "Moor."

6. Consider, for perspective, that this is a period longer than the history of the United States to date.

7. "Mozarab" refers to a Spanish Christian under allegiance to a Muslim ruler; "Mudejar," to a Muslim of Spanish Christian origin.

8. Note that Ibn Battuta lived *after* the Mongol invasions had disrupted the Islamic world, yet still had a sense of security within Dar al-Islam.

9. Termagant is the name given by the authors of medieval romances to one of the "Saracen" gods with a violent, overbearing character; sometime in the seven-

teenth century, it came to mean a quarrelsome, overbearing woman; a virago, vixen, or shrew (OED). The development of the meaning of this word is, therefore, intriguingly linked to the meta-narrative of the Muslim woman.

10. Thanks to Diane DeLauro for pointing this out.

11. One account of the fall of Caesarea in the First Crusade reports that women were found—how?—to have hidden gold coins in their genitals (Daniels 1975, 133).

12. A name probably chosen for its association with a work by that name recounting the life of Saint Juliana, a convert from paganism in northern Europe.

13. Medieval Cairo was called Babylon in Europe.

14. The situation bears some resemblance to the stereotype of Western women among Arab men in our day.

15. In *Maugis d'Aigremont*, a giant Saracen offers Maugis his huge, ugly, black daughter if he will convert, which is meant to parody the "white as swan" Saracen beauties.

16. Muslims did once occupy Orange, but it was before the historical William was born. This poem preserves the memory of Muslims, not as distant foreigners, but as rulers in the home of Europe.

17. One might compare what would happen if an Arab feminist held up Margaret Thatcher or Golda Meir as a model.

18. To the credit, at least, of the oft-maligned medieval mind.


## Chapter 3

1. An expression more convenient than accurate, since slave trade had been a constant feature in world history to this point. I have capitalized it to indicate that this is the slave trade whose consequences are still most relevant today, the specifically European mass importation of black Africans primarily for heavy gang labor, primarily to the Americas.

2. As in Dante's *Commedia*, many of whose organizing concepts have been linked to Islamic sources by, for example, Miguel Asin Palacios (*Islam and the Divine Comedy*).

3. Perhaps similarly to the ways in which "Western" structures of thought permeate the postmodern world?

4. Arabia was an Ottoman backwoods; most of North Africa was under the Turks; the Moghul and Persian kingdoms were the peers of the Ottomans, but not of immediate concern to Europe. The Iberian kingdoms became the empire's main rivals when they struck from the rear at its monopoly on Asian trade.

5. Philip Stubbes, for example, castigated women's cosmetics in *The Anatomie of Abuses* (1583), and Counter-Reformation moralists such as Francois de Sales denounced hedonistic aristocratic dress and sexual ethics in his *L'introduction à la vie dévote*.

6. This is Edward Fairfax's translation (1600), which, having gained acclaim in

the Elizabethan and Stuart courts, is valuable in itself as an expression of the Renaissance imagination. The numbers refer to canto and stanza.

7. The death of Clorinda also has unavoidable classical resonances of the slaying of the Amazon Penthesilea by Achilles.

8. Technically, there were no more Moors in Spain after this. After conversion the neophytes were called Moriscos, meaning "little Moors" and really implying "beaten Moors." Slippage between the terms Moor and Morisco in *Don Quixote* show that this metamorphosis was not quite complete.

9. For example, Spain captured Algiers in 1510, then lost it in 1516 to the privateer brothers Barbarossa, who gave it to the Turks in return for governorship and continued their energetic assaults on Spanish shipping in the Mediterranean. Muslim seamen off North Africa not only raided the northern Mediterranean coast regularly, but attacked Spanish galleons carrying concentrated wealth from New World mines and took Spanish captives for sale as slaves in Algeria, "inflicting enormous damage" (Chejne, 10). Khayr al Din Barbarossa finagled admiralship of a Turkish fleet, "became the hero of Western Islam by ferrying 70,000 Moors from inhospitable Spain.... raided town after town on the coasts of Sicily and Italy, and took thousands of Christians to be sold as slaves" (Durant, 696). The Captive mentions Barbarossa in his story (chap. 39). At the same time, the Spanish Crown's despotism over Spain and its Muslim/Morisco population was formidable and irrefutable.

10. Sophronia, an Eastern Christian maiden in *Gerusalemme Liberata*, is approvingly cited as veiled:

And forth she went, a shop for merchandize,
Full of rich stuff, but none for sale exposed
A veil obscur'd the sun-shine of her eyes. (2.18)

11. Garces reaches this conclusion through an elaborate argument equating the pearls heaped on Zoraida's body with phallic Medusan snakes representing the Freudian uncanny, which finally constitute Zoraida as a phallus substitute or fetish in the form of a Mariological divinity. Not only is a less tortuous path to this conclusion available, but Zoraida's pearls, rather than affiliating her with baroque images of the Madonna in pearls, may equally connect her to the fabled sensuality of Arabian riches, and thus to the aspect of sexuality which the Captive wants to deny. While there is no allusion to the image of the pearl-encrusted Madonna in *Don Quixote*, chap. 16 alludes to the "*preciosas perlas orientales*" and the "*oro de Arabia, cuyo resplandor al del mesmo sol escurecía*" (350) (precious pearls from the Orient [and the] gold of Arabia, whose brightness obscured that of the sun [157]).

12. Juan Latino, an Ethiopian, was professor of Latin in the University of Grenada in 1573, for example (L. Johnson, 67).

13. And Othello's mother, as well as the Egyptian sorceress who gave her the magic handkerchief he now possesses.

14. The Jewish Jessica (*The Merchant of Venice*) and Abigail (*The Jew of Malta*) play a strikingly similar role.

15. See, for example, Hayklut's and Dallam's travel writings. Both have early descriptions of seraglios. (Dallam was sent by Elizabeth to charm the sultan with an ornate wooden organ.)

16. Similarly, the "haremization" of women in the ancient world occurred with the rise of urban centers and strong states (Ahmed, 11).

17. She is referring to the common English use of the black Ethiope as an emblem on tavern signboards.

18. Oriana is pregnant at this point.

19. The phrase "white devil" was commonly used in seventeenth-century sermons for a person who pretends sanctity as a cover for corruption (Lucas' notes on Webster, 193).

20. Darkness hides Vittoria's blush and women of her ilk are like "curst dogges" (I.i); she has "a soule so blacke;" she is the "picture" of the devil; as a "whore" she is a "deadly poison" (III.ii). Zanche "haunts" the play's villain like a "devill," is a "Witch," like a "wolf" (V.i), and "infernall" (V.iii).

21. Similarly, an earlier black Zanthia in John Marston's *Sophonisba* (1606), set in ancient Carthage, betrays her ladylike mistress to a sexual pursuer, who happens to be a Negro general.

22. As he dies; *The White Devil* is, as the title states, a "tragedy," while *The Knight of Malta* is not.

23. A handbook for extermination of witches (published 1487).

24. Clorinda's father, though Christian, also "mew'd up" his wife out of a jealous sense of property in her (*Gerusalemme Liberata*, canto 12). The issue of "mewing up" women is prior to and independent of the seraglio as *topos*, and does not necessarily evoke Islamic associations.

25. E.g., *Women Beware Women* (Middleton); *The Woman's Plot* (Massinger); *The Insatiate Countess* (Marston), etc.

26. Molière's *turquerie*, his comic ballets replete with Moorish dancers (*Le Sicilien*), faux Turkish dignitaries (*Le Bourgeois Gentilhomme*), and phony Turkish phrases, are a breezy paring-down of the once-dread Turkish peril. The Moors in Corneille's *Le Cid* (1637) hover at the end of the conflict as a lurking danger which a gust of wind might still bring back ("*Le flux les apporta, le reflux les remporte*" (IV.iii.1318) (Brought by the tide, now the ebb takes them to sea). Thirty years later Molière hangs a "kick me" sign on the behind of the Turk—almost literally, for he wrote *Le Bourgeois Gentilhomme* at the king's request after a particularly pompous Turkish ambassador had left Paris.

27. Racine may have had in mind Roxelena, an influential concubine who in 1530 convinced Suleiman the Lawgiver, probably the most powerful Ottoman sultan, to marry her, against the custom of the Ottoman rulers, and to release or distance the other women. She moved the women's quarters into the administrative palace and remained one of the greatest power brokers of his reign until her death. There was also a struggle in 1651 between Kosem (whose son, Bayazid, was killed,

like his namesake in Racine's play, by his brother Al-Murad) and her daughter-in-law Turhan over the de facto regency. The whole era from 1541 to 1687 is known in Ottoman annals as "The Reign of Women," a fact which did not escape the attention of European ambassadors and travel writers (Croutier, 115–120, 208).

28. *"Lieux"/"yeux"* being one of the most common rhymes in Racine.

29. Intellectual movements among noblewomen.

## Chapter 4

1. Adam Smith's famed phrase.

2. It must be said that these elements have had a century to percolate and gain authority through prototypical references marginal and central in the writings of merchants, academics, and ambassadors from Hayklut, Ben Jonson, and Sir Paul Rycaut to Chardin, Tavernier, and Jean Dumont (*Nouveau Voyage du Levant*, 1694), in addition to the literary texts I have examined.

3. The Turks suffered disastrous losses. (Abbott, 2:162–163).

4. Written by Barthelemy d'Herbelot, it was published after his death by Galland.

5. The word appeared in English in 1779; in French in 1799.

6. He initiates his discussion of this deployment by citing *Les Bijoux indiscrets*, Diderot's tale of a Muslim sultan whose magic ring makes the genitals of his women speak and reveal their secrets.

7. (That is, over the Spanish Succession, the Austrian Succession, etc.)

8. (Whose mission to mediate between the sultan and Emperor Charles VII "utterly failed" [Melman, 79]).

9. Favorite of the former emperor, now living outside the seraglio.

10. Lady Mary eloped, foregoing the negotiation of her wifely "portion" that was the woman's only security in aristocratic marriages (Melman, 88).

11. When Romantic painter Jean-Auguste Ingres copied passages from this letter to paint *Le Bain Turc*, he skipped this part, naturally.

12. Charles Jervas, London portrait painter.

13. Except when it comes to descriptions of sumptuary luxury. She is defensive about these descriptions: "This is but too like (says you) the Arabian tales; these embroidered napkins, and a jewel as large as a turkey's egg! . . . But I depend on your knowing me enough to believe whatever I seriously assert for truth . . ." (110).

14. There was a production of *Bajazet* in Paris in 1718.

15. Giovanni Marana launched the genre of a pseudo-Muslim traveler critiquing European customs in the seventeenth century with *Letters Writ by a Turkish Spy*.

16. William Beckford's lethargic and relentlessly erudite Oriental fantasy, *Vathek* (1786), is clearly the progeny of works such as *Lettres Persanes* in its treatment of the harem as metaphor for despotic government and in its scopophilic erotica.

17. This goes beyond classical liberalism's legalistic definition of freedom,

which Montesquieu espouses in the work that has always been regarded as his substantive contribution to political theory, *De l'esprit des lois* (1748). The latter, a product of his disenchanted old age, is a profoundly pessimistic work of conservative authoritarianism, positing virtue as self-renunciation and liberty as submission to the laws.

18. Even though he modified many of these positions decades later in *De l'esprit des lois*.

19. Montesquieu's view, expressed in the fifth book of *De l'esprit des lois*, that the Eastern female's innate concupiscence makes her dangerous and justifies her seclusion, sustains his preoccupation and desire for the enslaved Muslim woman.

20. The mullah has "*la science du Paradis*," similar to the pope's "keys to the kingdom of heaven." The "*neuf choeurs des Puissances célestes*" or "nine celestial choirs" which Usbek mentions in his address to the mullah come from medieval Christian iconography. Even the mullah's closing prayer, "May Mohammed be in your heart," smacks of Christian rather than Muslim pietism.

21. One wonders if they distinguished between the actual climates of places like Tahiti and Turkey; the latter is quite temperate.

22. Ellipses his.

23. Tight clothing aggravated his urinary problems.

24. He bases this on such accurate documentation as the folktale trope of the sudden fall from greatness in "Oriental stories." Bloom, in translating Émile, surmises that this refers to the *Thousand and One Nights*.

25. John McClure, written comment on my paper, "The Harem Drama of Orientalist Literature," submitted in March 1988.

26. Having been part of the Ottoman Empire since the late middle ages, Greece gained independence in 1830 after a protracted war in which Britain, France, and Russia participated.

27. Ironically, Zuleika (as Byron knows and notes) is the Arabic name for the biblical Potiphar's wife, a woman of aggressive sexuality famous for having tried to seduce Joseph. Islamic love poetry rehabilitates Zulaikha as an older, wiser, repentant woman who continues to love Joseph, but as a mystical, spiritual lover.

28. Obviously, the terms are not always neatly inverted; some voyeurism remains in some Romantic texts, just as one could locate some fetishism in earlier texts, but there is a shift in the *predominant* mode of scopophilia.

29. "Giaour," according to Byron, is a Turkish word for "infidel."

30. It is amazing how alive this paradigm is in twentieth-century film and how precisely it informs that genre. From Alexander Korda's 1942 *The Thief of Bagdad* to Disney's 1992 *Aladdin*, the scopic competition structures the entire conflict from opening sequence to closing scene, and the Romantic material lives even in the continued use of the name Jaffar for the villains.

31. Percy Shelley's *The Revolt of Islam* contains undifferentiated throngs of Muslim women "outraged and polluted long," but he calls this "a tale illustrative of such a revolution as might be supposed to take place in an European nation" and

does little to activate Islamic material besides making the women generically oppressed (77, 44).

32. "After Byron had published the tale, public rumor about his implication in
the affair it records prompted him to request a certain Lord Sligo to substantiate
his relation to the story" (Meyer, 674).

33. Translation by John L. Sullivan (Williams, 49).

34. Actually, this is an example of combined fetishistic and voyeuristic visual
pleasure. Nevertheless, the excessive reverence attached to the body of the silenced
Muslim woman, combined with such recurrent imagery, makes it clear that she is
a fetish-object.

35. Translation by Frank S. Mahony (Williams, 50).

36. The translations of this line and the following one are mine.

37. Marginalia on the Muslim woman are provided by Madame de Stael in
*Corinne*; Elizabeth Barrett Browning in *Aurora Leigh*; Charlotte Brontë in *Jane Eyre*.

38. Meaning "pure."

39. The convention of a secret education in Christianity imparted to the Muslim woman by someone in her household recalls Zoraida, who was similarly instructed by her Christian slave.

40. There are interesting parallels here to the angelic daughters of treacherous
Jews in *The Merchant of Venice* and *The Jew of Malta*.

41. In *Les bijoux indiscrets* (1748).

42. In *Vathek* (1786).

43. Spivak suggests, in relation to *Jane Eyre*'s Bertha but just as possible here, that
the suicide be read in connection to British policies on sati, Hindu widow self-
immolation. There are parallels and intersections between the woman of sati and
the woman of the harem in Western discourse.

44. The "dark lady" in Nathaniel Hawthorne's novels has been celebrated as a
resolute, tragically sexual, erotically forceful woman; she has demonstrable roots in
Hawthorne's interest in Arabiana and is definitely related to the Romantic Muslim woman. See Luther Luedtke, *Nathaniel Hawthorne and the Romance of the Orient*.

45. The damsel in distress and the villainess, respectively, in Samuel Taylor
Coleridge's poem "Christabel."

## Chapter 5

1. See, for example, Rana Kabbani, *Europe's Myths of Orient*.

# Bibliography

Abbott, Wilbur Cortz. 1927. *The Expansion of Europe: A Social and Political History of the Modern World, 1415–1789.* Vols. 1 and 2. New York: Henry Holt.

Ahmed, Leila. 1992. *Women and Gender in Islam: Historical Roots of a Modern Debate.* New Haven: Yale University Press.

Armstrong, Nancy. 1987a. *Desire and Domestic Fiction.* Oxford: Oxford University Press.

———. 1987b. "The Rise of the Domestic Woman." In *The Ideology of Conduct.* Ed. Nancy Armstrong and Leonard Tennenhouse. New York: Methuen.

*Aucassin et Nicolette.* 1984. Ed. Jean Dufournet. Paris: Flammarion.

Bartels, Emily C. 1990. "Malta, the Jew, and the Fictions of Difference: Colonialist Discourse in Marlowe's *The Jew of Malta.*" *English Literary Renaissance* 20:1–16.

Barthes, Roland. 1977. *On Racine.* Trans. Richard Haword. New York: Octagon.

Beckford, William. 1923. *Vathek.* London: Chapman.

Behdad, Ali. 1989. "The Eroticized Orient: Images of the Harem in Montesquieu and His Precursors." *Stanford French Review* 13:109–126.

Bell, Susan Groag. 1973. *Women from the Greeks to the French Revolution.* Stanford: Stanford University Press.

Berman, Marshall. 1970. *The Politics of Authenticity: Radical Individualism and the Emergence of Modern Society.* New York: Atheneum.

Bitton-Jackson, Livia. 1982. *The Jewish Woman in Christian Literature: Madonna or Courtesan?* New York: Seabury.

Boccaccio, Giovanni. 1975. *Il Decameron.* Ed. Natalino Sapegno. 1956. Reprint. Torino, Italy: Capretto.

———. n.d. *The Decameron.* Trans. anonymous. London: Bibliophilist Society.

Bolton, W. F. 1970. *History of Literature in the English Language: The Middle Ages.* London: Barrie & Jenkins.

Bowers, Fredson., ed. 1992. *The Dramatic Works in the Beaumont and Fletcher Canon.* Vol. 8. Cambridge: Cambridge University Press.

Brault, Gerald J. 1978. *The Song of Roland: An Analytical Edition.* University Park: Pennsylvania State University Press.

Brontë, Charlotte. 1962. *Jane Eyre.* New York: Macmillan.

Browning, Elizabeth Barrett. 1979. *Aurora Leigh.* Chicago: Academy Chicago.

Burshatin, Israel. 1985. "The Moor in the Text: Metaphor, Emblem, and Silence." *Critical Inquiry* 12:98–118.

Bush, M. L. 1967. *Renaissance, Reformation and the Outer World.* New York: Humanities.

Busia, Abena. 1989–1990. "Silencing Sycorax: On African Colonial Discourse and the Unvoiced Female." *Cultural Critique* 14:81–104.

Byron, Lord (George Gordon). 1879. *The Poems and Dramas.* Vol. 1. New York: Arundel.

————. *Byron's Don Juan*. 1957. Ed. Truman Guy Steffan and Willis W. Pratt. Austin: University of Texas Press.

Castle, Terry. 1986. *Masquerade and Civilization: The Carnivalesque in Eighteenth-Century English Culture and Fiction*. Stanford: Stanford University Press.

*Cambridge Modern History, The New*. 1965. Vol. 9. *War and Peace in an Age of Upheaval*. Ed. C. W. Crawley. Cambridge: Cambridge University Press.

————. 1967. Vol. 10. *The Zenith of European Power*. Ed. J. P. T. Bury. Cambridge: Cambridge University Press.

Cervantes, Miguel de. *Don Quixote*. 1964. Trans. Walter Starkie. New York: Signet.

————. 1990. *El ingenioso hidalgo Don Quijote de la Mancha*. Ed. Justo García Soriano and Justo García Morales. Madrid: Aguilar.

Chance, Jane. 1986. *Woman as Hero in Old English Literature*. Syracuse: Syracuse University Press.

*La Chanson de Roland*. 1881. Ed. Leon Gautier. Tours: Alfred Mame et Fils.

Chaucer, Geoffrey. 1989. *The Complete Poetry and Prose of Geoffrey Chaucer*. Ed. John H. Fisher. New York: Holt, Rinehart and Winston.

Chejne, Anwar G. 1983. *Islam and the West: The Moriscos, a Cultural and Social History*. Albany: State University of New York Press.

Chew, Samuel C. 1937. *The Crescent and the Rose: Islam and England during the Renaissance*. New York: Oxford University Press.

Christoph, Siegfried Richard. 1981. *Wolfram von Eschenbach's Couples*. Amsterdam: Editions Rodopi N.V.

Coleridge, Samuel Taylor. 1959. *The Ancient Mariner, Kubla Khan, Christabel*. New York: Macmillan.

Cook, Robert Francis. 1987. *The Sense of the Song of Roland*. Ithaca: Cornell University Press.

Croutier, Alev Lytle. 1989. *Harem: The World Behind the Veil*. Ed. Alan Axelrod. New York: Abbeville.

Damico, Helen, and Alexandra Hennessey Olsen, eds. 1990. *New Readings on Women in Old English Literature*. Bloomington: Indiana University Press.

Daniels, Norman. 1975. *The Arabs and Mediaeval Europe*. London: Longman Group, and Beirut: Librairie du Liban.

————. 1984. *Heroes and Saracens: An Interpretation of the Chansons de Geste*. Edinburgh, U.K.: Edinburgh University Press.

Defoe, Daniel. 1931. *Roxana, The Fortunate Mistress*. New York: Bibliophilist Society.

Diderot, Denis. 1995. *Les bijoux indiscrets*. Arles, France: Actes Sud.

Djait, Hichem. 1985. *Europe and Islam*. Trans. Peter Heinegg. Los Angeles: University of California Press.

Djebar, Assia. 1986–1987. "Forbidden Sight, Interrupted Sound." *Discourses* 8: 38–55.

Dresen-Coenders, Lene. 1987. *Saints and She-devils: Images of Women in the Fifteenth and Sixteenth Centuries*. Trans. C. M. H. Sion and R. M. J. van der Wilden. London: Rubicon.

Dunn, Ross E. 1989. *The Adventures of Ibn Battuta: A Muslim Traveler of the Fourteenth Century*. Berkeley: University of California Press.

Durant, Will. 1957. *The Story of Civilization*. Vol. 6. *The Reformation: A History of European Civilization from Wycliffe to Calvin 1300–1564*. New York: Simon and Schuster.

Ellis, George. 1848. *Sir Bevis of Hamptoun. Specimens of Early English Metrical Romances*. London: Henry G. Bohn.

Ellis-Fermor, Una M. 1974. "Marlowe's *Tamburlaine*." In *Christopher Marlowe's Tamburlaine. Part 1 and Part 2: Text and Major Criticism*. Ed. Irving Ribner. Indianapolis, Ind.: Odyssey Press.

El Saffar, Ruth. 1984. *Beyond Fiction: The Recovery of the Feminine in the Novels of Cervantes*. Berkeley: University of California Press.

Evans, Hilary. 1979. *Harlots, Whores, and Hookers*. New York: Dorset.

Ewing, Elizabeth. 1978. *Dress and Undress: A History of Women's Underwear*. New York: Drama Book Specialists.

Faugere, Annie. 1979. *Les origines orientales du Graal chez Wolfrom von Eschenbach: État des Recherches*. Stuttgart: Kummerle Verlag.

Fisher, Sheila, and Janet E. Halley, eds. 1989. *Seeking the Woman in Late Medieval and Renaissance Writings*. Knoxville: University of Tennessee Press.

Fletcher, John, Nathan Field, and Philip Massinger. 1992. *The Knight of Malta*. In *The Dramatic Works in the Beaumont and Fletcher Canon*. Ed. Fredson Bowers. Vol. 8. Cambridge: Cambridge University Press.

*Floire et Blancheflor, Le Conte de*. 1980. Ed. Jean-Luc Leclanche. Les Classiques français du Moyen Age. Paris: Librairie Honore Champion.

Flynn, Carol Houlihan. 1987. "Defoe's Idea of Conduct: Ideological Fictions and Fictional Reality." In *The Ideology of Conduct*. Eds. Nancy Armstrong and Leonard Tennenhouse. New York: Methuen.

Foucault, Michel. 1978. *The History of Sexuality*. Vol. 1. Trans. Robert Hurley. New York: Pantheon.

———. 1977. *Language, Counter-Memory, Practice: Selected Essays and Interviews*. Ed. Donald F. Bouchard. Trans. Donald F. Bouchard and Sherry Simon. Ithaca: Cornell University Press.

Galland, Antoine. 1745. *Les milles et une nuits: contes arabes*. Paris: Compagnie des libraires.

Garces, Maria Antonia. 1989. "Zoraida's Veil: 'The Other Scene' of the Captive's Tale." *Revista de Estudios Hispánicos* 23(1):65–98.

Giamatti, A. Bartlett. 1966. *The Earthly Paradise and the Renaissance Epic*. Princeton: Princeton University Press.

Gibbs, Marion E. 1972. *Wiplichez Wibes Reht: A Study of the Women Characters in the Works of Wolfram von Eschenbach*. Pittsburgh: Duquesne University Press.

Gilbert, Sandra M., and Susan Gubar. 1979. *The Madwoman in the Attic: The Woman Writer and the Nineteenth-Century Literary Imagination*. New Haven: Yale University Press.

Goldenberg, Rita. 1984. *Sex and Enlightenment: Women in Richardson and Diderot.* Cambridge and London: Cambridge University Press.

Grunebaum, Gustave E. von. 1953. *Medieval Islam.* 2d ed. Chicago: University of Chicago Press.

Hallissy, Margaret. 1987. *Venomous Woman: Fear of the Female in Literature.* New York: Greenwood.

Hartman, Geoffrey, and David Thorburn, eds. 1973. *Romanticism.* Ithaca: Cornell University Press.

Hodgen, Margaret T. 1971. *Early Anthropology in the Sixteenth and Seventeenth Centuries.* Philadelphia: University of Pennsylvania Press.

Hourani, Albert. 1991. *A History of the Arab Peoples.* Cambridge, Mass.: Belknap Press of Harvard University.

Hugo, Victor. [1829] n.d. *Les orientales. Oeuvres complètes de Victor Hugo.* Vol. 17. Paris: J. Hetzel.

Johnson, Lemuel. 1971. *The devil, the Gargoyle, and the Buffoon: The Negro as Metaphor in Western Literature.* Port Washington, N.Y.: National University Publications, Kennikat Press.

Johnson, Samuel. 1971. *The History of Rasselas, Prince of Abissinia.* Ed. Geoffrey Tillotson and Brian Jenkens. London: Oxford University Press.

Jones, George Fenwick. 1963. *The Ethos of the Song of Roland.* Baltimore: Johns Hopkins University Press.

Kabbani, Rana. 1986. *Europe's Myths of Orient.* Bloomington: Indiana University Press.

Kerber, Linda. 1996. "The Republican Mother: Women and the Enlightenment— An American Perspective." *American Quarterly* 28: 187–295.

Knudson, Charles A. 1969. "La thème de la princesse sarrasine dans *La Prise d'Orange.*" *Romance Philology* 22(4):449–462.

Lawner, Lynne. 1987. *Lives of the Courtesans: Portraits of the Renaissance.* New York: Rizzoli.

Lee, Stephen J. 1978. *Aspects of European History 1494–1789.* New York: Methuen.

Luedtke, Luther S. 1989. *Nathaniel Hawthorne and the Romance of the Orient.* Bloomington: Indiana University Press.

Lewis, Bernard. 1973. *Islam in History.* New York: Literary Press.

Marlowe, Christopher. 1963. *The Complete Plays of Christopher Marlowe.* Ed. Irving Ribner. New York: Odyssey.

Marly, Diana de. 1985. *Fashion for Men: An Illustrated History.* New York: Holmes & Meier.

Marston, John. 1856. "Sophonisba." In *The Works of John Marston.* Ed. J. O. Halliwell. London: John Russell Smith.

Mason, Eugene. 1931. *Aucassin and Nicolette and Other Mediaeval Romances and Legends.* 1910. Reprint. London: J. M. Dent & Sons.

Massinger, Philip. 1845. *The Plays of Philip Massinger.* Ed. W. Gifford. London: Henry Washbourne.

McEvedy, Colin. 1985. *The Penguin Atlas of Medieval History*. 1961. Reprint. New York: Penguin.

Melman, Billie. 1992. *Women's Orients: English Women and the Middle East, 1718–1918: Sexuality, Religion, and Work*. Ann Arbor: University of Michigan.

Metlitzki, Dorothee. 1977. *The Matter of Araby in Medieval England*. New Haven: Yale University Press.

Meyer, Eric. 1991. "'I know thee not, I loathe thy race': Romantic Orientalism in the Eye of the Other." *ELH* 58:657–699.

Michaut, Gustav. 1934. *Aucassin et Nicolette*. In *Medieval French Literature: Representative Selections in Modernized Versions*. Eds. Thomas Rossman Palfrey and William Collar Holbrook. New York: D. Appleton-Century.

Miles, Margaret R. 1986. "The Virgin's One Bare Breast: Female Nudity and Religious Meaning in Tuscan Early Renaissance Culture." In *The Female Body in Western Culture*. Ed. Susan Rubin Suleiman. Cambridge, Mass.: Harvard University Press.

Montesquieu, Charles-Louis de Secondat. 1930. *Lettres Persanes*. Paris: Le Musée de Libre.

———. 1964. *The Persian Letters*. Trans. George R. Healy. Indianapolis: Library of Liberal Arts.

Mulvey, Laura. 1975. "Visual Pleasure and Narrative Cinema." *Screen* 16(3): 6–18.

Palacios, Miguel Asin. 1968. *Islam and the Divine Comedy*. Trans. Harold Sutherland. London: Frank Cass.

Passage, Charles E. See Wolfram, von Eschenbach.

Pico della Mirandola, Giovanni. 1998. *On the Dignity of Man*. Indianapolis, Ind.: Hackett.

Pizan, Christine de. 1982. *The Book of the City of Ladies*. Trans. Earl Jeffrey Richards. Foreword by Marina Warner. New York: Persea Books.

Prior, Mary, ed. 1985. *Women in English Society 1500–1800*. London: Methuen.

Racine, Jean. 1947. *Bajazet*. Ed. Xavier de Courville. Paris: Editions du Seuil.

Reinert, Stephen W. 1987. Course lectures from "The Crusades." History Department, Rutgers University, New Brunswick, N.J. Spring.

Ribner, Irving. Introduction to *The Complete Works of Christopher Marlowe*. New York: Odyssey.

Richardson, Alan. 1988. "Romanticism and the Colonization of the Feminine." In *Romanticism and Feminism*. Ed. Anne K. Mellor. Bloomington: Indiana University Press.

Richardson, Samuel. 1971. *Pamela or, Virtue Rewarded*. Boston: Houghton Mifflin.

Roche, Thomas P., Jr. 1977. "Tasso's Enchanted Woods." In *Literary Uses of Typology from the Late Middle Ages to the Present*. Ed. Earl Miner. Princeton: Princeton University Press.

Rodinson, Maxime. 1987. *Europe and the Mystique of Islam*. Trans. Roger Veinus. Seattle: University of Washington.

Rogers, Katherine M. 1966. *The Troublesome Helpmate: A History of Misogyny in Literature.* Seattle: University of Washington.

———. 1986. "Subversion of Patriarchy in *Les Lettres Persanes*." *Philological Quarterly* 65:61–78.

*Romance of the Sowdone of Babylone and of Ferumbras his Sone who conquerede Rome.* 1969. *The English Charlemagne Romances.* Part 5. Ed. Emil Hausknecht. The Early English Text Society. 1881. Reprint. London: Oxford University Press.

Ross, Marlon B. 1988. "Romantic Quest and Conquest." In *Romanticism and Feminism.* Ed. Anne K. Mellor. Bloomington: Indiana University Press.

Rousseau, Jean Jacques. n.d. *The Confessions of Jean Jacques Rousseau.* New York: Modern Library.

———. 1889. *La Nouvelle Heloise.* 6 vols. Paris: Librairie des Bibliophiles.

———. 1960. *Les Reveries du Promeneur Solitaire.* Paris: Garnier Frères.

———. 1968. *La Nouvelle Heloise. Julie, or the New Eloise.* Trans. Judith H. McDowell. University Park: Pennsylvania State University Press.

———. 1979a. *Émile, or On Education.* Trans. Allan Bloom. New York: Basic Books.

———. 1979b. *The Reveries of the Solitary Walker.* Trans. Charles E. Butterworth. New York: New York University Press.

———. 1989. *Politics and the Arts. Letter to M. D'Alembert on the Theatre.* Trans. Allan Bloom. Ithaca: Cornell University Press.

Rowbotham, Sheila. 1973. *Hidden from History: Rediscovering Women in History from the Seventeenth Century to the Present.* New York: Vintage.

Said, Edward. 1979 *Orientalism.* New York: Vintage.

Schelling, Felix E. 1908. *Elizabethan Drama.* Boston: Houghton Mifflin.

Seaton, Ethel. 1974. "Marlowe's Map." In *Christopher Marlowe's* Tamburlaine. *Part 1 and Part 2: Texts and Major Criticism.* Ed. Irving Ribner. Indianapolis, Ind.: Odyssey Press.

Shaw, Ezel Kural, and C. J. Heywood. 1972. *English and Continental Views of the Ottoman Empire, 1500–1800.* Los Angeles: University of California.

Shelley, Mary. 1992. *Frankenstein.* Ed. Johanna M. Smith. New York: St. Martin's.

Shelley, Percy. 1974. *The Poetical Works of Shelley.* Cambridge ed. Ed. Newell F. Ford. Boston: Houghton Mifflin.

Short, Ian. 1973. *The Anglo-Norman Pseudo-Turpin Chronicle of William de Briane.* Anglo-Norman Text Society. Oxford: Basil Blackwell.

*Song of Roland, The.* 1970. Trans. Robert Harrison. New York: New American Library.

Southern, R. W. 1953. *The Making of the Middle Ages.* New Haven: Yale University Press.

———. 1962. *Western Views of Islam in the Middle Ages.* Cambridge, Mass.: Harvard University Press.

Spivak, Gayatri Chakravorti. 1985. "Three Women's Texts and a Critique of Imperialism." In *"Race," Writing, and Difference.* Ed. Henry Louis Gates. Chicago: University of Chicago Press.

Stael, Anne-Louise-Germaine Necker, Mme de. 1979. *Corinne, ou, L'Italie*. Paris: Des Femmes.

Stafford, Pauline. 1983. *Queens, Concubines, and Dowagers: The King's Wife in the Early Middle Ages*. Athens: University of Georgia Press.

Stephens, Walter. 1989. "Saint Paul among the Amazons: Gender and Authority in *Gerusalemme liberata*." In *Discourse of Authority in Medieval and Renaissance Literature*. Hanover, N.H.: University Press of New England.

Stuard, Susan Mosher, ed. 1976. *Women in Medieval Society*. Philadelphia: University of Pennsylvania Press.

Tasso, Torquato. 1963. *Jerusalem Delivered*. Trans. Edward Fairfax. New York: Capricorn.

Trumpener, Katie. 1987. "Rewriting Roxane: Orientalism and Intertextuality in Montesquieu's *Lettres Persanes* and Defoe's *The Fortunate Mistress*." *Stanford French Review* 11:177–191.

Vickers, Nancy J. 1986. "This Heraldry in Lucrece' Face." In *The Female Body in Western Culture*. Ed. Susan Rubin Suleiman. Cambridge, Mass.: Harvard University Press.

Warren, F. W. 1914. "The Enamoured Moslem Princess in Orderic Vital and the French Epic." *PMLA* 29:314–358.

Webster, John. 1937. "The White Devil." *Complete Works of John Webster*. Ed. F. L. Lucas. New York: Oxford University Press.

Williams, Henry L., ed. 1907. *Poems of Victor Hugo, Translated into English by Various Authors*. Vol. 9. New York, Philadelphia, and Chicago: Nottingham Society.

Wolfram, von Eschenbach. 1977. *The Middle High German Poem of Willehalm by Wolfram of Eschenbach*. Trans. Charles E. Passage. New York: Frederick Ungar.

———. 1961. *Parzival by Wolfram von Eschenbach*. Trans. Charles E. Passage and Helen M. Mustard. New York: Vintage.

Wollstonecraft, Mary. 1992. *A Vindication of the Rights of Women*. Ed. Miriam Brody Kramnick. Harmondsworth, England: Penguin.

Woodruff, William. 1981. *The Struggle for World Power 1500–1980*. New York: St. Martin's.

Wortley-Montagu, Mary. 1970. *The Selected Letters of Lady Mary Wortley-Montagu*. Ed. Robert Halsband. Harlow, England: Longman.

# Index